Before You Go
to Great Britain

BEFORE YOU GO TO

GREAT BRITAIN

A Resource Directory and Planning Guide

James W. Brown
Shirley N. Brown

Library Professional Publications • 1986

© 1986 by James W. Brown and Shirley N. Brown.
All rights reserved. First published in 1986 as a
Library Professional Publication, an imprint of
The Shoe String Press, Inc., Hamden, Connecticut 06514.
Printed in the United States of America

Library of Congress Cataloging-in-Publication Data
Brown, James W. (James Wilson), 1913 Sept. 18-
Before you go to Great Britain.

Bibliography: p.
1. Great Britain—Description and travel—
1971-   —Information services—Directories.
2. Great Britain—Description and travel—
1971-   —Guide-books—Bibliography. 3. Travel—
Information services—Directories. I. Brown,
Shirley N. II. Title.
DA650.B9   1986   914.1'04858   86-15195
ISBN 0-208-02088-8

This royal throne of kings, this scepter'd isle,
This earth of majesty, this seat of Mars,
This other Eden, demi-paradise,
This fortress built by Nature for herself
Against infection and the hand of war,
This happy breed of men, this little world,
This precious stone set in the silver sea,
Which serves it in the office of a wall
Or as a moat defensive to a house,
Against the envy of less happier lands,
This blessed plot, this earth, this realm, this England.

SHAKESPEARE, *Richard II.*

Contents

Abbreviations

Abbreviations in the entries have been used in the
following instances:

ann.	annually
comp.	compiler
distr.	distributor
mins.	minutes
mm.	millimeter
mo.	month
nd.	no date available
np.	no pagination, or pages un-known
q.	quarterly
semi-ann.	semi-annually (semi-annual)
tr.	translator
wk.	weekly

Preface

This book is intended to be what its title and subtitle say it is: a resource directory and planning guide for use *before* you go to Great Britain. Properly used, it will help you make the most out of a visit to places that are somehow pleasantly familiar even while they are excitingly foreign. It is expected that much of this use will be made in a library, but of course considerably further use of it could be made at home as well. The book will steer you to a variety of sources—travel books, guidebooks, directories, newspapers and magazines, organizations, private businesses (such as airlines, tour companies, renters of canal boats), motion pictures, audiotapes, and videotapes—all associated with topics related to Great Britain. If you start your planning early enough, you will have time before you depart to read and also to write directly to many of the suggested addresses to request materials or to seek answers to specific questions you may have about your trip.

Our directory and planning guide has nine chapters. Chapter 1 introduces Britain and refers you to facts about its present-day characteristics and its past. Also, it puts you in touch with sources that outline the range of sightseeing locations available within its comparatively small geographic boundaries. Chapter 2 tells you how to make sure that "getting there is half the fun," and about some services and aids that will help you to ensure such results materialize. Chapter 3 tells you about guidebooks, general and special or specific, and sources of maps, while chapter 4 details ways in which you may use modern library resources and services to add enjoyment and intellectual stimulation to a well-planned trip. Many types of general reference books, periodical guides, and audiovisual sourcebooks are listed and described, as are several computerized information bases applicable to the world of travel. Chapter 5 tells about ways to get around Britain, and as with all other activities covered in the book, sources and referrals of many kinds are given to aid readers in obtaining the specific kinds of help they need. Chapter 6, about food and drink, offers leads to information about all manner of participatory activities from eating and tea drinking to pub-crawling and visiting distilleries in Scotland!

Chapters 7 and 8 provide insights into two very disparate areas in which the British excel: the world of sports—from team to individual (soccer to bird-watching); and the world of the arts—from London's fabulous theatres and museums to folk dancing. Chapter 9 may be one of the most interesting of all, for it contains a list of suggested activities for which plenty of advance information is required for their fullest enjoyment. One of these considers "Literary Site Sleuthing"—or the planning of visits to places made memorable by stories, poems, and plays by British authors through the centuries; another presents information about tracing your British ancestors; and still another about "antiquing" and other collecting.

Our book ends with a directory of sources: an alphabetical listing of producers, publishers, distributors, and other agencies for which, for quick reference, we supply names and addresses. Because this directory contains full addresses for all publishers whose books are cited in the bibliographies, locations for publishing houses are omitted from bibliographic citations.

The organization of information is similar from chapter to chapter, with lists of sources in each one related to the chapter topics. Information for audiovisual materials includes identification of media type, production date, running or playing time, and notes on content.

Where British-published books have U.S. distributors, the British publisher is listed first, followed by a slash (/), and the name of the U.S. publisher or distributor.

Access to the audiovisual materials listed can often be gained through one or more of the following channels: (1) nearby college and university audiovisual libraries that rent items in their collections and sometimes provide them for preview purposes; (2) audiovisual collections in public libraries which usually circulate their materials free of charge or for very low service fees; (3) certain other college or university film rental libraries that are members of the Consortium of University Film Centers (CUFC). This organization may be reached c/o Audiovisual Services, Kent State University, 330 Library, Kent, Ohio 44242. Tel: (216) 672-3456.

Whether you have bought your own copy of this book or are consulting a copy borrowed from a library, we recommend that you arrange an early conference with a library reference staff member to discuss reading, listening, and viewing opportunities in connection with your British trip plans. This book will serve as a source of specific titles geared to a greater enjoyment of your trip, but the librarian will have additional good ideas as well, and will help you to put your hands on materials that will give you the most satisfaction and help.

We wish to acknowledge the help of a number of persons in the preparation of the manuscript: representatives of the British Tourist Authority (BTA) offices in New York City and Los Angeles, who made suggestions for our original outline and supplied numerous valuable publications for our use; Ms. Katharine Read McCormack, of the Anglo-File organization (Tarzana, California), who prepared British history materials; Professor Richard Adams, of Oxford, England, who, while serving as a visiting professor at San Jose State University, critiqued and made certain editorial improvements for us; British Library personnel (London) who assisted us through a computer search for appropriate book titles; Harrods' department store (London) whose excellent book department saved us hours of time in locating entries; Foyle's Bookstore (London), which provided a similar service; the San Jose State University Library; and numerous bookstores in San Jose, Los Gatos, Los Altos, San Francisco, Los Angeles, Palo Alto, Boston, and New York. Virginia Mathews, of Library Professional Publications (the Shoe String Press, Inc.), helped us greatly in the organization and emphases of the book. Rosalie Gailey typed the manuscript.

Finally, we recommend that you spend some time with this book before you make final plans with your travel agent. A trip, long or short, to Great Britain, lends itself well to individualization—the better it is tailored to fit you, your interests, and the things that are important to you, the better the tour will be. A great part of the customizing will be up to you, and this book was prepared by us to help you do it. *Bon Voyage!*

MAP OF GREAT BRITAIN
SHOWING REGIONS

From *Great Value Great Britain 1984*, p. 109
Used by permission. British Tourist Authority.

THE THAMES AND CHILTERNS
Berkshire
Oxfordshire
Buckinghamshire
Bedfordshire
Hertfordshire

THE SOUTH EAST, SOUTHERN
ENGLAND, AND THE ISLE of WIGHT
Surrey
Sussex
Kent
Hampshire
Isle of Wight

WEST COUNTRY
Cornwall
Devon
Somerset and Avon
Dorset
Wiltshire

WALES
North Wales
Mid-Wales
South Wales

HEART OF ENGLAND/
EAST MIDLANDS
The Cotswolds
Shakespeare
   Country—Warwickshire
The Welsh Border
Staffordshire and West Midlands
Gloucestershire, Herefordshire,
   Worcestershire

EAST ANGLIA
Essex
Suffolk
Cambridgeshire
Norfolk

YORKSHIRE AND HUMBERSIDE
South and West Yorkshire
Yorkshire Dales
North York Moors
The Wolds and Humberside
York

NORTH AND NORTH WEST
Lancashire
Cheshire and the Peak District of
   Derbyshire
Merseyside and Greater
   Manchester

CUMBRIA AND NORTHUMBRIA
Cumbria
Northumbria

SCOTLAND
Borders and Lowlands
Central Scotland
Highlands
The Islands

Introduction
to Great Britain

Great Britain has figured importantly in the lives of the people of the United States ever since colonial times. Much of what we are nationally can be traced to British origins—our principal language, the bases of our laws, our court system, many of our customs and traditions, and much, much more. Despite large disagreements such as those which erupted into the Revolutionary War and the War of 1812, and many smaller ones since then, the United States and Great Britain have stood together to fight the two great world wars and have otherwise developed ties that express the special quality of their relationship. The people of the United States and Britain are very different, yet they have much in common; they have long had an interest in visiting each other's countries to marvel at ways of life that are at once so alike and so unlike. In 1985 alone, more than three million Americans visited Great Britain; that same year nearly a million persons from Britain came as visitors to the United States. But perhaps the most compelling evidence of kinship lies in the fact that approximately sixty million U.S. citizens trace their ancestry to some place in Britain.

SOME FACTS AND FIGURES ABOUT BRITAIN

Britain is comprised of England, Scotland, and Wales. The United Kingdom of Great Britain and Northern Ireland adds the latter to the first three to form the sovereign state frequently referred to as

1

the United Kingdom, or, even more briefly, as "the U.K." Together, the political subdivisions of England, Scotland, and Wales (which are the concern of this book) include an area of about 88,000 square miles, which is slightly less than that of the state of Oregon. London, the capital city, has 6.7 million inhabitants. Great Britain as a whole is 30 percent arable, 50 percent meadow and pasture, 12 percent waste or urban, 7 percent in forest, and 1 percent land water. It is well down the list of countries in size (about seventieth in the world); less than 2 percent of the world's people live there. Still, its population is large in relation to its land mass, and its influence and power have been vastly out of proportion to its size and population. Blessed with few natural resources of their own, the British nevertheless contrived to bring the world's resources to their shores, and with them led the world in the industrial revolution while building the most far-flung empire the world had ever seen.

Great Britain is, of course, an island country, and it has flourished as such. No part of the country is more than about 100 miles from the seas that surround it—the seas that, before the age of flight, provided some of the best fortifications any country ever had.

The greatest distance from north to south in Great Britain is approximately 600 miles; east to west it is around 300. In all, the area has some two thousand miles of coastline. The population of Great Britain is approximately 54.5 million, which averages a little more than 610 persons to the square mile. (Our own ratio in the United States is one tenth that, or sixty-four persons to the square mile.) Approximately 46.5 million of the 54.5 million persons live in England, which has a population density of about 925 to the square mile. Relative populations of the geographic divisions of Great Britain tell us where people are concentrated:

England	46.50 million persons
Scotland	5.13 million persons
Wales	2.73 million persons
Other (Channel Islands, etc.)	.20 million persons

Within these geographical divisions, the greatest population concentrations in England occur in and around London, Bristol, Portsmouth, Birmingham, Sheffield, Liverpool, Manchester, Leeds, and Newcastle-Upon-Tyne; in Scotland in and around Edinburgh and Glasgow; in Wales in and around Swansea and Cardiff.

Generally speaking, summers in Britain are cool and winters are mild. It is somewhat colder in the north than in the south, as one might expect. Air reaching Britain's western shores is warmed by the Gulf Stream, which originates in the warm waters of the Gulf of Mexico. This helps account for the fact that although southern England is at approximately the same latitude as Quebec or Newfoundland, one may find healthy palm trees and other subtropical vegetation growing in places. Although it may sometimes snow in winter, the snow does not lie for any length of time on the ground except at the higher altitudes. The English summer may produce a number of dry sunny days, but there are some rainstorms, too. The average July temperature in London is 64 degrees Fahrenheit (17.6 degrees Celsius); in Edinburgh it is 59 degrees Fahrenheit (14.8 degrees Celsius). Annual rainfall varies from 100 inches in the mountains of north Wales and western Scotland to less than 20 inches in the driest areas surrounding the estuary of the River Thames in southeastern England.

The lists of organizations and associations, books, and audiovisual materials that follow contain many sources of further information about the physical, political, and sociological characteristics of England, Scotland, and Wales. Among them are numerous items that will help to fill out the backgrounds of those who contemplate a well-prepared trip to those areas.

Organizations and Associations

British Information Services. 845 Third Avenue, New York, NY 10022. Supplies factual data about the United Kingdom and the British Commonwealth.

British Tourist Authority. This organization supplies travel information, assistance, and literature and background information to individuals planning trips to Great Britain. Contact the nearest office: 40 West 57th Street, New York, NY 10019; John Hancock Center, Suite 3320, 875 North Michigan Avenue, Chicago, IL 60611; 612 South Flower Street, Los Angeles, CA 90017; or Plaza of the Americas, 750 North Tower, LB 346, Dallas, TX 75201.

English Tourist Board. 4 Grosvenor Gardens, London SW1W ODU. Provides general tourist information and services.

Institute of Travel and Tourism. 53-54 Newman Street, London W1 4JJ. Seeks to advance the cultural and educational aspects of travel.

Institute of British Geographers. 1 Kensington Gore, London SW7 2AR. Promotes geographic research.

National Tourist and Information Centre and Bookstore. Victoria Station Forecourt. London SW1. See entry in chapter 2.

Royal Geographical Society. 1 Kensington Gore, London SW7 2AR. Strives to advance the study of geographical science; finances geographical surveys; publishes.

Scottish Tourist Board. 23 Ravelston Terrace, Edinburgh EH4 3EU. General tourist information and services. See entry in chapter 2.

Wales Tourist Bureau. Brunel House, 4 Fitzalan Road, Cardiff CF2 1UY. General tourist information and services.

Books

Britain: This Beautiful Land. Philip Clucas. Colour Library International. 1983. Word and color photo presentation of the country's moods: its mountains, canals, lakes, islands, uplands, lowlands, and much more.

The Changing Countryside. John Blunden and Nigel Curry, eds. Croom Helm/Longwood Publishing Group. 1985. Examines the changing face and the future of Britain's countryside—industrial, upland, lowland, coastal, and conservation areas.

The Countryside Explained. John Seymour. Penguin. 1979. Fascinating reading for British "country lovers"; information on farming, geology, rural history, architecture, transport, and folklore.

David Gentleman's Britain. David Gentleman. Dodd, Mead. 1983. Full-color sketches (chiefly in watercolor, some in black and white) of nearly the whole of the British Isles. A beautiful book to "look at"; some text.

Discovering Britain and Ireland. Jonathan B. Tourtellot, ed. National Geographic Society. 1985. Profusely illustrated (full color), with interesting and accurate verbal commentaries and text. Discusses London, the English Heartland, the West Country, the Southeast, East Anglia and the Fens, the Midlands, the North Country, Wales, the Scottish Lowlands, Highlands and Islands, the East of Ireland, the the West of Ireland.

England by the Sea. Elizabeth Gundrey. Severn House. 1982. England's maritime heritage (early history); seaside resorts and life; seaside wildlife, shore life, walks, lighthouses, commercial ports. Includes directories for sources of further information.

Everyman's England. Bryn Frank. Harper and Row. 1984. Personal impressions of English people and places; practical and helpful information about the country. Especially good for the armchair traveler.

The Matter of Wales: Epic Views of a Small Country. Jan Morris. Oxford University Press. 1985. Reveals the character of Wales and its people through an expose of their history, religion, poetry and music, industry, agriculture, politics, geography, and architecture.

Modern England: From the Eighteenth Century to the Present (2d ed.). Robert K. Webb. Harper and Row. 1980. Emphasizes changes in the social and industrial fabric of Britain from the Second World War to 1968. Also describes the political climate, the rise of democracy and prosperity. Bibliography of reading appended.

On Britain. Ralf Dahrendorf. British Broadcasting Corp. 1982. An analysis of Britain's economic, social, and political conditions.

Reading the Celtic Landscapes. Richard Muir. Michael Joseph/ Merrimack Publishers Circle, distr. 1985. Guide to studying the English landscape—the people, the villages, prehistory, Roman times, the homes, towns, hamlets, religion.

The Scots. Clifford Hanley. Sphere Books. 1982. Discusses the Scots through the years; as they are, and sometimes as they would like to be regarded. Records some of their achievements in the context of history and customs. A humorous approach.

This Is Historic Britain. Miroslav Sasek. Macmillan Ltd. 1974. Beautifully illustrated panoramic tour of Britain. Includes Trafalgar Square, a Cheshire village, Windsor Castle, Stonehenge, Stratford, Canterbury, and others. Also in this series for young children: *This Is London,* and *This Is Edinburgh.*

West of England Market Towns. Maggie Colwell. Batsford/David and Charles. 1983. Market days in Gloucestershire and Oxfordshire and their links with the past.

Whatever Happened to Britain? John Eatwell. Oxford University Press. 1984. Analyzes Britain's economic decline since the Industrial Revolution.

Audiovisual Materials

The British Isles. Society for Visual Education. nd. 35mm sound filmstrip set (six film strips and three cassettes). Contains the following titles: "London and the Mother of Parliament,"

"Bath and the English Countryside," "Scotland: A Separate Way of Life," "The Orkneys: Isolated Islanders," "Wales: Land of the Red Dragon," and "Ireland: A People Divided."

Capital City: London. International Film Bureau. nd. 16mm sound film or video cassette, 27 mins. The economic workings of the city of London, historical commentaries, the Commodity Exchange, wholesale food markets, Lloyd's, and other businesses within the heart of the city.

English Family: Life in Sheffield. Encyclopaedia Britannica Educational Corp. 1983. 16mm sound film, 22 mins. Gives viewers glimpses of life and typical activities in a millworker's home in North Country England where the world's finest steelware is made.

Geography of Europe Series: The British Isles—United Kingdom and Ireland. National Geographic Society. 1984. 35mm sound filmstrip (with audio cassette). In set of three filmstrips (with "Low Countries," "Belgium and Luxembourg," "France and Monaco"). General overview of the British Isles and Ireland.

Great Britain: European Neighbor. Encore Visual Education, Inc. 1974. 35mm sound color filmstrip series. Titles in the series: "Britain: Island Nation," "Feeding Britain's People," "Britain, Industrial Pioneer," "Britain; World Trade," "Britain's Cultural Heritage," "Living in Britain Today." Each filmstrip 34 to 40 frames, with accompanying audio cassette.

Great Britain: The Island That Was an Empire. Encyclopaedia Britannica Educational Corp. 1982. 35mm sound filmstrip (with audio cassette). An overview of Great Britain today—its industries, its people, its problems, and its future.

London: The Urban Giant. Encyclopaedia Britannica Educational Corp. 1983. 35mm sound filmstrip (with audio cassette). A review of the present-day importance and the chief activities and landmarks of the city of London.

A Traveler's Map of Britain and Ireland. National Geographic Society. 1985. Developed to accompany the National Geographic Society book, *Britain and Ireland*. Also includes (on reverse side) graphs and charts on the historical past of the British Isles.

Two Cities: London and New York. Simon and Schuster Communications. nd. 16mm sound film, 23 mins. Investigates the texture of life in two large metropolitan areas and explores reasons why differences exist.

We Are Americans. National Center for Audio Tapes. nd. audio cassettes, 30 mins. Explores America's international heritage through music of persons who have populated the country. Includes the titles: "England," "Scotland."

.Your Personal Guide to London. Tours by Tape. 1985. audio cassettes, two cassettes, 120 mins. For use on a Sony Walkman or any portable tape cassette playback. A BBC narrator offers explanatory information about various landmarks and sections of London. A map of London, keyed to the tape, and a small reference book, are also provided.

Magazines and Newsletters

In Britain. British Tourist Authority. Box 1238 Allwood, Clifton, NJ 07012. mo. Contains articles on various places and current activities in Britain; features a calendar of forthcoming events; includes excellent photographs, many in full color; includes addresses of British Tourist Authority and other information-offering agencies related to Great Britain.

London Planner. British Tourist Authority. Box 1238 Allwood, Clifton, NJ 07012, mo. Regular listings of information about some of London's places of interest, tours and travel, galleries and museums, pageantry and special events, plays and musicals, ballet performances, and concerts and recitals.

This England. Expediters of the Printed Word Limited, 527 Madison Avenue, New York, NY 10022. q. Color photos, poetry, and stories of the land and the people provide warm and vivid impressions of England.

FIRST DECISIONS ABOUT SIGHTSEEING IN BRITAIN

Early in your planning of a trip to Britain you will need to narrow the field of possible places to visit and things to do. After all, the typical traveler has only so much time to devote to these endeavors, and it behooves everyone to make the best use of available opportunities.

The books and audiovisual materials listed below will provide help with making informed choices. Many of them contain detailed maps and full descriptive information about areas of special interest in Great Britain. Two of them (AA's *Where to Go in Britain* and

Discovering Britain) give organized presentations on several hundred top sightseeing attractions, and include information about indigenous flora, fauna, and folklore. The three geographical subdivisions of Great Britain—England, Scotland, and Wales—are represented in the readings mentioned. Special attention is also given to London, and to the variety of possible short trips from that location.

Books

An American's Guide to Britain. Robin W. Winks. Scribner's. 1984. This revised and updated version gives detailed trip guides, both long and short, out of London; covers cathedrals, castles, country houses, gardens, galleries, national parks, and shopping areas all over Britain.

Atlas of Royal Britain. H. J. M. Massingberd. Windward. 1984. An illustrated guide to more than 750 palaces, houses, villages, battlefields, cities and towns of royal heritage; covers 1,000 years of British history; index and gazetteer included.

The Blue Plaque Guide to London. Caroline Dakers. W. W. Norton. 1982. An annotated list of all blue plaques, historic markers, attached to places in London; arranged alphabetically by individual name.

Britain '85: Land with a Regal Heritage. British Tourist Authority. 1985. General overview of England, Scotland, Wales, and Northern Ireland, as well as various British islands; considerable information about London—where to go, what to see, easy journeys from there, and more. Contains specific information on the year's drama and music, and art. Details of various sections of Britain (England's West Country and East Country, the North Country, and more); a year's calendar of interesting events for the tourist. Available free from BTA.

The Companion Guide to London. 6th ed. David Piper. Prentice-Hall. 1983. A series of guides giving narrative descriptions of little known areas of London; lists hotels and restaurants in areas by price category at end of book. Black-and-white illustrations abound.

Daytrips from London by Rail, Bus, or Car. Earl Steinbicker. British Tourist Authority. 1984. Information on some fifty trips within a day's reach of London. Each trip description contains text and photos, street map, transportation information, and suggestions for eating and refreshments along with other background details.

Discover Scotland. British Tourist Authority. 1984. Describes eight main areas of Scotland and sights to see; maps and illustrations enhance the basic descriptions.

Discovering Britain. Automobile Association (AA)/W. W. Norton. 1983. A guide to more than five hundred selected British sites; includes color photos, maps, and details of flora, fauna, geology, and folklore of the regions.

Explore the Heart of England: The Cotswolds, Shakespeare Country, The Welsh Borderland, Staffordshire, and the West Midlands. Heart of England Tourist Board/New Enterprise Publications. 1984. Maps, descriptive sightseeing information, and names and addresses (with accompanying advertisements) of village, town, and city commercial establishments.

Heritage Tours and Holidays: 1985. British Tourist Authority. 1985. Tours and special interest holiday arrangements related to many different aspects of Britain's heritage, including its famous people and locations given. Full information is provided for each tour.

Richard Binns' Best of Britain. Richard Binns. Atheneum. 1985. The author's favorite haunts in fifteen different areas of Britain described; original maps enhance the text.

Scotland: 1001 Things to See. Automobile Association (AA)/Merrimack Publishers Circle, distr. 1985. Lists all of Scotland's major attractions with pertinent details for each.

Where to Go in Britain. Rebecca King, ed. Automobile Association (AA)/Merrimack Publishers Circle, distr. 1983. This colorfully illustrated paperback includes over four hundred "best places" to visit in Britain; also street plans, maps, hours of opening for stately homes, castles, museums, cathedrals, and scenic areas.

The Whole Europe Escape Manual: UK/Ireland. Kerry Green and Charles A. Leocha, eds. World Leisure Corp. 1984. Offbeat information about people, places, and things to do in the United Kingdom. Includes information about how to catch glimpses of the Loch Ness monster, how to lay siege to castles, how to be a proper guest at a medieval feast, how to translate "Britishisms" (unusual words with unusual meanings), and more. Each page includes a photo or map.

Audiovisual Materials

Audience Planners, Inc. 1 Rockefeller Plaza, New York, NY 10020. Distributes 16mm motion pictures to travel agents (and for review by agency customers as well) to be used in generating client interest in visiting Britain. Titles range in length from fourteen to thirty minutes. Films are offered in five categories, as indicated by the following selected titles: (1) "Bing's Britain," "Britain: Kingdom of the Seas," "Britain's Royal Heritage: Destination Britain," "Gardens of Britain," "Landscape with Castles," "Royal Britain," "The Face of Britain"; (2) (London) "City for All Seasons," "Covent Garden," "Curtain Up! On London Theatre," "This Must Be London"; (3) (England) "Cotswolds Journey," "Dorset—Thomas Hardy Country," "Josiah Wedgwood and the English Potteries," "Midland Country," "Northumbria Magic," "Spell of the Lakes," "Lake District: Wordsworth Country," "Open Secret of East Anglia," "Yorkshire of the Brontë Sisters," "Wells Cathedral"; (4) (Scotland) "Fishing in Scotland," "Sean Connery's Edinburgh," "Treasures of Scotland," and (5) (Wales) "Land of Harmony," "The Wales of Dylan Thomas," "The Welsh Connection," and "Wales—Heritage of a Nation."

Glasgow. Learning Corporation of America. 1980. 16mm sound film, 25 mins. Noted psychiatrist R. D Laing leads viewers through Glasgow—a city of stark, clashing contrasts in commerce, industry, learning, and people.

London. Learning Corporation of America. 1980. 16mm sound film, 28 mins. Jonathan Miller, British television and theatre personality, guides viewers through an unusual visit to London on the North London line from Broad Street to Kew.

SELECTED BRITISH HISTORY RESOURCES

The traveler to Great Britain is almost immediately aware of having entered a country that is especially rich in historical heritage. Official agencies at national and regional levels and in almost every country and city of any size are committed to aiding the preservation of much of that heritage and in helping casual tourists as well as more serious scholars to gain access to preserved or restored facilities and to useful information resources. Reading or seeing or hearing some audiovisual materials about Britain's history before traveling there will help visitors obtain a truer flavor of the country.

The books and audiovisual materials included in the listings that follow are recommended as sources of interesting and helpful, but for the most part not academically oriented, historical information that will contribute to that purpose. NOTE: Books marked with asterisks (*) are considered to be especially suitable for children.

Organizations and Associations

Association of Contemporary Historians. London School of Economics, Aldwych, London WC2A 2AE. Promotes study of contemporary history, especially British history, and represents persons engaged in that effort.

English-Speaking Union. 16 East 69th Street, New York, NY 10021. Founded in 1920; thirty-one thousand members and eighty-seven local groups functioning within the United States. Seeks "to foster mutual understanding and friendship among English-speaking peoples worldwide and to enlarge channels of communication." Maintains an eight thousand-volume library; offers a speakers program; publishes *English-Speaking Union News* (q.).

English-Speaking Union of the Commonwealth. 37 Charles Street, Berkeley Square, London W1X 8AB. Promotes "mutual trust, understanding, and friendship between peoples of the Commonwealth and the United States."

Institute of Contemporary History. 4 Devonshire Street, London W1N 2BH. Seeks to further research into contemporary history.

National Trust. 36 Queen Anne's Gate, London SW1H 9AS. Administers certain properties (castles, estates, and other historic buildings) which have been purchased and are being maintained by the National Trust organization for the general benefit of the public.

Social History Society of the United Kingdom. Centre for Social History, The University of Lancaster, Lancaster LA1 4YG. Encourages study of the history of British society.

Standing Conference for Local History: National Council for Social History. 26 Bedford Square, London WC1B 3HU. Publishes *The Local Historian* (q.); will help to put interested persons in contact with local historians in Great Britain.

Books

The Age of Dickens. Patrick Rooke. Putnam. 1970. Shows the social reforms Dickens was concerned with in his stories related to life in the Victorian period, especially on the streets of London; one of Putnam's "Documentary History Series." Other titles include: *Medieval Pilgrims, Reformation of the Sixteenth Century, Plague and Fire, Origins of World War I,* and *Origins of World War II.*

Alfred the Great: The King and His England. Eleanor S. Duckett. University of Chicago Press. 1958. Story of the ninth century life and times of the only king that England called "great."

All Our Working Lives. Peter Pagnamenta and Richard Overy. British Broadcasting Corporation. 1984. A vivid history of British working life since 1914.

Battle of Britain: Then and Now. Winston Ramsey, ed. Battle of Britain Prints International. 1982. Full details, including grave photos, personal data, of Royal Air Force airmen killed during the Battle of Britain. The book contains many thousands of accurately verified facts about the affair.

Book of British Villages: A Guide to Seven Hundred of the Most Interesting and Attractive Villages in Britain. Automobile Association (AA)/W. W. Norton. 1981. Gives a brief history and description of each village with essays on village crafts, buildings, lost villages, names of villages; also includes thirteen maps.

Britain in Our Century: Images and Controversies. Arthur Marwick. Thames and Hudson/W. W. Norton. 1985. An historian's view from 1900 to the present of the changes in British life and culture; illustrated with photos.

Britain: A World by Itself: Reflections on the Landscape by Eminent British Writers. John Fowles, et al. Little, Brown. 1984. Large sized, pictorial book with comments by various well-known British authors.

British Folk Customs. Christina Hole, ed. Paladin. 1978. Describes folk customs now in use and also those that have disappeared from the British scene; alphabetically arranged by custom or celebration.

British Folklore, Myths and Legends. Marc Alexander. Weidenfeld and Nicolson. 1982. Examines folklore legends and beliefs handed down in the British heritage. The evolution of British folk beliefs is detailed with numerous maps locating sites to be visited.

Changing World: Rural Life in Victorian and Edwardian England. Sadie Ward. Schocken. 1985. Shows the effect of technological change upon the educational, social, and leisure life of the ordinary people of Britain; illustrated with old photos.

A Concise History of England. F. E. Halliday. Thames and Hudson. 1980. English history from Stonehenge to the present day— 4500 years in all. Includes 225 illustrations.

David Gentleman's London. David Gentleman. Dodd, Mead. 1985. A brief history of the city illustrated profusely with watercolor sketches. Places featured are the River Thames, the East End, Westminster, St. James, the parks, the West End, and the villages and suburbs.

The Discovery of King Arthur. Geoffrey Ashe. Doubleday/Anchor. 1985. Examines the writings of historians and reconstructs the story of Arthur's life and accomplishments; attempts to verify the existence of this legendary figure. Bibliography and index included.

The First Elizabeth. Carolly Erickson. Summit Books/Simon and Schuster. 1984. An easy "read" about the Elizabethan period and its impact on British history.

*For Queen and Country: Victorian England. Margaret Drabble. Clarion/Houghton Mifflin. 1979. A look at British culture during Queen Victoria's reign, showing the development of a social welfare system to deal with problems of overcrowding, poverty, and disease. Illustrated with color plates and with an extensive bibliography. This is one of many titles in the "Cultural History" series from Clarion for young people, aiming to teach history through story and illustration. Other titles include: *Beyond the Inhabited World: Roman Britain; Green Blades Rising: The Anglo-Saxons; A Strong Hand and A Sturdy: Life in Medieval England; The House of Hanover: England in the Eighteenth Century;* and *A Mighty Ferment: Britain in the Age of Revolution, 1750-1850.*

Iron Bridge to Crystal Palace. Asa Briggs. Thames and Hudson, 1979. The impact and images of the Industrial Revolution.

Great Britons. David Howarth, et al. Viking/British Broadcasting Corp. 1978. Details of lives of famous British people based on the BBC series of the same name. Includes Nelson, Thomas Cook and Son, Florence Nightingale, Robert Burns, Marlborough, and Lloyd George. Illustrated with photos.

Great Harry: The Extravagant Life of Henry VIII. Carolly Erickson. Summit Books/Simon and Schuster. 1984. Carefully researched narrative biography of this notorious king.

*A History of Everyday Things in England. Marjorie and C. H. B. Quennell. David & Charles. 1978. Originally published by Batsford in London, these books cover a period from the twelfth century through the nineteenth century, describing with words, drawings, photos, and diagrams various aspects of everyday life in England. This appealing story teaches history to young people through exposure to ordinary things: costumes, customs, food, agriculture, wars, clothes, shipbuilding, furniture, medicine, dance, tithes, crafts, and even crime and punishment.

History of the English Speaking Peoples. Winston Churchill. Henry Steele Commager, ed. Greenwich. 1983. A one-volume version arranged by Commager of Churchill's portraits of leaders, historical description of wars and political conflicts; illustrated, with maps appended.

Ilustrated Guide to Britain. Automobile Association (AA)/W. W. Norton. 1979. Details the discovery and making of Britain, well-illustrated in color and featuring West Country legends, gardens of England, defenders and invaders, pageants and ceremonies, the markets of London, Hadrian's Wall, and more.

Industrial Heritage. British Tourist Authority. 1985. pamphlet. Essential information regarding Britain's past industrial history and development of the Industrial Revolution. Available free from BTA.

The Intelligent Traveller's Guide to Historic Britain. Philip A. Crowl. St. Martin's/Congdon and Weed. 1983. A narrative history of Britain with chronological accounts of Britain's past; organized according to remaining sites which may still be visited.

An Introduction to Anglo-Saxon England. 2d ed. Peter Hunter Blair. Cambridge University Press. 1977. Discusses the foundations of England, Britain, the Viking, the church, government, economy, and British letters. A general history covering events and effects of seven formative centuries of British life. A standard reference on this subject.

Kirgs and Queens of England and Scotland. David Piper. Faber and Faber/Muller. 1984. Written by the former Keeper of the National Portrait Gallery, this work presents photo portraits of all the English and Scottish monarchs from Saxon times to the 1980s. A brief biography accompanies each portrait.

The Last Plantagenets. Thomas B. Costain. Doubleday. 1962. One in a series covering the history of England called *The Pageant of*

England. Other titles are: *The Conquerors, The Magnificent Century,* and *The Three Edwards.*

*Life in Roman Britain. Peter Quennell, general ed. Batsford/ Putnam. Various dates in the 1960s and 1970s. This is one volume in the "English Life Series"; well illustrated works showing children a glimpse of English life at various time periods. Other titles include: *Life in Norman England, Life in Tudor England, Life in Elizabethan England, Life in Britain Between the Wars,* and several more.

Life in Victorian London. L.C.B. Seaman. David & Charles. 1973. Covers sixty-four years of life in London, its development problems, London transport expansion, river and rail travel, shopping, women and their place in home and society, the growth of theatre and music hall entertainment, and more. Further reading lists appended at end of each chapter.

Majesty. Robert Lacey. Harcourt, Brace, Jovanovich. 1977. A classic biography of Elizabeth II and a history of the House of Windsor; details private lives of Princess Margaret and others from World War II to the present (1977).

The Making of the English. Barry Cunliffe. British Broadcasting Corporation. 1973. Story of the British peoples during the first one thousand years, A.D.

A New History of England 410-1975. L.C.B. Seaman. Barnes and Noble Imports. 1982. Written by a leading historian, this narrative history gives one a clear picture of British life, its wars, and religious revolutions in one compact volume.

Nicholson's Historic Britain. Robert Nicholson. Automobile Association (AA)/Merrimack Publishers Circle, distr. 1986. A guide to what is worth seeing in Britain, with historical connections; includes facts, maps, line drawings, and photos.

The Origins of Britain. Lloyd and Jennifer Laing. Academy Chicago. 1983. A prehistory of Britain before the conquest, this work discusses significant sites, artifacts found, and social and cultural changes. Written by an archaeologist and an ancient history expert, it is illustrated profusely with photographs. Other books of early Britain by the Laings are *Celtic Britain* and *Anglo-Saxon England.*

The Oxford Illustrated History of Britain. Kenneth O. Morgan, ed. Oxford University Press. 1984. A compilation of facts, fully interpreted, illustrated with photographs of medieval treasures and reproductions of paintings and posters from each period.

Pax Britannica: The Climax of an Empire. James Morris. Harcourt/ Penguin. 1979. Deals with the rise and fall of the Victorian Empire and concentrates primarily on the times of Queen Victoria in 1897. This author of travel books describes the areas in question well and gives a complete picture of life in those thrilling times.

Pitkin Pictorial Guides and Souvenir Booklets. Pitkin/British Tourist Authority. Regularly revised and updated, paperback books. An inexpensive series of color pictorials on most of the sights in Britain such as: cathedrals, famous cities and places, royal pageantry, royal history, and famous people.

The Prime Ministers. George Malcolm Thomson. Secker and Warburg. 1980. Vignettes of the forty-nine prime ministers who have led the British government, up to and including Margaret Thatcher.

Royal England: A Historical Gazetteer. Alan and Veronica Palmer. Methuen. 1983. Lists all the places associated with royalty in towns, villages, houses, and historic castles in England.

Scotland Story: A New Perspective. Tom Steel. William Collins Sons. 1984. A television-related (BBC) history of Scotland—a twenty-four-part documentary series. Excellent background information on the Scottish people and land.

Shell Guide to the History of London. W.R. Dalzell. W. W. Norton. 1981. An illustrated guide from Roman times to the present; maps, practical information, indexed.

Traveller's History of Great Britain and Ireland. Richard Muir. Michael Joseph/Merrimack Publishers Circle, distr. 1983. An armchair traveler's guide to Britain through the eyes of this author and photographer. Also includes a section on useful equipment and techniques for photographing landscapes and antiquities.

Understanding Britain. John Randle. Basil Blackwell. 1981. A history of the British people and their culture.

The Weaker Vessel: Women's Lot in Seventeenth-Century England. Antonia Fraser. Knopf. 1984. A look at women in the seventeenth century, their domination by men and the gradual awakening of their talents, courage, survival instincts, and intellectual development. Gives accounts of women from all walks of life and men's attitudes towards them at that time. Includes a bibliography of sources for further reading and research.

William the Conqueror. David C. Douglas. University of California

Press. 1964. Causes and character of the impact of the Norman incursions upon eleventh-century England.

Audiovisual Materials

Anglo-Saxon England. International Film Bureau. nd. 16mm sound film, 22 mins. Background for the study of early English literature and the history of the English language.

Battle of Britain. U.S. National Audiovisual Center. nd. 16mm sound film, 55 mins. Story of Britain's stand alone while the German air force bombed her cities during World War II; the "great fire blitz." Basis for Churchill's statement: "Never in the field of human conflict was so much owed by so many to so few."

Battle of Culloden. Films, Inc. 1966. 16mm sound film, 72 mins. Objective reenactment, filmed in Culloden Moor, of the 1746 battle that ended the cause of Bonnie Prince Charlie, his Jacobite rebellion, and the royal House of Stuart.

The British Isles: The Land and the People. Encyclopaedia Britannica Educational Corp. 1982. 16mm sound film, 21 mins. Traces the physical geography of England, Wales, Scotland, and Northern Ireland. Reveals ways in which the land has influenced the way of life and national character of the British people.

Cromwell: The Great Independent. Encyclopaedia Britannica Educational Corp. 1982. 35mm sound filmstrip (with audio cassette). Cromwell's activities in the political life of early England.

Crystal Year. Indiana University. 1966. 16mm sound film, 30 mins. Focuses on the year 1851 in English history. Contrasts the smug serenity of the Victorian middle class with the smoldering resentments of factory workers. Erection of the Crystal Palace reflects society's confidence in the triumph of the Industrial Revolution.

Elizabeth: The Queen Who Shaped an Age. Society for Visual Education. 1982. 35mm sound filmstrips with audio cassettes. Spans the forty-five-year reign of Elizabeth I, revealing her strategies, the storms of intrigue surrounding her as she transforms a bankrupt land into a powerful nation.

England in the Middle Ages. Encyclopaedia Britannica Educational Corp. 1982. 16mm sound film, 30 mins. The history of England in the middle ages—with a delineation of the main historical developments between 1066 and 1453 A.D., including the Norman invasion, the Peasant Revolt, the rise of the universities, the fourteenth-century religious revolts, cultural achievements of the period, and the Hundred Years' War.

The England of Elizabeth. International Film Bureau. nd. 16mm film or video cassette, 26 mins. Emphasizes the glory and the greatness of sixteenth-century Elizabethan England which included Drake's voyage around the world, the defeat of the Spanish Armada, the Tudor reformation, Caxton's printing press, and Queen Elizabeth I herself.

Fire Over England. Waldenbooks Video Film Classics. 1937. video cassette, 89 mins. About the war between England and Spain in the 1500s; political intrigue; Vivien Leigh's last English film before going to Hollywood.

Fourteenth-Century Nobleman. International Film Bureau. nd. 35mm sound filmstrip (with audio cassette). Life of an English nobleman from the start of the Hundred Years' War (1338) to the end of the fourteenth century.

Great Episodes in British History. Encyclopaedia Britannica Educational Corp. 1982. 35mm sound filmstrips (with audio cassettes). A set of six productions covering important segments of British history: "The Norman Conquest," "Magna Carta," "The Spanish Armada," "The Puritan Revolution," "The Bill of Rights," and "The Industrial Revolution."

Great Explorers: Cook. National Geographic Society. 1978. 35mm sound filmstrip. An account of Captain James Cook's travels and exploration to the Pacific Islands and in Alaska.

Great Explorers: Drake. National Geographic Society. 1978. 35mm sound filmstrip (with audio cassette). An account of Sir Francis Drake's explorations aboard the *Golden Hind.*

Horatio Nelson (1758-1805). Jeffrey Norton Publishers. nd. audio cassette. Commemorates the memory of one of England's greatest heroes and his exploits in opposition especially to Napoleon Bonaparte.

The Industrial Revolution. International Film Bureau. nd. 16mm sound film or video cassette, 23 mins. The nature and significance of the Industrial Revolution and how it changed the lives of all who lived at the time. Features Watt's steam engine, Kay's flying shuttle, Crompton's mule spinner, and Bessemer's steel converter.

The Magna Carta, Part I and Part II. Encyclopaedia Britannica Educational Corp. 1982. 16mm sound films, 16 mins. Traces the history of England from the Norman invasion (1066 A.D.) to the crowning of King John (1199 A.D.) and dramatizes events which brought the conflict between king and barons to a climax and the drafting of the Magna Carta on which Britain's unwritten constitution is founded.

Medieval England. National Geographic Society. Map, 23″ × 30″, 1979. Contains descriptive notes and illustrations.

Medieval England: The Peasants' Revolt. Society for Visual Education. 1982. 35mm sound filmstrips with audio cassettes. An account of peasants' storming of London in 1381; concessions obtained; the beginning of the end of Feudalism.

The Private Life of Henry VIII. Waldenbooks Video Film Classics. 1933. video cassette, 92 mins. Stars Charles Laughton, Elsa Lanchester, Merle Oberon, and others. Laughton's portrayal of this sixteenth-century monarch won him an Oscar.

Queen Elizabeth II. National Center for Audio Tapes. nd. audio cassette, 30 mins. History of the British monarchy; genealogy of the present queen; biographical data on her life.

Queen Victoria; A Profile in Power. Simon and Schuster Communications. nd. 16mm sound film, 26 mins. Portrays Queen Victoria as the proud ruler of the British nation and commonwealth of nations.

Queen Victoria and British History (1837-1901). International Film Bureau. 1974. 16mm sound film, 28 mins. An impressionistic evaluation of the nineteenth-century history of Great Britain, stressing events in the life of Queen Victoria.

Second Battle of Britain. Carousel Films. 1976. 16mm sound film, 49 mins. Reports social and economic developments in Britain, growth of labor unions, decay of private industry, welfare-state policies in effect at the time, interviews with various British people.

Sir Francis Drake: The Rise of English Sea Power. Encyclopaedia Britannica Educational Corp. 1982. 16mm sound film, 30 mins. Episodes in Drake's life and how he persuaded the British people to "look to the sea for their strength."

Will There Always Be an England? Carousel Films. 1977. 16mm sound film, 24 mins. Examines the economic decline of Great Britain; commentary by Milton Friedman, Nobel laureate.

2 Planning for Travel

There are many practical matters to be considered in getting ready to leave the country for a trip to Britain—or anywhere else, for that matter. If you have made all these arrangements and coped with such details before, you know that the more carefully you organize before you go, the more carefree and satisfying things will be when you finally get under way. The information resources included in this chapter are offered to help you have a more enjoyable, and perhaps a more economical, trip.

Trip planning to Britain will be helped by checking into details of the several items discussed in this chapter. Each is approached through provision of a list of printed and audiovisual resources that may be found in public libraries, obtained on loan from nearby film centers, or purchased or obtained free from U.S. or British sources. The topics treated include traveling smart; sources of British publications and information; London bookshops; travel tour agencies; specialized tours; computerized personal travel information; airlines to Britain; ships to Britain; discount travel; travel for disabled persons; a place to stay; shopping in Britain; learning to live with British English; and some unique travel opportunities.

TRAVELING THE SMART WAY

There are several important matters related especially to traveling "the smart way" to Britain or anywhere. Those of greatest concern to most persons are:

- Money
- Health, including possible accidents abroad
- Passports and other necessary documents
- Home, security; care of pets
- Electrical power (of different voltage from U.S.)

Three books, in particular, offer good information about these matters: (1) Fodor's *Great Britain*, (2) Birnbaum's *Great Britain and Ireland*, and (3) American Express's *The American Express Pocket Guide to England and Wales*. All of them are described in greater detail in the "General Guidebooks" section of chapter 3.

Books and Pamphlets

Avoiding the Hassels of Travel. Eugene Fodor. Fodor's Travel Guides. 1984 (booklet). Helpful small publication with tips for traveling on a budget while avoiding many of the problems sometimes associated with that activity.

The American Express Pocket Guide to England and Wales. John Tomes and Michael Jackson. Simon and Schuster. 1986. Its first chapter, "Basic Information," includes these topics: before you go, getting around, on-the-spot information, useful addresses, money and other conversion tables, and emergency information.

Fodor's Great Britain. Fodor's Travel Guides. 1986. An excellent presentation of the basic facts one needs to undertake travel to Britain, presented under these headings: planning your trip, getting to Britain, staying in Britain, traveling in Britain, useful information (including tips for the handicapped), and leaving Britain (matters of customs and duties).

Great Britain and Ireland Nineteen Eighty-Six. Stephen Birnbaum. Houghton Mifflin. 1986. This author's "Getting Ready to Go" section (the first in the book) presents readable information about when and how to go, preparing for the trip, affairs "on the road" (checks, tipping, shopping, and the like), and useful sources of information and assistance.

Know Before You Go. U.S. Customs Service. 1984. pamphlet. Discusses in some detail the special regulations pertaining to U.S. Customs for travelers abroad.

101 Tips for the Mature Traveler. Grand Circle Travel, Inc. 1985. pamphlet. Clearly presented outline of details that must be taken care of in planning for, conducting, and returning from a trip abroad.

Toll-Free Travel/Vacation Phone Directory. Celebrity Publishing. 1982. A directory of 800 numbers related to travel to make your planning, before you go, much easier, less expensive, and more efficient.

Magazines

Travel Smart. Communications House. 40 Beechdale Road, Dobbs Ferry, NY 10522. 12/yr. General information about travel, primarily in Europe, with suggestions for money saving, time saving shortcuts.

Travel Smart for Business. Communications House. 40 Beechdale Road, Dobbs Ferry, NY 10522. 12/yr. Directed toward frequent business travelers. General information about travel, chiefly in Europe, including travel opportunities, car rentals, currencies, airport travel, and the like—varying with each issue.

SOURCES OF BRITISH PUBLICATIONS AND INFORMATION IN THE UNITED STATES AND CANADA

Various publications related to Great Britain, such as those of the British Tourist Authority, the Automobile Association, the Royal Automobile Club, and certain other organizations, including those of regular publishers, may be obtained in the United States and Canada. The suppliers listed below are examples of the many available sources to which one may turn for help in obtaining specific publications of interest to Britain-bound tourists.

Organizations and Associations

Academic Press Canada. 55 Barber Greene Road, Don Mills, Ontario MC3 2A1, Canada. Will fill mail orders for British-related publications. Write for titles and prices.

Berkshire Traveller Press. Stockbridge, MA 02162. Most British Travel Authority publications are available from this source, as well as publications of the Automobile Association (of Great Britain).

Book Passage. The Market Place, Tamal Vista Boulevard, Corte Madera, CA 94925. Offers a special collection of books and several small publications about Britain.

British Gifts. Box 26558, Los Angeles, CA 90026. Sponsors the sale of many British Tourist Authority (BTA) publications. Fills mail order only. Write for titles and prices.

British Information Services. 845 Third Avenue, New York, NY 10022. Does not handle tourism matters, but does supply factual data about the United Kingdom and the British Commonwealth.

British Market. 2366 Rice Boulevard, Houston, TX 77005.

British Publications, Incorporated. 11-03 46th Avenue, Long Island City, NY 11101.

British Tourist Authority (BTA). Apply at any of the following locations: 40 West 57th Street, New York, NY 10019; John Hancock Center, Suite 3320, 875 North Michigan Avenue, Chicago, IL 60611; 612 South Flower Street, Los Angeles, CA 90017; Plaza of the Americas, 750 North Tower, LB346, Dallas, TX 75201. Supplies many publications free; makes charges for others.

British Travel Bookshop. 40 West 57th Street, New York, NY 10019. Fills mail orders for British Tourist Authority publications.

Britrail Travel International. Contact the office most convenient for you: 630 Third Avenue, New York, NY 10017; 510 West Sixth Street, Los Angeles, CA 90014; 333 North Michigan Avenue, Chicago, IL 60601.

The Complete Traveller Bookstore. 199 Madison Avenue, New York, NY 10016. Described as "one of the most complete sales locations for travel books in the country," rivaling Forsyth's (see below).

Forsyth Travel Library. Box 2975. Shawnee Mission, KS 66201. Source for a large number of travel guides, maps, and travel information generally, including: American Express pocket guides, Baedeker guides, Fodor guides, Arthur Frommer guides (including *Dollarwise*), Michelin red and green guides, Berlitz pocket phrase books, rail travel guides, audio foreign language courses, the *Thomas Cook Continental Timetable, Airport Links,* Michelin road maps of Britain and British cities, and much more. Write for free catalog. Also arranges for purchase of Britrail passes.

Fowler Brothers Bookstore. 717 West Seventh Street, Los Angeles, CA 90017. Maintains a wide selection of British books and maps. Fills mail and phone orders.

ITN Bookshelf. 2120 28th Street, Sacramento, CA 95816. Fills mail orders for Britain-related publications.

Le Travel Store. 1050 Garnet Avenue, San Diego, CA 92109. Innovative and hard-to-find travel gear, books, maps, and other items of interest to travelers going abroad.

Merrimack Book Services. 99 Main Street, Salem, NH 03079. Trade distributors for BTA and other publications.

David Morgan. Box 70190, Seattle, WA 98107. Specializes in Welsh materials of a touristic or historical nature; will procure Welsh publications on demand.

Sandmeyer's Bookstore. 714 South Dearborn Street, Chicago, IL 60605. Good selection of travel materials.

Travel Books Unlimited. 4931 Cordell Avenue, Bethesda, MD 20814.

Traveller's Bookstore. 22 West 52nd Street, New York, NY 10019.

Travel Market. Golden Gateway Commons, 130 Pacific Avenue Mall, San Francisco, CA 94111. A travel bookstore where one can get the latest in travel books about Britain, as well as luggage, maps, language tapes, and other necessities.

Wayfarer Books. Box 1121, Davenport, IA 52805.

Wide World Books and Maps. 401 Northeast 45th Street, Seattle, WA 98105.

SOURCES OF BRITISH PUBLICATIONS AND INFORMATION IN BRITAIN

A similar list of sources of British publications and information is available from Britain itself. In addition to those that appear below, there are in most cities and sizeable towns of interest to tourists local information centers (identified with a prominent "i") from which publications and directive assistance may be obtained.

Organizations and Associations

Automobile Association (AA). Fanum House, Basingstoke,Hants RG21 2EA, England. Maintains a nationwide service, publications, and accommodations rating program for its subscribers.

English Tourist Board. 4 Grosvenor Gardens, London SW1W ODU. Primarily provides service to telephone inquiries. Maintains public information offices in Harrods' department store, with a good selection of publications, complimentary or for a small charge. Also makes bookings for tours and shows, and gives travel guidance and information.

Heart of England Tourist Board. Box 15, Worcester, WR1 2JT, England. Promotes tourist interest in the area of England which includes The Cotswolds, Shakespeare's Country, the Welsh Borderland, Staffordshire, and the West Midlands. Maintains a publications program of booklets and brochures on sightseeing and hotel/motel accommodations in this part of the country.

London Tourist Board. 26 Grosvenor Gardens, London SW1W ODU. Handles both written and telephoned requests for information for London and other parts of England. Also has auxiliary centers at Selfridges, Harrods, Heathrow Airport, and the Tower of London.

National Tourist Information Centre and Bookstore. Victoria Station Forecourt, London SW1. Offers a great variety of specific and general material about London and Great Britain as a whole, including walking tour books and tapes, street maps and road maps; posters, and booklets on such subjects as cycling, restaurants, stately homes and gardens, museums, tracing your ancestors, and others. The centre provides many other services to tourists: help in obtaining bed and breakfast and other hotel accommodations, sightseeing bookings, and much more.

Royal Automobile Club (RAC). Box 100, Landsdowne Road, Croydon, England. This organization is competitive with the Automobile Association (AA). It maintains publications, service, and accommodations rating programs for the benefit of its subscribers.

Scottish Tourist Board. 23 Ravelston Terrace, Edinburgh, EH4 3EU. Also: 19 Cockspur Street, London, SW1Y 5BL. Tourist materials and information on Scotland.

Wales Tourist Board. 3 Castle Street, Cardiff, CF1 2RE, Wales, or 2-3 Maddox Street, London W1. Tourist materials and information on Wales.

Magazines and Newsletters

British Travel News. British Tourist Authority. 239 Old Marylebone Road, London NW1 5QT. q. Britain's only tourist business magazine; directed toward related trades and industries: hotels and catering, transport and travel, car rental, entertainment, and other facets of the field.

In Britain. See entry in chapter 1 under "Magazines and Newsletters."

London Planner. British Tourist Authority. 239 Old Marylebone

Road, London NW1 5QT. mo., free. A guide listing events and sightseeing information such as: theater, music and dance, sports events, pageantry, shows and trade exhibitions, art galleries and museums, and tours and travel specialties.

This England. See entry in chapter 1 under "Magazines and Newsletters."

LONDON BOOKSHOPS

You will find it easy and worthwhile to add to your collection of books and pamphlets about Britain and other related subjects you are interested in after you reach London. The following list of bookshops is a good sample of those that are available to you for this purpose. Hunter Davies presents an especially concise and informative list of them in his *London at Its Best*.

Bookshops

BBC Bookshop. Broadcasting House, Portland Place, London W1A 1AA. Specializes in publications on a variety of subjects, which grew out of recent BBC television and radio productions.

Children's World. 229 Kensington High Street, London W8. A place to buy interesting children's books.

Dillon's University Bookshop. One Malet Street, London WC1. Books on a wide variety of subjects. It specializes (but not exclusively) in academic publications.

Foyle's. 119-125 Charing Cross Road, London, WC2. Said to be the world's largest bookstore. It is jam-packed with books—recent and not so recent. You may have trouble finding what you want, but the clerks are helpful.

Harrods' Bookshop. Brompton Road, London SW1. A well-organized collection of mostly recent books—including many on British travel—that are easy to find and to review. Conveniently located in a department store which you'll certainly be visiting for many other purposes as well.

HMSO Bookshop. 49 Holborn Street, London WC1. The British equivalent of our Government Printing Office known locally as Her Majesty's Stationery Office. Specializes in official British government publications; its collection of maps is especially good.

Travel Bookshop. 13 Blenheim Crescent, London, W11. Wide selection of travel books, both old and new.

Books

The Bookshops of London. Martha Redding Pease. Salem House Ltd./Merrimack Publishers Circle, distr. 1983. A revised and expanded edition of this work has great appeal for booklovers. Shops are arranged by district within the city, with addresses, types of books stocked, services, catalogs, and publication connections.

Bookshops of London. Dianna Stephenson. Bradt Enterprises. 1984. A revised edition of this basic guide to the booksellers of London; includes subject areas, locations, and specialty lines.

London at Its Best: The Essential Guide. Hunter Davies. Pan Books. 1984. Lists bookshops, addresses, and services; includes children's art, and other specialist bookshops. For a complete annotation see chapter 3 under "London Guidebooks."

TRAVEL TOUR AGENCIES

Following is a list of travel agencies selected because they plan and promote regular tours to the United Kingdom. Each will supply, free of charge upon request, illustrated and annotated folders or catalogs describing the nature and costs of such tours, and detailed information about them.

American Express	CIE Tours, International
American Express Plaza	590 Fifth Avenue
New York, NY 10004	New York, NY 10036
Barclay Travel, Limited	Thomas Cook Travel
261 Madison Avenue	380 Madison Avenue
New York, NY 10016	New York, NY 10017
Caravan, Incorporated	Esplanade Tours
401 North Michigan Avenue	38 Newberry Street
Chicago, IL 60611	Boston, MA 02116
Cartan	Fourways Travel
One Crossroads of Commerce	950 Third Avenue
Rolling Meadows, IL 60008	New York, NY 10022

Arthur Frommer Holidays, Inc.
770 Broadway
New York, NY 10003

Globus-Gateway
105-114 Gerrard Place
Forest Hills, NY 11375

Grand Circle Travel
555 Madison Avenue
New York, NY 10022

Great Britain Vacations
590 Fifth Avenue
New York, NY 10036

Heritage Travelers
41 East 42nd Street
New York, NY 10017

Insight International Tours
441 North Newport Boulevard
Newport Beach, CA 92663

Maupintour
Massachusetts Street
Lawrence, KS 66044

Olson Travel
(consult your local travel agent)

Passage Unlimited, Inc.
48 Union Street
Stamford, CT 06900

Saga International Holidays
120 Boylston Street
Boston, MA 02116

Siemer and Hand Travel
Two Embarcadero Center,
Suite 1655
San Francisco, CA 94111

Trafalgar Tours
30 Rockefeller Plaza
New York, NY 10020

Travel Corporation of America
Chicago, IL and
Newport Beach, CA
(consult your local travel agent)

Unitours
8 South Michigan Avenue
Chicago, IL 60603

Yugo Tours
350 Fifth Avenue
New York, NY 10018

SPECIALIZED TOURS

Numerous organizations, of which the following may be regarded as somewhat typical, confer with clients in the development of customized tours of various parts of Great Britain. Write or call for further information.

The Anglo-File. 5923 Corbin Avenue, Tarzana, CA 91356. A consultation-by-mail service for independent travelers to Britain. Among about twenty-five features offered are choices of car itineraries for one, two, or three weeks; an outline of what to see by train and coach; accommodation recommendations; budget London; descriptions of "hidden corners"; and travel tips. Information is concise and comes in a form which is easily carried. Prices and further details upon request.

Institute of Travel and Tourism. 53-54 Newman Street, London W1 4JJ. Seeks to advance cultural and educational studies through various travel-related activities.

A Taste of Britain. 2000 Center Street, Suite 1380, Berkeley, CA 94704; (415) 893-5639. Specializes in unique, leisurely tours to Britain with a limit of eighteen people per group; "English Gardens, Country Inns & Stately Homes" is the featured tour for the current year, led by Paul Coopersmith, landscape artist and author, and Christopher Baker, travel writer.

Travelways, Incorporated. 100 Spear Street, Lobby, San Francisco, CA 94104. Conducts specialty tours to English destinations, such as to James Herriot's area in the Yorkshire countryside. Cooperates with a British tour operator, Your Host.

Wilson and Lake. One Appian Way, Suite 704-8, South San Francisco, CA 94080. (415) 589-0352. Offers historical tours of England and Scotland to small groups with first class lodgings, food, and transportation. Each tour emphasizes a particular literary figure or group of writers (such as "In the Footsteps of the Brontës"). Individual extended stays can also be arranged.

COMPUTERIZED PERSONAL TRAVEL INFORMATION

Those who own personal computers are beginning to be able to retrieve basic travel information from "for fee" data bases such as: Bibliographic Retrieval Services (BRS), CompuServe, DIALOG, or the Source. There are several advantages to using them: (1) data are available night and day and on weekends as well, (2) information is generally more complete than that obtained from other sources, (3) facts are also more up-to-date, (4) facts are likely to be less biased than those obtained from other sources (from airlines, for example), and (5) the electronic system makes it easier to meet specific needs quickly.

Prices for these services vary, depending upon the length of time they are used and other factors. Soon to be added to some electronic data bases will be theater ticket reservation systems, currency exchange rate information, and sightseeing information.

Organizations and Associations

BRS Information Technologies. 1200 Route 7, Latham, NY 12110. (800) 227-5277. Maintains several data bases that include travel information. A new one, TOUR, scheduled to come on line in spring, 1986, features travel and tourism data generally, with considerable emphasis upon Britain and Commonwealth nations. Leading travel magazines are included in the system's materials. Fees range from $6 to $35/hour.

CompuServe. 5000 Arlington Centre Boulevard, P.O. Box 20212, Columbus, OH 43220. (800) 848-8199. Offers "TWA Travel Shopper" service as well as the Official Airline Guide listings. Data bank holds information of names, addresses, telephone numbers of hotels, worldwide; money exchange rates.

DIALOG Information Service. 3460 Hillview Avenue, Palo Alto, CA 94304. (800) 334-2564. Offers Official Airline Guide service, including the capability to make plane reservations, hotel reservations, worldwide; displays fares in U.S. dollars; art history, galleries, and museums; *Magazine Index.*

The Source. 1616 Anderson Road, McLean, VA 22102. (800) 336-3366. Offers numerous on-line data base systems that pertain to travel, including a travel service that schedules and permits the booking of airline tickets (from unbiased information) anywhere in the world. Also offers International Hotels guide and reservation service; rent-a-car service; weather information; and "Let's Go" travel tips service.

AIRLINES TO BRITAIN

The following airlines provide service between the United States and Britain. They will also send you free travel literature that may be useful in planning your trip. Many of these airlines have 800 numbers which are available from Directory Assistance.

AerLingus (Ireland)
122 East 42nd Street
New York, NY 10168

Air India
345 Park Avenue
New York, NY 10154

Air New Zealand
Suite 1020
9841 Airport Boulevard
Los Angeles, CA 90045

British Airways
245 Park Avenue
New York, NY 10167

British Caledonian Airways
10700 North Freeway
Suite 700
Houston, TX 77037

Delta Air Lines
Hartsfield International Airport
Atlanta, GA 30320

El Al (Israeli)
850 Third Avenue
New York, NY 10022

Icelandair
630 Fifth Avenue
New York, NY 10111

KLM
437 Madison Avenue
New York, NY 10022

Kuwait Airlines
430 Park Avenue
New York, NY 10019

Northwest Orient Airlines
Minneapolis/St. Paul International
   Airport
St. Paul, MN 55111

Pan American
Pan Am Building
New York, NY 10016

People Express
North Terminal
Newark International Airport
Newark, NJ 10158

Trans World Airlines
605 Third Avenue
New York, NY 10158

World Airways
Oakland International Airport
Main Terminal
Oakland, CA 94614

SHIPS TO BRITAIN

Although going to Britain by ship from the United States is still possible, comparatively few people do it these days because of the greater cost in time and money. Nevertheless, the Cunard's *Queen Elizabeth II* does make the transatlantic crossing from New York to Southampton approximately every two weeks from April through October. There are two classes of service (expensive and more expensive!) now known as "transatlantic" and "first" class. A call to the Cunard line 800 number from anywhere in the United States except Alaska and New York enables one to obtain price and availability information and/or make a booking.

Far less luxurious than the QE II is travel to Britain by freighter, which is still a possibility. This type of travel is not for people on fixed schedules: extra stops may be added, extra time may be taken, or other changes made. Information about such trips is provided in the references that follow.

Organizations and Associations

Air Marine Travel Service. 501 Madison Avenue, New York, NY
   10022.

Cunard Lines. 555 Fifth Avenue, New York, NY 10017. (800) 221-4770. Write for brochure on the QE-II sailings, costs, and accommodations.

Books and Magazines

Ford's Freighter Travel Guide and Waterways of the World. Ford's Travel Guides. Box 505, 22151 Clarendon Street, Woodland Hills, CA 91365. 2/yr. Information on steamship lines that operate ships having room for a few passengers. Provides names, addresses, and information about facilities, services, costs, and schedules.

Freighter Travel News. Freighter Travel Club of America, Salem, OR 97309. mo. A newsletter which publishes personal accounts from tourists sailing on freighters plus evaluations of the various lines.

Pearl's Freighter Tips. 175 Great Neck Road, Great Neck, NY 11021. Offers services and sells publications related to freighter travel all over the world.

Trip Log Quick Reference Guide. c/o Pearl's Freighter Tips. 175 Great Neck Road, Great Neck, NY 11021. Information about freighter trips abroad.

DISCOUNT TRAVEL

Practical travelers often take advantage of "deeper discount" fare prices. Companies that offer regular travel services may be reluctant to discuss this phenomenon, but it exists, nevertheless. The way it works is quite simple. Travel operators who have booked specific spaces (airline seats, hotel rooms, cruise space, or other) need to have them filled and sold—if not at full price, then at the best price the market affords. This sometimes means that, more or less at the last minute, the operator will "release" certain space to discount agents whose operations make it easy for them to get in touch with people who have paid the necessary small listing fee and are willing to "buy and go—in a hurry." They are aided in this effort through widespread use of repeating audio tape recordings (24 hours a day), and, if time permits, newsletters. Discounts often range from 15 percent to as high as 65 percent. Most frequent users of the service appear to be retirees and others free to leave on short notice and to stay for varying lengths of time. In such instances, the key to being a successful discount ticket user is: be flexible.

Organizations and Associations

Adventures on Call, Inc. Baltimore, MD. (301) 356-4080. Specializes in air charter tours with all accommodations; includes plans for London. Charges a fee.

Destinations 2001. 28-29 Southampton Street, Covent Garden, London WC2E 7JA. This company specializes in trips from London to all parts of the world; discount prices on airline tickets, tours, hotel, train, and boat fares as well. Write two or three months in advance or stop in when you get to London.

Discount Travel International. The Ives Building, Suite 205, 114 Forrest Avenue, Narberth, PA 19072. (800) 253-7824. Membership $45. Telephone-available (800 line) information and cut-rate bookings for trips almost anywhere in the world. Frequent availabilities to London and the British Isles.

Intercontinental Navigation. Box 49954, Los Angeles, CA 90049. Offers, in cooperation with British Airtours (charter division of British Airways), full service flights to London and return at reduced prices.

Moments Notice. 40 East 49th Street, New York, NY 10164. (800) 221-4737. A travel discount company offering reduced rates available from commercial tour operators and vacation travel providers. Members (a fee is charged) dial a special telephone number to discover what is available and for what dates. For further information and for reservations for any in which they are interested, they dial a second number and talk directly with the agent.

Vacations to Go. 1377 K Street N.W., Suite 864, Washington, D.C. 20005. (800) 624-7338. Operates branches in many cities throughout the United States. Charges a fee.

Spur-of-the-Moment Tours and Cruises, Inc. 4315 Overland Avenue, Culver City, CA 90230. (800) 343-1991. A discount travel club that gives more attention to low-priced tour reservations than others.

Stand-Buys, Ltd. 311 West Superior Street, Suite 414, Chicago, IL 60610. An annual fee-based organization that offers travel and travel-related accommodations at reduced prices on a strictly stand-by basis. Savings up to 65 and 75 percent recorded.

Members also receive other benefits (such as second night free in selected motels and hotels). Cruises, all-expense package tours, and round-trip charter flights also offered.

WEXAS (World Expeditionary Association) International Ltd. 45 Brompton Road, Knightsbridge, London SW3 1DE. Specializes in adventure vacations from London and in both regular and discount travel. Membership required.

Worldwide Discount Travel Club, Inc. 1674 Meridian Avenue, Miami Beach, FL 33139. (305) 534-2082. Travel opportunities, often at half normal prices, and sometimes on air fares alone. Destinations vary according to vacation season. Members are advised on availabilities by frequent mailings of *Travelog* (newsletter). Charges an annual fee.

Books

Free, or Nearly Free, London. London Transport. 1982. Organized on the basis of free, or nearly free, London sites which young people would be interested in visiting. Describes four days of sightseeing, numerous side trips, what to do on evenings out, and various sightseeing tours one might take.

Free Stuff for Travelers. Tom Grady, ed. Meadowbrook Books. 1984. Provides full data regarding travel-related items costing $1 or less.

How to Fly for Less. Travel Information Bureau. 1984. Covers 600 charter operators that use both scheduled and unscheduled domestic and international airlines, including some offering one-way service.

How to Travel Inexpensively. Kevin Kelly. Nomadic Books, nd. Includes evaluations of several different books, plus a number of personal suggestions drawn from travel experiences about how to save travel money—at home and abroad.

1001 Sources for Free Travel Information. Jens Jurgens, ed. Travel Information Bureau. Lists 1200 tourist information agencies— embassies, consulates, missions, state chambers of commerce, and other information sources on an international basis.

TRAVEL FOR DISABLED PERSONS

The British welcome to disabled travelers is a genuinely warm one. Many special arrangements and facilities are made for them. Those involved are advised to inform carriers, hotel personnel, and others of intended plans as far in advance as possible. There is usually no charge for the special services provided.

Organizations and Associations

Guide Dogs for the Blind Association. 9-11 Park Street, Windsor, Berkshire, England. Trains dogs for the blind and blind people in the use and care of these animals; also raises funds for this work.

Rehabilitation International. 1123 Broadway, New York, NY 10010. Concerned with restoring disabled persons to participate in the normal activities of life, including travel and transportation problems involved.

Rehabilitation World. 20 West 40th Street, New York, NY 10018. Gathers and disseminates information intended to assist disabled travelers to get around with minimum difficulties.

The Society for the Advancement of Travel for the Handicapped. Suite 1110, 26 Court Street, Brooklyn, NY 11242. Serves as an educational forum for the exchange of knowledge and information on how best to serve needs of handicapped travelers and to publish and distribute such information to those who have use for it.

Books

Access to the World. Louise Weiss. Facts on File. 1983. A complete travel information guide for handicapped persons. Lists transportation, specialized travel agents, and tour operators giving attention to the needs of handicapped persons, and numerous tips for better travel.

Frommer's Guide for the Disabled Traveler: United States, Canada and Europe. Frances Barish. Simon and Schuster. 1984. Recommends hotels and restaurants which can be reached by wheelchair; information on transportation, sightseeing, and entertainment.

London for the Disabled Visitor. London Tourist Broad. nd. pamphlet. Lists facilities and accommodations for disabled travelers. Available free from LTB.

A Travel Guide for the Disabled: Western Europe. Mary Meister Walzer. Van Nostrand Reinhold. 1982. A comprehensive guide to Europe for the disabled. Includes a number of pages (approximately twenty-five) on disabled person provisions in England, Scotland, and Wales. The book lists hotels, restaurants, entertainment, shops, sights, and other places that disabled travelers (e.g., persons in a wheelchair or with limited walking ability) may enjoy without encountering architectural barriers.

A PLACE TO STAY

No matter what your eventual plans for housing may be, most people recommend that you make advance arrangements for at least the first few nights after you arrive in Great Britain. Your travel agent will help you with this, but several calls (usually within the U.S., but sometimes to Great Britain itself) may have to be made. If you handle this matter yourself, you will be helped by using this list of 800-numbered hotel chains that maintain facilities in Britain:

Best Western	800-528-1234
Hilton	800-445-8667
Holiday Inn	800-HOL-IDAY
Hyatt	800-228-9000
Marriott	800-228-9290
Sheraton	800-228-3535
Trust House Forte	800-223-5672

Whether you handle the reservations yourself or have it done by your travel agent, you will speed things along by locating the numbers of two or three London hotels that sound promising. For this purpose use the hotel listings in one or more of the general or London guidebooks (Fodor's, Birnbaum's, *American Express Pocket Guide to England and Wales,* Baedekers, or other) included in chapter 3 or the specific London guidebook publications listed below. U.S. representatives of some of the more posh London hotels are often to be found in ads of such magazines as *Travel and Leisure* and the *New Yorker*.

Books

Hotels and Restaurants in Great Britain, Ireland, and Overseas. The Official Guide. British Hotels, Restaurants, and Caterers Association. ann. Lists over sixteen hundred hotels and restaurants with pictures, map references, prices, meals, opening dates and times, and other accommodations. "How to use this guide" section is in English, French, German, and Spanish.

London Hotels and Inexpensive Accommodation. London Tourist Broad/British Tourist Authority. 1986. An official guide to hotels, bed and breakfast units, guesthouses, group and youth accommodations, apartments, and camping sites in London. Includes prices and descriptions of facilities.

Michelin (Red Guide): Greater London: Hotels and Restaurants— Plan. Michelin Tyre Public, Limited, Company. 1984. An extract from the *Michelin (Red Guide): Great Britain and Ireland.* Lists and rates London hotels and restaurants; classified; includes further information on car dealers and automobile repair shops. Provides detailed maps of London boroughs.

SHOPPING IN BRITAIN

Despite the fluctuating value of the pound against the dollar, shopping in Great Britain remains an exciting and often economically rewarding adventure. Good values do exist, and good quality remains the hallmark of innumerable British products. The range of shops and goods in the larger cities, especially in London, is stupendous.

Information about shopping in Great Britain appears briefly in three of the general guidebooks mentioned earlier. In the *American Express Pocket Guide to England and Wales,* for example, two pages of useful information are provided; and Fodor's *Great Britain: 1986* and Birnbaum's *Great Britain and Ireland* provide similar treatments. See full descriptions of these books in chapter 3. Hunter Davies's *London at Its Best* has a better, very detailed section on shopping—specialty stores, antiques, and street markets. See full citation in chapter 3 under "London Guidebooks."

Books

A Guide to London's Best Shops. Automobile Association (AA)/ Merrimack Publishers Circle, distr. 1983. Lists a thousand of London's best shops with complete information on types of merchandise and locations. Also available through the BTA bookshops.

Harrods: The Store and the Legend. Tim Dale. Pan Books. 1981. A history of this famous store with illustrations, and floor-by-floor descriptions.

London Shopping Guide. British Tourist Authority. Penguin. nd. A guide for all shopping tastes and for active participants or armchair travelers.

London Street Markets. Kevin Perlmutter. Wildwood House. 1983. A complete guide to street markets arranged by areas of London, with a subject index.

London Street Markets. London Tourist Board. 1984. A list of some of London's better known, most heavily patronized street markets, with addresses and open hours.

The Royal Shopping Guide. Nina Grunfeld. Morrow. 1984. Sheds an interesting light on royal living; describes some 450 of the shops that hold a royal warrant; tells about places where Diana shops and where Prince William's clothes are made.

Shopping in London. British Tourist Authority. Distribution Services Corporation. nd. Describes London's most important shopping areas such as Regent Street, Piccadilly, King's Road, Carnaby Street, and others. Helpful discussion of British currency and clothing sizes, store hours, banking practices, customs affairs, and more of interest to the shopping visitor.

LEARNING TO LIVE WITH BRITISH ENGLISH

While we both speak a language called English, there are differences between the English language spoken by the British people and our own. We are, of course, quite familiar with some variations in spelling from reading English fiction as well as histories, biographies, reports of conferences, and the like. Thus we know that certain words ending in "or" in the U.S. have an extra "u" in them in Great Britain, to say nothing of "organise" for our "organize," "programme" for "program," and so forth. It sometimes takes a little detective work, however, and a few seconds of uncertainty to be sure of the meaning of "bonnet" as part of an automobile (the hood), or where tickets "in the stalls" would seat one in the theatre (the orchestra). The list of books that follows contains many items that will help you explore this subject further and to understand more fully how similar and yet how different are our two versions of the same basic language.

Books

American English; English American Phrase Book. Abson Books. 1984. A two-way glossary of a hundred or more words (English

and American; American and English) that are used on both
sides of the Atlantic, selected because of their potential to
confuse or to cause misinterpretations in ordinary conversation
or writing.

British/American Language Dictionary. Norman Moss. National
Textbook. 1984. Compares meanings of the same and different
words in use in Britain and the United States. Useful for
tourists, business people, and students of English the world
over.

Britishisms: A Dictionary of British English. Lawrence Holofeener.
Partners Press. 1984. The revised edition of this small dictionary of words and expressions used by the British is a good
guide to the language for first-time tourists to the country.

Cockney Dialect and Slang. Peter Wright. Batsford. 1981. This
authority on Cockney speech discusses the history and future
of the rhyming slang language, including ordinary slang, gram-
mar, and pronunciation.

*Cockney Past and Present: A Short History of the Dialect of
London.* Williams Matthews. Routledge and Kegan Paul/Gale
Research. 1970 (reprint of 1938 edition). Details history of
cockney from the sixteenth century to the present; includes
music hall cockney performers, mannerisms and familiar slang
terms, and a guide to pronunciation—much of which remains
the same today. Extensive bibliography of sources appended.

English English: A Descriptive Dictionary. Norman W. Schur. Verbatim Books. 1980. Explains in American English typically
British word usage, slang, and colloquialisms that add spice to
the basic English language.

Morris Dictionary of Word and Phrase Origin. William Morris and
Mary Morris. Harper and Row. 1977. Information about origins
and development of various words and phrases in the English
language.

SOME UNIQUE TRAVEL OPPORTUNITIES

The magazines and newsletters listed here offer subscribers sources
of information regarding many unique vacation opportunities in
various parts of the world, including but by no means limited to
Great Britain. Most of the information provided can be relied upon
as having been verified by publishers themselves or by subscribers'
own comments on subjects discussed.

Entree. Box 5148, Santa Barbara, CA 93108. 12/yr. Assesses hotels, restaurants, shops, and tours. Reviews are based on the editors' personal experiences and visits.

The Hideaway Report. Harper Associates, Inc. Box 300, Fairfax Station, VA 22039. 12/yr. Self-described as "a connoisseur's guide to peaceful and unspoiled places." Assessments and descriptions of resorts, hotels, and other lodging places in unusual, often remote, locations.

International Living. 824 East Baltimore Street, Baltimore, MD 21202. 12/yr. Directed towards individuals who wish to travel or live in a foreign environment. Information on tours of particular value, the status of foreign currencies, houses and estates for sale in countries worldwide; how to get around in specific foreign cities, vacations abroad, and more.

International Travel News. Martin Publications Incorporated. 2120 28th Street, Sacramento, CA 95818. 12/yr. Tabloid size. Contains many first-person reports by individuals who have actually visited (recently) the places they describe and evaluate. Also includes staff-written articles, surveys, and descriptions of unusual travel opportunities.

Passport. Enterprise Publications. 20 North Wacker Drive, Chicago, IL 60606. 12/yr. Directed toward sophisticated travelers for whom expense is no particular obstacle. Accompanied each month by an "extra"—often a short report of special travel opportunities, such as one on 132 unusual European museums.

The Pleasure Traveler. American Travel Press. 3690 North Peachtree Road, Chamblee, GA 30341. 12/yr. Information on unusual, often very economical, travel bargains worldwide. Sometimes distributed free through travel agents.

Very Special Places. Box 3885, New York, NY 10185. Offers "independent, confidential reports on inns, resorts, hotels, and hideaways of exceptional character."

Voyager International. Argonaut Enterprises, Inc., Box 2777, Westport, CT 06880. 12/yr. New worldwide travel magazine sent to subscribers interested in out-of-the-way places and unusual travel experiences. Detailed descriptions of travel and tours.

3

Guides to Great Britain

In this chapter we bring together information about several different kinds of guidebooks, as well as maps, that are of prime concern to anyone planning to travel to Britain. To make the listings more useful and accessible we have divided them into the following categories: (1) general guides—those that deal with all or most of Britain, (2) special kinds of guides—hotel guides, trip guides, county-by-county guides, and others that also deal with all or most of the country, (3) London guides of several different types, (4) England guides, Scotland guides, and Wales guides that deal only with those separate areas, and (5) a collection of maps of Britain.

GENERAL GUIDEBOOKS

The books described here are the best we have found that deal generally with England, Scotland, and, often, Wales as well. We believe that anyone who intends to make an extensive trip around Britain should choose one or more of these titles to study carefully in advance of the trip and during plan making, and to take with them to refer to for day-to-day sightseeing and accommodations questions. All of the books that are listed should be generally available in the United States so that they can be used before you go.

Baedeker's Great Britain. Baedeker. (Baedeker's Travel Series.) Prentice-Hall, 1984. One of the traditional Baedeker guides to

European locations (the series has been published for 150 years), *Baedeker's Great Britain* is produced from familiar, reliable, comprehensive and up-to-date information from "detailed, first-hand knowledge of the country concerned," which tells you where to go, how to get there, and what to see. It is well illustrated with full-color pictures, numerous maps, and street plans specially drawn for the book. A gazetteer is included, and the book offers principal features of architectural, artistic, and historical interest for every name that appears in it. The main scenic and sightseeing attractions are identified and rated as to value and importance based on the number of asterisks accorded. A "Practical Information" section at the back of the book tells where to go to engage in a variety of leisure activities, and gives a number of useful addresses.

Britain at Its Best. Robert S. Kane. Passport Books. 1986. Arranged by sections of the country with separate London, Wales, and Scotland descriptions; presents the author's choices in best hotels, restaurants, shops, and sights. A mini A-Z introduction to everything you need to know before you go.

Dollarwise Guide to England and Scotland: 1986-1987. Darwin Porter. Frommer-Pasmantier. 1986. A two-part guide to finding the best food, overnight accommodations, sightseeing, and diversions in England and Scotland. There is included a chapter on London restaurants, pubs, and wine bars, and a "what to see and do in London" treatment. Major areas of England that are included in the text are Windsor, Oxford, and the Home Counties; Kent, Surrey, and Sussex; Hampshire and Dorset; Devon and Cornwall; Wiltshire, Somerset, and Avon; The Cotswolds; Stratford and the Heart of England; Cambridge and East Anglia; East Midlands; Cheshire, Liverpool, and the Lakes; and Yorkshire and Northumbria. Treatment of Scotland covers: Southern Scotland; Edinburgh and Central Scotland; Northeast Scotland; and Highlands and the Islands.

England and Scotland on $25 a Day: 1985-1986. Darwin Porter. Frommer-Pasmantier. 1985. Provides listed ratings of economical but good hotels, restaurants, and sightseeing locations, organized by districts in England and Scotland in accordance with the plan used in Frommer's *Dollarwise Guide to England and Scotland*.

Fisher Annotated Travel Guide—Britain: 1985. Edward Antrobus. Fisher Travel Guides. 1985. Planning the trip; getting around

London in one, two, three or more days; London hotel ratings, trips out of London to Stratford Country, West Country, North of England, Scotland, Wales, Channel Islands. A special section covers "Inside Today's Britain," "The Cultural Scene," and "British Food and Drink." Employs a one to five asterisk rating for hotels, restaurants and sightseeing attractions.

Fodor's Budget Britain: 1986. Fodor's Travel Guides. David McKay. 1986. Eugene Fodor has been publishing his travel guides since 1936, and they now number 100. Reportedly, their accurate and true reflection of the local scene results from the fact that some 300 persons provide information for the Fodor organization about the places where they live and write. Most of the Fodor guides, including this one, are updated every year and completely revised every four years. After a first section which answers practical questions about planning a trip to Britain, getting there and getting around, a second section introduces "The British Scene," and includes a British native's perspective on the kind of place Britain is, a minihistory, a review of historic houses, its performing arts, and its food and drink. The third section, "Exploring Britain," is more predictably a travel book, with maps, principal sightseeing attractions, and practical information. London is fully covered with names, addresses, and relative costs for hotels and restaurants. Presentation of travel information for other parts of Britain, while considerably less detailed than that for London, is useful and interesting. The areas for which materials are included are: Southeast (Kent, Sussex, Surrey); South (Hampshire, Isle of Wight, Dorset, Wiltshire); Southwest (Somerset, Devon, Cornwall, the Isles of Scilly); Channel Islands; Cotswolds and the Thames (Oxfordshire, Berkshire, East Anglia, Essex, Suffolk, Cambridgeshire); Herts, Bucks, and Beds (Hertfordshire, Buckinghamshire, Bedfordshire); Midlands (Northhamptonshire, Warwickshire, West Midlands, Hereford and Worcester, Shropshire, Staffordshire, Leicestershire); North Midlands (Nottinghamshire, Derbyshire, Cheshire); The Industrial Centers (Merseyside, West Yorkshire, South Yorkshire, Humberside); Northeast (Northumbria, Cleveland and Tyne and Wear, Durham County, Northumberland); Northwest (Cumbria, Lancashire, Isle of Man); Wales; and Scotland. The guide's index is divided in two parts: topical and geographical.

Great Britain and Ireland: Nineteen Eighty-Six. Stephen Birnbaum.

Houghton Mifflin Company. 1985. A combination general travel guide to Britain and the Irish Republic that is "different from the rest." It is a treatment in depth for those who want a really meaty and satisfying encounter with Britain. It deals broadly with the usual traveler interests, rather than laying out information in encyclopedic fashion. The critical reader will sometimes find it difficult to locate specific information, but even so, Birnbaum's is a commendable, innovative approach to the whole picture of what Britain's special attractions are and how to savor them. The "Getting Ready to Go" section is characterized as a "mini-encyclopedia of practical travel facts" which is "a sort of know-it-all companion that provides all the precise information you need to go about creating a trip" and tells you what things are apt to cost and how to avoid problems.

The section called "Perspectives" serves as background, discussing in a somewhat jaunty and understandable manner the people of Britain, their past and present, their architecture, literature, music and dance, and food and drink. A section on "The Cities" reports on fourteen cities in the U.K. (plus seven in the Irish Republic) and is designed to be used on the spot in Bath, Belfast, Brighton, Bristol, Cambridge, Canterbury, Cardiff, Chester, Edinburgh, Glasgow, London, Oxford, Stratford, and York. These "short-stay" guides are immensely valuable. Another section reports "Diversions," an interesting roundup of places to enjoy and ways to enjoy them, being "a wide collection of physical and cerebral activities."

The final segment of Birnbaum's book is his collection of nineteen itineraries grouped under the heading "Directions." This is the only section that is organized geographically, with a plan of touring highlights that will spare the tourist "exhaustion." It includes a cost and quality guide to food and accommodations, and activities in addition to sightseeing in which to engage. The author's advice is to "pick and choose" needed information from the book's various sections, using them as building blocks to put together the best possible personalized trip. The details about the Republic of Ireland do not particularly complicate the book's use by persons interested chiefly in Great Britain; in most cases, intermixed data can be sorted out quite easily.

Let's Go: Britain and Ireland 1986. Harvard Student Agencies, Inc. St. Martin's Press. 1986. A definitive budget guide to Britain and Ireland with descriptions and evaluations of good but relatively inexpensive accommodations and restaurants of special interest to students. Comprehensive; covers all areas of major interest in an array of towns and villages as well as cities. This publication series has been in existence for more than twenty years. Also covers Scotland and Wales.

Michelin Red Guide to Great Britain and Ireland. Michelin Tyre Public Company, Ltd. ann. Multi-lingual (English, French, Italian, German) guide to hotels, restaurants, and road information in Britain and Ireland; provides fully coded ratings in understandable, space-saving manner.

Nagel's Encyclopedic Guide to Great Britain. Nagel Encyclopedia Guides Series. Hippocrene Books. 1983. Offers highly detailed, mile-by-mile British itineraries, with special attention to sightseeing, hotel accommodations, and restaurant facilities. Infrequently updated; contains no prices.

SPECIAL KINDS OF GUIDES

In this section we review briefly the contents and style of several different kinds of specialized guidebooks that deal with the particular interests of those who plan to visit Great Britain. Among these titles are those that deal with hotel, castle, bed-and-breakfast, and restaurant accommodations; places to go for a variety of kinds of holidays—in the active as well as the more passive categories—and much more.

Books

Activity and Hobby Holidays. English Tourist Board. 1984. Advertisements and general information regarding hundreds of opportunities to spend a few days in fresh surroundings, on holiday, exploring different parts of Britain. Activities in which one may engage (at special centers, colleges and universities, hotels, or guest houses) include courses in sports (archery, cricket, etc.); programs of special interest to children (arts and crafts, pony-trekking, etc.); and special interest (amateur radio, bridge, driving, and motor racing).

Adventure Holidays: Britain and Abroad. David Stephens, ed. Vacation-Work. 1985. Provides brief descriptions of several hundred outings (most in Britain, many in the rest of Europe) by types of activities (surfing, canoeing, etc.).

Britain. Rand McNally. 1982. What one needs to know for an enjoyable trip to Britain: places of interest, transportation, history, art and architecture, shopping, food and drink, sports, entertainment, and more.

Britain: The Landscape Below. Philip Clucas. Colour Library International/British Gifts, distr. 1984. Lavishly illustrated; views of Britain from the air, as seen from a light aircraft. Includes maps of areas covered as well as a complete text related to the pictures. Printed in large format (11 × 12³/₄ inches).

Egon Ronay's Lucas Guide: 1986. Egon Ronay Organization. St. Martin's. 1985. Lists hotels, restaurants, and inns of Britain and Ireland; includes a discussion and listing of economy evening meals and economy hotels in London and bargain weekends in the British Isles.

English, Welsh, and Scottish Country Inns and Castle Hotels. 2d ed., rev. Karen Brown and June Brown. Travel Press. 1985. Describes and pictures some hundred hotels, inns; outlines details of ten interesting itineraries connected with them.

Historic Country House Hotels in Great Britain and Ireland. Sigourney Welles, ed. U.K.H.M. Publishers. 1985. Evaluative and descriptive data regarding hotels and other overnight accommodations; rates, history of the area in which facilities are located. Another version of this same title but distributed in the United States by East Woods is *Historic Country House Hotels, the Finest Forty-Five.*

Hotels and Restaurants in Britain. Automobile Association (AA). British Tourist Authority. 1986. A guide to over five thousand eating and lodging establishments in Britain, including London, which are inspected and approved by the AA; prices and facilities given along with a star rating of one to five.

The New Shell Guide to Britain: A County by County Guide. George Speaight, ed. Salem House/Merrimack Publishers Circle, distr. 1985. A gazetteer of the most interesting and beautiful places to visit in each British county; keyed to full color maps.

Nicholson's Guide to England and Wales. Robert Nicholson. Robert Nicholson Publications. 1986. Covers all the major areas of the two countries; gives attention, among other things, to archaeology, bird-watching, zoos, and museums. Others of interest in this series are *Historic Britain* and *Guide to English Churches.*

1985: Commended Country Hotels, Guest Houses and Restaurants. British Tourist Authority. 1984. A listing of 375 "commended" (by the British Tourist Authority) hotels, guest houses, and restaurants. Each has been anonymously inspected and judged worthy of displaying the distinctive silver, red, and blue plaque awarded for this honor. Criteria include good food, attentive, courteous service, atmosphere, comfort, cleanliness, and certain extra touches (flowers in the room, toiletries in the bathroom, etc.). Some buildings are centuries old, others recently built. They vary considerably in size and in prices charged, but each must represent a good value for the money. Most units listed will be found to have fifty or fewer rooms only. Establishments listed have made formal application for such consideration and have met BTA requirements for the rating.

1984 Heritage Britain: Where to Visit, Where to Stay. Farm Holiday Guides. 1984. Provides pictures, names, addresses, telephone numbers of board and room accommodations for visitors at National Trust Properties throughout Great Britain (England, Wales, and Scotland). Includes, in addition, advertisements of some listed establishments. Accommodations are alphabetical, by shire. Similar publications are available for ensuing years.

Short Breaks in Britain: Let's Go. British Tourist Authority. 1984. A year-round hotel (with meals) guide to all of Britain, featuring inexpensive two-day stays.

Staying Off the Beaten Track. Elizabeth Gundrey. Automobile Association (AA)/Merrimack Publishers Circle, distr. 1986. The author has stayed at every one of the 100 places chosen for presentation in this book: inns, farmhouses, small hotels, and country hotels. Details about each, including illustrations.

Traveller's Britain: Data File for People on the Move. M. J. Cottingham, ed. George Thorn/Hippocrene Books. 1985. A handbook for travelers in the British Isles; advice on transportation, accommodations, and eating establishments.

Treasures of Britain: A Traveller's Guide to the Riches of Britain and Ireland. Drive Publications/W. W. Norton, distr. 1981. A gazetteer of treasures from Roman times to the twentieth century; alphabetically arranged by town, village, place, or site. Each treasure is keyed to maps and related to architects, sculptors, men of letters, and other famous people. Also indexed by collections—with a glossary of architectural terms illustrated with sketches. (Originally published by the Automobile Association (AA).)

Audiovisual Materials

Bath: England's Roman Spa. International Video Network. 1986.
video cassette, 29 mins. Narrated by Sir Michael Holdern.
Bath's Assembly Rooms, Roman remains, Royal Crescent,
Pultnay Bridge, afternoon teas (in the Pump Room), and more
sights of the city included.

LONDON GUIDES

The excitement and variety of the London scene are reflected in the
myriad of available "guidebook" publications that deal with the
many facets of that city. Among those we have included here are
titles that deal with largely photographic presentations of its pageantry and color, London from the air, regular guidebooks such as
the *American Express Pocket Guide to London,* directories of
various types, especially those dealing with restaurants and hotels,
historical guides to the city, and tourist information generally.

Books

Above London. Robert Cameron and Alistair Cooke, eds. Cameron
& Co. 1980. A "coffee table" sized book (14 × 11 inches); a
color album of the British capital from the air. Includes 150
pictures with detailed captions.
Access in London. Gordon Couch and William Forrester. Automobile Association (AA)/Merrimack Publishers Circle, distr. Robert Nicholson Publications. 1984. General information needed
to get around in Britain. Identifies accommodations, historic
buildings; areas of special interest; churches; theatres; arts
complexes; museums and galleries; specialty shops; sports and
special events.
The American Express Pocket Guide to London. Michael Jackson.
Simon and Schuster. 1986. This highly portable book contains
as much or more information about London as many others
twice its size. Its claim to provide "all the information you need
to get the most out of your visit" is no exaggeration. In addition
to the "before you leave home" data everyone needs, it features a time-chart placing London in the mainstream of history,
and special features on architecture, literature, and the royal
family and its role in London and Britain. A "Calendar of

Events" and a "When and Where to Go" direct one to London-based activities and events. The useful "Walks in London" section offers clear maps and verbal commentaries. More than a hundred "Sights and Places of Interest" are given and fully and clearly annotated. These annotations and the lists themselves are of great help to the London tourist, as is the complete and classified list of good restaurants that follows, with coded information about food offerings and features of each. Cafés and tearooms are mentioned on one page; pubs occupy four pages. Entertainment—headed "Nightlife"—is classified under headings such as ballet and opera, bars, casinos, cinemas, concerts, folk, rock and jazz, music, nightclubs, and theatres. A section on shopping includes specifics about auctions and antique houses, and a unique feature gives thumbnail sketches of famous people who had close associations with London (Sir Francis Bacon, for example). Sports activities, "London for Children," and a list of excursions one may take out of London (a day's trip or so) round out the book. There is a two-part index: a general one and a gazetteer of street names. Both are excellent and highly useful.

A-Z Visitors' London Atlas and Guide. British Tourist Authority. 1985. A pocket guide with maps, street index, and location of major sightseeing destinations.

Barron's London in Your Pocket. Barron's Educational Series. 1982. A directory of restaurants, shops, theaters, sights, pubs, parks, hotels, movies, children's activities, and art galleries, plus much more. Handy pocket size.

Baedeker's City Guide: London. Baedeker. Baedeker's Travelers Series. Prentice-Hall, Inc. 1985. A pocket-sized, illustrated guide to sightseeing, hotels, shopping, and major places to visit; a detailed pull-out map included.

Berlitz Travel Guide: London. Berlitz, eds. Macmillan Ltd. 1985. History of London, eating out in London, London for children, London excursions, budgeting, and more.

The Best of London. Henry Gault and Christian Millau. Crown. 1984. Restaurant guide; guide to shopping; hotels; diversions; sights.

The Book of London. Michael Cady, ed. Automobile Association (AA)/British Tourist Authority. 1983. A large-format paperback guide to all aspects of London; fully illustrated and divided into sections on many subjects including pageantry, history, culture, churches, shops, parks, pubs, and other sights. Maps appended.

Companion Guide to London. David Piper. Prentice-Hall. 1983. Includes sightseeing information along with anecdotes about people and places; a good addition for the leisurely traveler.

Country London. John Talbot White. Routledge and Kegan Paul. 1984. An illustrated guide to the areas surrounding London, complete with detailed maps.

A Day Out of London, 1985. English Tourist Board. 1984. Pictures (full color) and annotations of more than 250 places within reach of a day's travel outside of London. How to get there by rail, bus, or auto.

Everybody's Historic London: A History and Guide. Jonathan Kiek. Salem House/Merrimack Publishers Circle, distr. 1985. A guide "to the rich tapestry of the history of London." More than a hundred photos, plans, and maps; twenty "self-serve" day tours on Roman, Tudor, Stuart, and other trails.

Fodor's Budget London. Fodor's Travel Guides. David McKay. 1986. Organized by various sections: planning your trip, practical information, street maps, hotels, restaurants; gives "best values" in accommodations for each section. Also lists children's activities, sports, transportation, and tours. Sightseeing highlights are presented for Trafalgar Square, Covent Garden, Westminster, South Bank, St. James's, Buckingham Palace, Soho, Oxford Street, Hyde Park, Chelsea, Knightsbridge, Kensington, The City, Tower of London, Greenwich, Hampton Court, and Windsor.

Fodor's Fun in London. Fodor's Travel Guides. David McKay. 1986. "A highly selective, quick and easy guide to the sights, activities, hotels, restaurants, and night life of historic and exciting London."

Fodor's London: 1986. Fodor's Travel Guides. David McKay. 1986. Introduces London; describes some of its better and more economical hotels, restaurants. Gives sightseeing and recreational highlights of central London and details of a few worthwhile one-day trips that may be taken just outside London.

Frommer's Guide to London. Darwin Porter. Simon and Schuster. ann. Revised each year; gives accurate information on sights, accommodations, and tourist activities.

In Search of London. H. V. Morton. Dodd, Mead. 1951. A view of London lovingly told from a personal point of view; includes

anecdotes and stories of famous people in London at the time.
A good "read" for the armchair traveler.

London. Stuart Rossiter, ed. Blue Guides Series/W. W. Norton.
1984. A comprehensive traveler's guide to London, with detailed atlas, town plans, and descriptive text.

London at Its Best. Hunter Davies. Pan Books. 1984. This is a book
based largely on the author's own opinions (clearly identified as
such) about many London sights and attractions to which he
believes visitors should either be guided, or dissuaded from
wasting time on. His rating system uses asterisks and other
symbols to mean "not to be missed," "highly recommended,"
or merely "interesting." Some listings have been included "for
reference" and to offer something for areas which might otherwise have nothing. The drawbacks of places to avoid are plainly
stated. The "Planning" chapter is filled with all sorts of useful
general information: how to use the phones, bank hours, post
offices hours and practices, pub licensing hours and laws,
getting help and advice (even with such matters as contracep-
tion), and what to do if you have an accident. A briefing on
London commences with a section on its history and continues
with London today—its government, postal zones, and thumbnail sketches of various areas of the city (such as Westminster,
Covent Garden, etc.).

Davies turns attention to transportation facilities: Green Line
Coach, the locations and features of the eight mainline railway
stations, driving in London, taxis, bicycles and motorcycles, as
well as walking. A chapter on "Sleeping, Eating and Drinking"
describes recommended hotels, restaurants, and pubs. There is
an interesting classification for the to-be-avoided boring ones!
The "top seven" traditional sights of London—the ones which
must be seen are identified with comments supporting his
opinion. The many forms of entertainment offered by the city
are examined—again with full information given (this complete-
ness of sources is one of the strengths of the book) and the
author's opinions: theater, ballet, opera, music (all kinds from
classical to rock), cinema, poetry, discos, dancing, nightclubs,
gambling, sex, strip clubs, gay London, and sports. As with
each section, full address and other information is provided. An
"Exploring" chapter gives an overview of London parks, gardens, the zoo, Thames-side, foreign areas of the city, open air
fairs, and some areas just outside the city. Another chapter

deals with cultural institutions: major and specialist museums, art galleries, homes that may be visited, libraries, churches, and statues. The main shops and shopping areas are laid out, and a final chapter gets at a number of "other things" to do, see, and savor: children's London, student London, free London, and more. A very good and useful nineteen-page index concludes the book.

The London Encyclopaedia. Ben Weinreb and Christopher Hibbert, eds. Adler & Adler. 1983. Hailed as "the most comprehensive book on London ever published." Provides general coverage of the city, with an index of people. More than five thousand entries, alphabetized, cross-referenced; mentions more than ten thousand individuals. Scholarly, yet highly readable.

London: The Biography of a City. Christopher Hibbert. Penguin. 1983. A history, social chronicle, and guidebook of London, its sights, treasures, and edifices from Roman times to 1968. Illustrated with photos, indexed, and a bibliography of source books appended.

London: 2000 Years of a City and Its People. Felix Barker and Peter Jackson. Papermac. 1983. London "in all its variety." A chronological story of its development.

Michelin Green Guide: London. Michelin Tyre Public Company, Ltd. 1983. One of the "green" tourist guides so highly respected in the world of travel. Michelin also produces the "red" guides which list and rate hotels and restaurants. Its convenient dimensions ($4^{3}/_{4} \times 10^{1}/_{4}$ inches) make it easy to carry and to thumb through; its attractive layout and use of clear, colorful maps and charts make it easy to use. An asterisk key is used to rate sightseeing attractions; the index (largely personal names and geographic locations) is helpfully detailed. The book opens to several pages of maps which show the locations of significant sights and important buildings. Practical information about transportation and other things is given. The development of London is traced, and a section gives answers to those who are curious about water supplies, lighting, and other life supports for the huge city. An interesting section on "Capital Citizens and Their Pursuits" tells something of the lives and work in London of painters, musicians, furniture designers, and other creators. A major part of the book is devoted, of course, to London's sights, listed alphabetically, each keyed to the maps mentioned above. Details of open hours and admission fees (if any) are given, as well as full information about the attraction (highlights of a museum, for example). "Ideas for an Excursion" outside of London are given, and a very complete index lists churches, squares, almshouses, pubs, the names mentioned in the text, place, street and building names, historical events, and lots of other terms.

Michelin Red Guide to London. Michelin Tyre Public Company, Ltd. ann. An authoritative guide to restaurants with Michelin's famous star rating system.

New Penguin Guide to London. F. R. Banks. Penguin. 1984. Winner of the London Tourist Board "guidebook of the year" award. Offers useful information on hotels, restaurants, museums, parks, transportation facilities, shopping, entertainment, galleries, sports, and historical sights of London.

Nicholson's Pocket Guides to London. Robert Nicholson. Automobile Association (AA)/Merrimack Publishers Circle, distr. various dates. These concise guides to many facets of visitor's London contain the latest practical information, prices, services, attractions, and more. Titles include: *Nicholson's Complete London Guide, Nicholson's Visitor's London, Nicholson's Student London, Nicholson's London Restaurant Guide, Nicholson's London Night Life,* and *London Arts Guide.* Each can be ordered from the British Travel Bookshop.

1985: This Is Your London. British Tourist Authority. 1984. A pocket guide to London, well-illustrated with maps, the Underground plan, bus routes; includes a street index; offers basic information on shopping, restaurants, entertainment, and important sightseeing locations.

Quick Guide to London. British Tourist Authority. 1983. Organized by London districts; where to find markets, museums, restaurants, sightseeing locations, scenic attractions, and places of entertainment.

Rothman's Concise Guide to London. George Hammond, ed. Rothman's Publications England/State Mutual Books, distr. 1981. A comprehensive guide, in color, to much that London has to offer. Includes information on accommodations, restaurants, sights, and more. Also available from BTA.

Traditional London. London Tourist Board. 1984. pamphlet. An alphabetically arranged, annotated description of many traditional ceremonies and customs of London. Cites dates ("first Tuesday in November," etc.) or indicates telephone numbers at which to inquire.

Audiovisual Materials

Berlitz Travel Kits: London. Macmillan Co., distr. 1985. cassette (60 mins.) Includes a *Berlitz Travel Guide,* the audio cassette with travel tips and an itinerary and planning map in one small package.

The Charm of London. International Video Network. 1986. video cassette, 26 mins. Narrated by Susannah York and Ron Berglas. A two-day tour of London: River Thames, Parliament, Tower of London, Changing of the Guard, Piccadilly, Covent Garden, Royal Opera House, and more.

London. Stephen Birnbaum. Waldentapes. 1985. two cassette tapes (70 mins. each). These audio tapes produced by Warner Audio give travel tips on hotels, restaurants, shopping, museums, nightlife; includes a city map as well.

ENGLAND GUIDES

For those who intend to spend most of their visit to Britain in England, selection of one or more of the books in the following list will be helpful. Of them, the *American Express Pocket Guide to England and Wales* offers the most comprehensive treatment of the subject.

Books

The American Express Pocket Guide to England and Wales. John Tomes and Michael Jackson. Simon and Schuster. 1985. One of this company's new series of twelve books offering an easy-to-use blend of essential travel information. Contains "before you go" data, supplemented by many useful addresses in easy-to-find form; also offers a special page of "emergency information" travelers are likely to need. Its historical time chart traces English and Welsh history in an understandable manner. Other special features covered: architecture, painting, literature, an events calendar, when and where to go data, a series of plans for short English and Welsh tours, and a detailed section on

"Accommodations, Food, and Drink" in England and Wales arranged, by name of city or town, on an A to Z basis. This latter section employs full use of symbols and informative writeups about these places—where to stay, shop, have fun, eat, what to see in each. City plan maps, with full details, are plentiful. The City of London features and offerings are particularly well covered. A special section, "England and Wales for Children," and another on "Excursions" (such as to the Islands of Guernsey or Jersey) round out the text. There is a combination (all-in-one) index and place name gazetteer that is quite complete with respect to the book's content. Easy-to-read colored maps of England and Wales are included in a special folio at the end of the book.

Companion Guide to the Shakespeare Country. Jonathan Keates. Prentice-Hall. 1983. A guide to the key sights to explore in this area plus stories of the literary inhabitants of long ago.

Country House Treasures. Arthur Foss. National Trust/Weidenfeld and Nicolson, Ltd. 1981. A guide to the artistic and historic contents of more than three hundred houses in Britain—all open to the public at least twenty days per year.

England. Stuart Rossiter, ed. Blue Guide Series. W. W. Norton. 1984. Very detailed guide to what is worth seeing and doing in England; arranged by areas; includes atlases, town plans, and practical information. Provides a mass of information on England's history, culture, and scenic resources, its historic buildings and sites, galleries and museums, the countryside, towns, villages, and cities.

Golden Hart Guides. British Travel Bookshop, distr. 1984–. A series of titles, fully illustrated, covering customs, ceremonies, festivals, historic buildings, inns, crafts, walking tours, and much more. Titles include: *London; Oxford—City and Countryside, Bath—City and Countryside, Devon, Cornwall, Traditional Britain, Historic English Inns, British Crafts, Stratford/Cotswolds, Cambridge, Ely & the Fens, The Lake District,* and *Stately Homes/Gardens.*

Michelin Green Guide: England, The West Country. Michelin Tyre Public Company, Ltd. 1984. Sightseeing, accommodations in England's West Country, including Avon, Bath, Bristol, Cornwall, Penzance, Devon, Dorset, and Somerset.

The New Shell Guide to England. John Hadfield, ed. Michael Joseph. 1981. Essays on English farming, rivers, woodlands, moorlands, gardens; includes details of what to see in each region of the country.

Shell Book of English Villages. British Travel Bookshop, distr. 1983. Describes more than a thousand English villages, with ratings, 120 black and white photos, 16 color photos, introductory chapters covering social, historical, and architectural character-istic of the villages discussed.

Villages of England. Brian Bailey. English Tourist Board. 1984. Describes in detail many picturesque villages and includes maps and diagrams showing location information; illustrated with over ninety photos in color and a hundred in black and white.

Scotland Guides

The guidebooks listed below provide more information about Scot-land than do any of the books that cover the entire United Kingdom or some combination of countries within it. *Fodor's Scotland* and *Blue Guides to Scotland* are especially highly regarded as informa-tion sources for the area.

Books

Fodor's Scotland 1986. Fodor's Travel Guides. David McKay. 1986. Splendid guide to the Scottish scene: history, arts, literature, clans and tartans, food and drink, sports and exploring.

Scotland 1986. Scottish Tourist Board/British Tourist Authority. David McKay. 1986. Includes a brief history, how the clans were born, shopping, holidays to spend in Scotland, getting around, staying and eating in Scotland, and more.

Scotland. John Tomes. Blue Guide Series. W. W. Norton. 1984. Good background information; discusses Scottish organiza-tions, important scenic areas and historic sites.

Scotland: The Light and the Land. Colin Baxter, photography. Salem House/Merrimack Publishers Circle, distr. 1985. Con-tains 88 full-color photographs portraying the natural beauties of Scotland.

Wales Guides

Although less numerous than those on England, several good guides to Wales are available. The Wales Tourist Board will supply addi-tional materials upon request.

Books

The American Express Pocket Guide to England and Wales. John
Tomes and Michael Jackson. Simon and Schuster. 1985. In-
cludes much useful information and suggestions for touring
Wales as well as England. See entry for this book under
"England Guides," in this chapter.

Going Places: A Motor Touring Guide to Wales. Wales Tourist
Board/British Gifts, distr. 1985. Describes twenty-three tours
which will take one through the best of Wales. Each tour is
illustrated and includes one or more maps; each region's historic background is described.

A Tourist Guide to North Wales. Wales Tourist Board/British Tourist
Authority. 1985. A guide to sights in this region; others available on *Mid Wales* and *South Wales* as well.

Wales. British Tourist Authority. 16 pp. 1984. Free. Valuable guide
for visitors to Wales includes: welcome (Land of Castles), how
to reach Wales, traveling around Wales, map of Wales, historical development of Wales, tracing one's ancestors in Wales,
industrial archaeology (including Welsh mining and quarrying),
Welsh activities and special interest holidays, museums and art
galleries, shopping opportunities, and where to stay and eat.

Wales. Wynford-Vaughn-Thomas. Michael Joseph/Merrimack Publishers Circle, distr. 1985. An autobiographical guide to travel in
Wales; beautiful, full-color photographs.

Wales: Hotels and Guest Houses. Automobile Association (AA)/
Merrimack Publishers Circle, distr. 1985. Lists establishments
in Wales with prices, locations, and facilities.

Wales: Where to Go and What to See. British Tourist Authority.
1985. Welcome to Wales, brief history, Christianity and culture
of Wales, public transportation, driving in Wales, Welsh holidays, staying in Wales, diary of events. Many other publications on Wales are available from the British Tourist Authority,
all periodically updated. Some of them are: *Wales: Going
Places, Wales: Where to Stay—Self Catering, Wales: Walking,*
and *Wales: Bed and Breakfast.*

MAPS OF BRITAIN

The list of maps and atlases that follows contains titles that will be of
considerable assistance to tourists going to Great Britain, especially
those choosing to see the country via private automobiles.

AA Big Atlas of Town Plans. Automobile Association. 1985. Plans of eighty historic towns and cities, descriptions of places of interest and historical sites; clear and detailed maps and plans.

AA Big Road Atlas of Britain. British Tourist Authority. 1986. Includes eight thousand places of interest, London section, ten town maps, parks and beaches, index for twenty-five thousand place names; large-format, scale: 4 miles to 1 inch.

AA Greater London Street Atlas. British Tourist Authority. 1985. Includes maps of the entire London area with a complete street index and guide.

AA Motorists' Atlas of Great Britain. Automobile Association. 1985. Town plans and index to all areas of Britain; scale of 1 inch to 5 miles.

AA Touring Map of Great Britain. Automobile Association. 1985. A detailed map of all areas of Britain including large scale maps of major city areas; a best-seller in Britain for motorists.

ABC London Street Atlas: Ordnance Survey. British Tourist Authority/Merrimack Publishers Circle, distr. 1985. A pocket-sized atlas with detailed street maps; maps in color with all major tourist sights marked.

A-Z Visitors' London Atlas and Guide. British Tourist Authority/Merrimack Publishers Circle, distr. 1985. A pocket guide to London and its sights; includes a detailed map of central London and a street index.

Britain: A Map for Travellers. British Tourist Authority/Merrimack Publishers Circle, distr. nd. Provides essential map information for road, airway trips of all types; also contains mileages, ferry information, route identifications.

British City Maps. Forsyth Travel Library, distr. Offers up-to-date British city maps for Bath, Birmingham, Brighton, Bristol, Canterbury, Cambridge, Edinburgh, Glasgow, Leeds, Liverpool, London, Manchester, Oxford, Stratford-upon-Avon, and Windsor.

British Isles: Traveler's Map. National Geographic Society. 1974. Map, 23 × 33 inches; developed on the scale of 1 inch to 26 miles, with descriptive notes.

Collins Road Atlas of Britain. Williams Collins. 1985-86. Book of large-scale maps (road atlas) of Britain.

Discover Scotland. Bryn Frank. John Bartholomew and Son. 1984. Maps of Scotland (by areas), beautifully illustrated with color photos, area road maps, index, general tourist information section. Also offers: "Whisky Map of Scotland," "Clan Map of Scotland," "Tartan Map of Scotland."

London A-Z Street Atlas. Geographers' A-Z Map Company/British Tourist Authority. 1985. Maps of the entire London area with a comprehensive index.

London Map. British Tourist Authority/Distribution Services Corp., distr. Four-color; an aid to moving around London, with surface and underground facilities clearly shown.

Michelin Main Maps. Michelin Tyre Public Company, Ltd. Detailed maps of individual countries and sections; may be used in conjunction with the *Michelin Green Guides* for sightseeing. Available for Great Britain are: *Great Britain and Ireland, Southern Scotland/North England, Wales/West England,* and *England/Midlands & Southeast.*

Ordnance Survey Maps: Tourist and Special Interest. British Tourist Authority. nd. various sizes. This series by the official British Government survey engineers is on a scale of 1 inch to 1 mile; also details places of interest, ancient monuments, camping sites, view-points. Areas include Dartmoor, Exmoor, Peak District, Lake District, North York Moors, and Hadrian's Wall.

Rand McNally Pictorial Atlas of Britain: The Land, The People, The Heritage. Arthur Marwick. Rand McNally. 1983. Looks at a number of aspects of Britain and British life illustrated by maps and stunning pictures. Portrays nature and landscapes, shaping the present, buildings and places, transport, and communications.

Rand McNally Road Atlas of Britain. Rand McNally, 1985. Large scale maps of Britain, twenty-eight detailed maps of Britain, close-ups of London, 28,000 places in Britain, road signs, route plans all included.

Scotland Touring Map. Scottish Tourist Board/British Tourist Authority. 1985. Marks each major tourist sight on a new edition of this reliable map.

Wales: Tourist Map. Wales Tourist Board/British Tourist Authority. 1985. A handy map for the tourist driving through small towns; includes suggested tours; scale 1 inch to 5 miles.

4 Using the Library

Activity associated with planning to go to Britain calls for some research in your local library on British subjects of special interest to you. Here we include general information about library organization and services that will help you to do this. We discuss (1) how the library catalog is arranged, (2) interlibrary loan service, (3) contributions of encyclopedias, (4) computerized data-base searching, (5) useful general reference guides, (6) periodical reference guides, (7) audiovisual reference guides, and (8) British periodicals.

If your community library is a medium or large one, your first approach no doubt will be to arrange an interview with a reference librarian. Bring to this conference a list of the specific questions you have. List the subject areas you would like to pursue and jot down reminders of other information you will need. The reference books to which you are likely to be referred (most of which are cited in this chapter) do not circulate outside the library, but there will be many other books suitable for your purposes that you can check out for more leisurely reading at home: histories, guidebooks, novels, personal experience accounts, and biographies of favorite authors, artists, musicians, and others.

The Library Catalog

Armed with specific subject headings suggested by your interview with the librarian, and perhaps a review of the *Sears Subject*

Headings guide or the Library of Congress subject headings list, you may then proceed to check the library's catalog to see what specific titles your library has that you might like to see. Some libraries still maintain card catalogs, but many now have their holdings in computer-produced book catalogs, a microfiche reader, a microfilm reader (the Com/Rom catalog) or, the ultimate, an Online Catalog system. All of these are usually arranged alphabetically in dictionary format (in one continuous alphabet) by author, title, and subject, with the holdings of the particular library system indicated.

Library research can be fun and rewarding, and you will be amazed at how much material is available on Great Britain on a local basis and how much more is available from other sources, much of it just for the asking.

Interlibrary Loans

If the titles you select are not in your library system, they may perhaps be borrowed from other systems through the process called "interlibrary loan." Materials from other sources may be listed via a printed or online union catalog which provides access to regional sources such as your state library, community college or university libraries, and special (often technical) libraries. Your librarian may be able to order the materials for you through a telex or telephone system and can either have books sent to your library or have photocopies of selected articles or specific chapters made for your use.

Encyclopedias as Sources of Information

Most general encyclopedias contain valuable entries for those who seek specific information in areas of British interest. *World Book* alone has signed articles by scholars in their respective fields on "The United Kingdom of Great Britain," "Scotland," "Wales," "Glasgow," "Liverpool," "Manchester," and hundreds of others. Of special interest are the short entries (often accompanied by photos) about writers, artists, dramatists, and others who have been cited in books, brochures, or other publications.

COMPUTERIZED DATA BASE SEARCHING

Another service provided by some libraries is access to biblio-graphic data bases such as DIALOG, *Bibliographic Retrieval Services (BRS), The Source,* and *CompuServe.* (These data bases were discussed earlier, in chapter 2, in connection with the subject, "Computerized Personal Travel Information.") For a relatively small fee your librarian can assist you in searching a data base with a list of descriptors similar to subject headings. If you have a home computer you can access *The Source,* an interactive search service, or *CompuServe,* which can give you up-to-date airline fares and schedules, and also State Department advice about travel to foreign countries.

GENERAL REFERENCE GUIDES

In your pursuit of information and background about Britain you may wish to use another especially helpful source—general refer-ence guides. The assistance you obtain through such use can lead you to materials that will stimulate your imagination and refresh your memory concerning places you may wish to visit and interests you may wish to pursue further when you are there. The following list suggests titles that are especially good for this purpose.

Books

Book Review Digest. H.W. Wilson. 10/yr. plus ann. cumulation. Available at most public libraries for your use; covers approxi-mately six thousand books per year, fiction and nonfiction, adult and juvenile, with excerpts from reviews and citations to reviews. Arranged alphabetically by author and title with all bibliographic data necessary for retrieval, this publication also gives title and subject access in a separate volume including "fiction themes," a biography section, and juvenile literature.

Books in Print. Bowker. ann. Lists nearly all books written in the English language that are still "in print." Listings are by author, subject, and title (in different volumes). The BIP listings are also available on Bibliographic Research Service (BRS) and DIALOG computerized data bases (for fees), and on microfiche.

Britain 1984: An Official Handbook. 35th ed. Her Majesty's Stationery Office. 1984. An overall view of Britain and its place in the European Economic Community. It includes information on government, land and people, overseas relations, defense, law and justice, agriculture, transport and communications, sports and recreation, and the arts. A map with products, natural resources and a list of government departments, and the responsibilities and functions of local governments included.

British Authors Before 1800. Stanley J. Kunitz and Howard Haycraft, eds. H.W. Wilson. 1952. A biographical dictionary with short sketches of literary figures of the British Isles before 1800. A companion guide to *British Authors of the Nineteenth Century.*

British Authors of the Nineteenth Century. Stanley J. Kunitz and Howard Haycraft, eds. H.W. Wilson 1973. Over a thousand biographical sketches of literary figures from nineteenth-century Britain; includes lists of their works, sources of criticisms, and some portraits. Also includes prominent figures in other fields whose writings have a place in British history.

British Books In Print. J. Whitaker and Sons. ann., updated monthly on microfiche. "A Reference Catalogue of Current Literature" which includes books in print and on sale in the United Kingdom; all bibliographic information provided along with a list of publishers and addresses and a book trade bibliography.

British Books in Print: Children's Books. J. Whitaker and Sons. ann. Over twenty-five thousand in-print titles arranged by author, title, and key-word; subject index with ninety-nine classifications, directory of publishers and distributors. These titles are published in English in Britain or published overseas and distributed in Britain.

British Paperbacks in Print. J. Whitaker and Sons. ann. Lists over sixty-five thousand titles with complete bibliographic data. List of publishers and distributors appended.

British Writers. (eight volumes). Ian Scott-Kilvert, general ed. Scribners. 1979-1984. Contains 153 essays about British writers who have contributed important works to English literature; covers the period from the fourteenth century to the present.

The Cambridge Guide to English Literature. Michael Stapleton, ed. Cambridge University Press. 1983. Three thousand one hundred entries arranged alphabetically by author, title, and subject in a dictionary format giving brief biographies, major works, and notes on great writers of the United Kingdom, Ireland, and others—three hundred authors covered in depth. Also includes an essay on the English language and the Bible.

Current Biography. H.W. Wilson. mo. Cumulates annually with a yearbook and index. To find articles on your favorite British personalities in the news such as Jeremy Irons or Anthony Andrews, check this publication. Includes biographical sketches, photos, bibliography of other references; indexed cumulatively.

Directory of British Associations. G.P. Henderson and S.P.A. Henderson. C.B.D. Research. 1982. A classified and alphabetical listing of names, addresses, telephone numbers, and key personnel of several thousand British associations. Copies may be inspected at British consulates throughout the United States. Also includes associations in Ireland.

Encyclopedia of Associations. Gale Research. ann., updated twice yearly. A guide to national and international organizations with up-to-date facts and figures and addresses. Accessed by a geographic and executive index as well.

Fiction Catalog. H.W. Wilson. 1980. Subscription includes four annual supplements for 1981, 1982, 1983, and 1984. Offers an author, subject, and title index plus a directory of publishers and distributors; an annotated list of over five thousand titles in-print and out-of-print which represent the best in fiction in the English language.

Great Writers of the English Language: Novelists and Prose Writers, Poets, Dramatists. 3 vol. James Vinson and Daniel Kirkpatrick, ed. St. Martin's/Macmillan Ltd. 1979. Alphabetical listings of biographies, works published, bibliographies, including critical studies and suggested readings about the writers.

The New Cambridge Bibliography of English Literature. George Watson, ed. Cambridge University Press. Organized in four separate volumes—vol. 1, 600-1660; vol. 2, 1660-1800; vol. 3, 1800-1900; vol. 4, 1900-1950. Classifies "the whole of English studies as represented by the literature of the British Isles," using "works by" as well as "works about" entries. An excellent blueprint of the field for serious researchers. A complete index is included in volume 4.

The Norton Anthology of English Literature. 5th ed. M.H. Abrams et al. eds. W.W. Norton. 1986. Volume one covers the Middle Ages and the Restoration through the eighteenth century; volume two covers the Romantic Period and the Victorian Age through the twentieth century. A good basic text for English literature and background reading of your favorite writer's works.

The Oxford Companion to Children's Literature. Humphrey Carpenter and Mari Prichard. Oxford University Press. 1984. A single volume encyclopedia of children's literature including the U.S. and Britain, concentrating on nineteenth- and twentieth-century writers and their works. The illustrated articles identify characters, summarize plots, and include short biographies of authors and illustrators.

Oxford Companion to English Literature. 5th ed. Margaret Drabble, ed. Oxford University Press. 1985. Alphabetically arranged by author, title, and subject—dictionary order—with brief sketches of life and works of the various writers. Essays on English copyright law and censorship are included.

The Penguin Companion to English Literature. David Daiches, ed. McGraw-Hill. 1971. A guide to the works of historians, philosophers, and writers in the English language, excluding the U.S. and Latin America. Alphabetically arranged by authors' names with a short sketch of life and works of each; critical works and bibliography appended.

Sears List of Subject Headings. 12th ed. Barbara Marietta Westby, ed. H.W. Wilson. 1982. Lists about one thousand five hundred subject headings including new ones on science and technology; based on Library of Congress headings but modified for use in smaller libraries. See section on Britain and England for research leads.

Subject Guide to Books in Print. Bowker. bi-ann. Lists and classifies the entire in-print nonfiction book world (more than six hundred thousand titles).

Subject Guide to Children's Books in Print. Bowker. bi-ann. Classifies approximately forty-five thousand books for children, giving full ordering and finding information.

Traveler's Reading Guides. Maggy Simony, ed. Freelance Publications. 1982. A series of travel reference books which cite travel literature and articles, background reading lists, and novels set in particular country areas. Three volumes are available: *Europe, Western Hemisphere,* and *Asia, Africa, Pacific,* each with semiannual updates. The up-to-date travel article lists culled from appropriate periodicals indexed in the *Reader's Guide* are especially valuable for the knowledgeable traveler who plans ahead.

Whitaker's Almanack 1985. 117th ed. J. Whitaker and Sons/Gale

Research. 1984. Includes an alphabetical list of members of Parliament; review of the year's British TV activities; also for cinema; diary of forthcoming British events and royal occasions; list of principal English cities; list of national parks and areas of outstanding natural beauty in Britain; castles, houses open to the public; museums and art galleries outside London; public and private buildings in London; "Literature of the Year," including those for opera and dance; principal book publishers; principal newspapers and trade, professional, and business journals; societies and institutions; archaeological societies.

Whitaker's Publishers in the United Kingdom and Their Addresses. J. Whitaker and Sons. ann. A selected list of British publishers, their full addresses and telephone numbers, telegraphic addresses, and telex numbers. Each listing carries indications of the types of subject matter dealt with in the books that are published.

Periodical Reference Guides

A second source of information, on a topical basis, is periodical articles accessed through *Reader's Guide to Periodical Literature,* the *Magazine Index,* or *Access.* Each of these tools is arranged by subject and lists many articles on Great Britain in current magazines, usually available on microfilm or by the photocopy process. The *New York Times Index* and the *Dow Jones News Retrieval* are sources of newspaper articles with full text on microfilm or by computer access and printout.

Books

Access. John Gordon Burke and Ned Kehde, eds. John Gordon Burke Publisher. 3/yr. (2 suppl. plus ann. cum.) An unofficial supplement to the *Reader's Guide to Periodical Literature.* With an author and subject index, this publication covers approximately 152 periodicals with an emphasis on regional and city magazines; titles in *Reader's Guide* are usually dropped from *Access* and the included titles are given in-depth subject indexing.

The Magazine Collection. Information Access. mo., cumulated.

Available on microfilm machines at your local library or online via DIALOG. A reference network including the *Magazine Index* which covers 370 of the most widely read periodicals; printouts available.

National Geographic Index: 1947-1983. Nelson Doubleday and C. Earl Cooley, eds. National Geographic Society. 1984. For exact references to over twenty-five thousand articles, arranged by author, subject, title, and photographer, covering 445 issues of the magazine; includes England, Northern Ireland, Scotland, and Wales subject matter.

New York Times Index. The New York Times. q., ann. cumulations. A guide to the *New York Times* which is reproduced on microfilm; abstracts and condensations of the most recent news articles giving one a short history of the world. Arranged by subject areas such as Great Britain.

Readers' Guide to Periodical Literature. H.W. Wilson. mo., plus q. and ann. cumulations. Available at your local library, this publication, arranged primarily by subject, can lead you to magazine articles covering nearly any subject you wish to research in the British Isles. Complete bibliographic data is given and most libraries will have the corresponding periodicals either on microfilm or in paper copies.

Ulrich's International Periodicals Directory. Bowker. ann. 2 vol. Lists and classifies periodicals available from all parts of the world, providing essential data about each.

AUDIOVISUAL REFERENCE GUIDES

To find specific subjects and titles for audiovisual materials such as 8mm and 16mm films, slides, filmstrips, and audio and video tapes, see such reference books as *The Educational Film Locator,* the *NICEM* (National Information Center for Educational Media) *Indexes,* and the *Video Source Book*. These works have subject indexes and all data needed for rental, purchase, or borrowing, including location, purchase/rental price, running time, color/black and white. Some local libraries have excellent collections of films and video tapes to lend, and often you may also rent similar materials from some colleges and universities. Your neighborhood travel agency or the library frequently presents slide/tape or film programs about places you may want to preview before you plan to go there.

Books

Directory of Spoken-Word Audio Cassettes. 3d ed. Gerald McKee. Jeffrey Norton Publishers. 1983. Lists seven hundred producer/ publishers, with addresses and phone numbers, arranged by subject, with an alphabetical index; prices included.

Educational Film Locator. 2d ed. Consortium of University Film Centers. Bowker. 1980. Locates sources and rental prices, gives content information, and other data regarding 16mm films distributed by a large number of university film libraries throughout the U.S.

NICEM Index to Educational Audio Tapes. 5th ed. National Information Center for Educational Media. 1980. Over twenty-eight thousand tapes listed and described in a variety of audio formats.

NICEM Index to Educational Video Tapes. National Information Center for Educational Media. 1985. Contains over sixty thousand titles including classics and documentaries on a variety of subjects; gives purchase price, running time, rental source, year of release, and an abstract of content.

NICEM Index to 16mm Educational Films. 8th ed. National Information Center for Educational Media. 1984. This edition of this valuable sourcebook describes and offers availability information and terms for some forty-eight thousand currently available 16mm educational films.

NICEM Index to 35mm Educational Filmstrips. National Information Center for Educational Media. 1985. Over forty thousand entries annotated and listed by title and subject; a comprehensive guide to currently available filmstrips.

The Video Source Book. National Video Clearinghouse. 1984. Describes more than thirty-four thousand prerecorded video programs on video cassette, video tape, and video disc, some of which deal with subjects related to the British Isles.

Video Tape and Disc Guide to Home Entertainment. National Video Clearinghouse. 1984. Fully indexed by tape title, subject, and other facets. Some titles deal with the British Isles.

British Periodicals

Most of the periodicals listed here can be subscribed to, and in some cases individual copies are available free for the asking. Often, they may also be consulted in libraries. A number of individual counties (e.g., Kent, Sussex) publish monthly magazines on life and events within their borders.

AA Travel Club Magazine. Automobile Association. Tallis Press, Ltd., 115 Old Street, London EC1. bi-mo.

About London. About London Publications. 60-62 Westbourne Terrace, London W2 3UJ. mo. Single copy free from above address.

American Guide to London. Dominion Press Ltd. 87-91 New Bond Street, London W1Y 9LA. 2/yr. Single copy free.

The Bookseller. J. Whitaker and Sons Ltd. 12 Dyott Street, London WC1A 1DF. wk. A magazine from the British book trade listing new titles, ordering information, and annotations; similar to *Publisher's Weekly* in the United States.

British Book News. The British Council. 10 Spring Gardens, London SW1A 2BN. mo. Reviews some two hundred books a month in all subject areas and lists over seven hundred forthcoming books with subject classification and annotation. Also reviews periodicals and lists paperback reprints; most likely found in academic libraries as a selection tool.

British Book News: Children's Books. The British Council. 10 Spring Gardens, London SW1A 2BN. 2/yr. Reviews and annotates the best in children's literature.

Commonwealth. Longman Group Ltd. Fourth Avenue, Harlow, Essex CM19 5AA. bi-mo. A news magazine which reports on politics, sports, economic affairs, science and technology, and the arts in Britain.

Country Life. IPC Magazines Ltd. 28th Floor, King's Reach Tower, Stamford Street, London SE1 9LS. wk. An exploration of English country life including book reviews.

The Economist. The Economist. Subscription Department, Box 904, Farmingdale, NY 11737. wk. Includes editorials, articles on world politics, current affairs, business, finance, and science; gives worldwide coverage. A highly respected periodical.

Geographical Magazine. IPC Magazines, Ltd. King's Reach Tower, Stamford Street, London SE1 9LS. mo. A publication of the Royal Geographical Society.

Illustrated London News. Illustrated London News and Sketch, Ltd. 10-16 Elm Street, London WC1X 0BP. mo. Book reviews, reviews of London films and plays.

In London.Parkway Publications. Linburn House, 350 Kilburn High Road, London NW6 2QJ. q. Single copy free.

Punch. Punch Publications, Ltd. 23-27 Tudor Street, London EC4Y 0HR. wk. Reviews books, films, and plays in addition to being a famous British humor magazine.

The Spectator. Spectator Limited, 56 Doughty St., London WC 1N 2LL. wk. Book, film, music and play reviews included in this classic publication on the British scene.

This England. Expediters of the Printed Word Ltd. 527 Madison Avenue, New York, NY 10022. q. Color photos, poetry, stories of the land and the people give the reader a glorious picture of England as it is and was; features such as "English Country Regiments," "England's Country Churches," and "English Heroes," add flavor; book reviews, a quarterly diary of events, and numerous biographical sketches round out an excellent publication.

This Is London: What, Where, and When for the Visitor. This Is London Magazine Ltd., 3 Heddon Street, London W1R 7LE. wk. Film, play, and book reviews.

In addition to the foregoing magazines, *London Week, City Limits,* and *Time-Out*—each covering current goings-on in London art-film-music-opera circles—are for sale at London newsstands.

5 Getting Around in Great Britain

There are many different ways to get around in Britain, and this chapter discusses a number of them. The resources listed in the pages that follow provide detailed information about (1) touring by coach or bus, (2) touring by rail, (3) taking walking tours, (4) hosteling, (5) bicycling and motorcycling, (6) canal boating, (7) camping and caravaning, (8) farm holidaying, (9) home exchanging, (10) self-catering, (11) bed-and-breakfasting, and (12) holidaying in the British Islands. Your enjoyment of any of these activities will be enhanced by appropriate "before you go" use of some of the resources and agency contacts listed with each section.

TOURING BY COACH OR BUS

There is a great difference between "coaches" and "buses" in Britain. Generally speaking, buses are for local transportation and not for long distance trips, and they are not very comfortable. Coaches, on the other hand, are relatively luxurious. Some of them are equipped with toilet facilities and offer hostess services, refreshments, and entertainment (film or video). Coaches resemble our own cross-country buses, traveling on main motorways on fairly tight, speedy schedules. It is possible to take short (usually less than a day long) excursions into surrounding areas with a local bus company, but for anyone touring for enjoyment, coaches are preferable. With them you may make your own arrangements for tickets, schedules, and accommodations along the route or use the services of one of the forty or more commercial coach touring companies that operate in Britain. (See below.) If the latter, some or all of your meals, lodging, sightseeing, and general comfort are arranged for you and you have only to "enjoy." See also the list of U.S. travel tour agencies included in chapter 2. Each of these will supply, on request, free brochures explaining and promoting their coach tour services in Britain.

Organizations and Associations

Anglo-World Travel, Ltd. 30 Stafford Street, Edinburgh EH3 7DB. Offers tours of Scotland, the borders, and central Scotland.

Britexpress, National Travel (NBC), Ltd. Victoria Coach Station, 164 Buckingham Palace Road, London SW1W 9TP. Sale source for Travelpass cards good for travel to some sixty cities and towns in England, Wales, and Scotland on a five- or ten-day limited basis. May also be purchased in the United States from The Kemwel Group, 106 Calvert Street, Harrison, NY 10528.

Bebb Travel. The Coach Station, Llantwit Fardre, Pontypridd, Mid-Glamorgan, Wales. Offers tours from Cardiff to Scottish destinations.

British Bus. Western House, Argyll Street, 237-239 Oxford Street, London W1R 1AB. Offers coach tours, guided sightseeing tours, day trips by scheduled coaches, and other travel opportunities in Britain.

Eastern Scottish. Holiday Tours Department, Bus Station, St. Andrews Square, Edinburgh EH1 3DU. Offers coach tours throughout eastern Scotland.

Evan Evans. Evan Evans Tours, Limited, 27 Cockspur Street, Trafalgar Square, London SW1Y 5BT. Offers coach tours throughout Britain.

Excelsior Holidays. Excelsior House, 22 Sea Road, Bournemouth, Dorset BH5 1DD. Offers holiday tours in North Wales, the English Lakes, Edinburgh, Warwick, and Stratford-upon-Avon.

Frames-National. Reservation Office, 33 Elizabeth Street (Victoria Coach Station), London SW1W 9RR. Coach tours throughout Britain.

Grey-Green. Tours Department, 53-55 Stamford Hill, London N16 5TD. Arranges tours.

In England. Galleon World Travel Limited, 45 Cathedral Place, London N16 5TD. Offers a variety of mini-tours (two to four days) throughout Britain.

London Transport Information Centre. 55 Broadway, London, SW1. Tel: 01-222-1234. Call for twenty-four-hour recorded information on bus schedules and trips.

National Travel. Victoria Coach Station, 164 Buckingham Palace Road, London SW1W, 9TP. Offers numbers of interesting coach trips to all parts of England.

Scottish Omnibuses. Bus Station, St. Andrews Square, Edinburgh EH1 7DB. Coach tours in Scotland.

Trafalgar Tours, Limited. 9-11 Bressenden Place, London SW1E 5DF. A large-scale coach tour operator in the United Kingdom and throughout Europe.

Victoria Coach Station. 164 Buckingham Palace Road, London SW1W 9TP. Information on coach and bus transportation in and around London, throughout England, and to the various airports.

Books

Stephen Birnbaum's *Great Britain and Ireland* and Fodor's *Great Britain* both contain helpful information on coach and bus travel.

England by Bus. Elizabeth Gundrey. Hamlyn Paperbacks. 1983. Practical advice on planning coach and bus trips to specific historic British towns, national parks, or literary or historical locations. Includes a "Dickens Trail," a "Lake Trip," and others. Also available from the British Tourist Authority.

The Illustrated Counties of England. James Bishop, ed. Facts on File. 1985. A useful book for those planning travel by car, bus, or rail.

Touring by Rail

Traveling by train is a very good method of getting around in Britain, whether for short trips or for a series of stop and go arrangements over a period of time. After all, the national railroad network operates fourteen thousand trains a day that reach some two thousand stations. Some of them (the Inter City units) travel at speeds up to 125 miles an hour. With such service, Edinburgh and London are just five hours apart, and the Bath Spa is only an hour from London. Most of these trains carry restaurant or buffet cars. You may purchase either a first-class or a second-class ticket. The former offers you greater privacy and more luxurious accommodations (wider seat, more leg room) than the latter. Sleeping cars are available on many trains. The following special fare ticketing arrangements are worth your consideration:

BritRail Pass. This popular pass for unlimited travel in a limited time period can *only* be purchased in the U.S. or Canada *before* going to Britain. It may be used for first- or second-class rail travel in England, Scotland, and Wales and also for Sealink ferries (sailing to Continental Europe), for trips to the Isle of Wight, and for Lake Windermere steamers in the Lake District. The pass may be purchased for periods of seven days, fourteen days, twenty-one days, or one month; the use period begins with the first day of travel, not the day of purchase. They are obtained from BritRail Travel International (see address below) in the U.S.

Britainshrinker tickets are also available for use out of London, and combine reduced rail fare with bus tours at your destination. Discounts are approximately one-third off regular prices. Inquire of the British Tourist Authority before leaving the U.S.

Organizations and Associations

British Rail Travel Centre. 4-12 Regent Street, London SW1. Also maintains offices at all railroad stations to provide all kinds of rail information.

BritRail Travel International, Inc. Department OV, 630 Third Avenue, New York, NY 10017. Offices are also located in the following cities: Department OV, 333 North Michigan Avenue, Chicago, IL 60601; Department OV, 510 West Sixth Street, Los Angeles, CA 90014; Department OV, 55 Eglington Avenue East, Toronto M4P 1G8, Ontario, Canada; and Department OV, 409 Granville Street, Vancouver VC6 1T2, British Columbia, Canada.

London Underground Railway Society. 6 Launceston Gardens, Perivale, Greenford, Middlesex UB6, 7ET, England. Studies railways of the London Transport system; preserves trains, models trains; supervises "roving" uses of the London Transport system (a plan that permits covering as many underground stations as possible in one day).

Narrow Gauge Railway Society. 15 Ham View, Upton-on-Severn, Worcester WR8 0QE, England. Concerned with all forms of narrow gauge railways—past and present, in the United Kingdom and overseas.

Railway and Canal Historical Society. 64 Grove Avenue, London W7 3ES. Supports the study of railway and canal history in Britain.

Railway Preservation Societies, Ltd. Sheringham Station, Norfolk NR26 8RA, England. Comprises a group interested in the preservation and restoration of historic railway facilities in the United Kingdom.

Books

Britain by BritRail: 1985-86. George W. Ferguson, ed. Burt Franklin. 1985. Organized according to provisions of the BritRail Pass and the Thomas Cook Continental Timetable. Tells how to see Great Britain comfortably and inexpensively, via British railways, following suggestions contained in more than forty trip entries.

Britain by Train. Patrick Goldring. British Tourist Authority/Merrimack Publishers Circle, distr. 1983. A complete guide to travel by BritRail with suggestions for enjoyable journeys throughout the British countryside.

Eurail Guide: 1986. Kathryn Saltzman Turpin and Marvin L. Saltzman. Eurail Guide Annual. 1986. Chapter 8 covers England, Wales, Scotland, and Northern Ireland and discusses British train passes, London rail stations, schedules, channel crossings, and over forty one-day excursions from London.

London's Historic Railway Stations. John Betjeman. Transatlantic Arts. 1978. Lavishly illustrated with black and white photographs; lists twelve major historic stations with myriad architectural details.

Preserved Railways. Shire Publications/British Travel Bookshop, distr. nd. A pocket guide to the old railways, some of which are being restored. A *Discovering Series* book. Available from the British Travel Bookshop.

TOURING BY CAR

Car rentals are as easy to arrange in Britain as they are in the United States, and only a little more expensive. With an automobile, of course, you have the maximum amount of freedom and independence to go where you want to and when you are ready. Car rentals may be arranged in the United States before you leave, or you may wait until you arrive in Britain to make your choice of vehicle and the dates you want the car. You may prefer to start your tour outside of London and thus avoid big city traffic (in Brighton, for example, which is only an hour's train trip south of London) and return the car there. British roads are for the most part good, and all of them free of tolls. You will soon get used to driving on the left side of the road with the steering wheel on the right. You may drive in Britain with a current driver's license from any state or obtain an International Driving Permit from your local automobile club. Speed limits are thirty miles per hour in built up areas, sixty miles per hour on regular roads, and seventy miles per hour on high speed motorways (thruways). All speed limits, parking regulations, and route numbers are well posted. The *Highway Code* which details travel regulations in the U.K. is available from AA, RAC, post offices in the U.K., and other outlets.

It is recommended that, if you are a member of an AAA-related organization, you inquire before going to Britain about reciprocal services available to you from the British Automobile Association (AA) or the Royal Automobile Club (RAC).

Organizations and Associations

Automobile Association (AA). Travel Services, 3 New Coventry Street, London WC2.; or Headquarters, Fanum House, Basingstoke, Hants RG21 2EA, England. Offers complete line of services to automobile owners in Britain similar to those offered by the American Automobile Association and its various affiliated state offices throughout the United States. Its list of publications is of special interest and usefulness to travelers in Britain.

Avis. Trident House, Station Road, Hayes, Middlesex, England, or *Avis Rent-a-Car System, Inc.* 900 Old Country Road, Garden City, NY 11530. Car rentals in Britain.

British Tour and Theater Center. 19 West 44th Street, Room 718, New York, NY 10036. Arranges car rentals in Britain.

Car Hire Centre International. 23 Swallow Street, London W1. Free reservation services for British and European car rental groups.

Godfrey Davis. Davis House, Wilton Road, London SW1. Rental of cars and vans.

Hertz Car Rentals. 35 Edgware Road, London W2.; or *Hertz,* 1272 London Road, London SW16. Car rentals in Britain.

Royal Automobile Club (RAC). Associate Motoring Section, RAC House, Box 100, Landsdowne Road, Croydon CR9 2JA, England. Tel: 01-686-2525. Similar in many purposes to the Automobile Association (or the American Automobile Association). Offers publications, motoring advice, insurance, and other automobile-related services.

Tranquil Roads Travel. Box 5536, Valencia, CA 91355. Offers escorted, chauffeur-driven car tours in the British Isles; preplanned or individually designed programs for not more than five passengers. Drivers are multilingual.

Books

AA Alternative Routes in Britain. British Tourist Anthority/Merrimack Publishers Circle, distr. 1982. Describes twenty-six routes covering over six thousand miles of the British countryside; detailed maps of out-of-the-way areas in England, Scotland, and Wales.

AA Britain: A Country Compass. Automobile Association. 1983. An exploration of the British countryside with a glimpse at the history and wildlife of the areas; beautifully illustrated.

AA: If Your Car Won't Get You There, We Will. Automobile Association. 1984. Details of automobile breakdown services provided by AA.

AA Members' Handbook. Automobile Association. 1986. A general information handbook for members of the Automobile Association (British). Contains directories of agencies from which AA members may obtain various required services.

AA Scotland: Where to Go, What to Do. Automobile Association. 1983. Includes accommodations, maps, town plans, sights to see, and fourteen one-day tours in all areas.

AA The Second Touring Guide to Britain. British Tourist Authority. 1985. Gives eighty illustrated tours in Britain recommended for drivers seeking the "best of Britain."

AA Touring Guide to Britain. Russell Beach, ed. Automobile Association. 1983. Full color, well-illustrated, containing many maps; organized by regions of the United Kingdom; contains 112 tours accessible to the motoring public.

AA/BTA: The Touring Book of Britain. British Tourist Authority. 1984. A planning book describing over two thousand places to see, forty major sections in important towns and cities, special features on historical areas, fifty day tours included; thirty-page atlas.

Avis Rent-A-Car has a new set of brochures on special interest tours for the traveler to Britain. The list of personalized tours includes "Best of Britain," "Ancient Britain," "Stately Homes," "Royal Heritage," "British Gardens," "Welsh Castles," "Craftsmens' Britain," "Maritime Britain," "Golfer's Britain," "Collector's Britain," and "Literary Britain." When making a reservation, either through Avis or your travel agent, you may request one or two of these trip printouts. Also included with the plan will be maps giving details of trips of 100 to 300 miles per day of one day to one month, and a list of hotels, sights to see, interesting restaurants, and pubs in the area.

Britain and Ireland On Your Own. J. and R. Choco. Country Road/ Forsyth Travel Library, distr. 1982. A guide to travel through the countryside of the British Isles; car hire information, driving routes, sights to see, and lists of bed and breakfast recommendations.

Driving in Britain: What the Guide Books Don't Tell You. Charlene Ferris Palm. Bittersweet Press. 1984. A personal account with tips on driving through Britain. Suggestions on reading, planning, advance bookings, renting a car, tourist information, parking, and roundabout driving.

Going Places: A Motor Touring Guide to Wales. British Tourist Authority/Merrimack Publishers Circle, distr. 1985. Lists twenty-three tours in Wales with historic backgrounds; illustrated with maps and a list of sights to see.

Off the Motorway. Christopher Peck. Cadogan Books/Hippocrene Books. 1984. Places in England of outstanding interest on or near the M-1, M-5, M-6, M-9, M-50, M-62, and M-90 motorways.

Offices Abroad. American Automobile Association. 1985. Describes the many reciprocal services available abroad to members of AAA-affiliated local automobile clubs. Includes those for Great Britain.

Peter Brereton's Touring Guide to English Villages. Mitchell Beazley, ed. Prentice-Hall. 1986. Arranged by region with twelve areas covering 300 villages; detailed descriptions of each with historical, architectural, folkloric, and literary associations. Appended are twelve maps which locate sights, accommodations, eating establishments, hotels, and pubs.

Through Britain on Country Roads. Peter Brereton. Crown. 1982. Describes eighteen tours which one may take on less well-traveled, sometimes remote, back roads of England, Scotland, and Wales. Includes historical notes, local stories and legends, data regarding available country inns, maps, driving conditions, and other details.

Traveller's Britain. Arthur Eperon. Pan Books (with BBC). 1981. A guide to twelve routes in England, Scotland, and Wales; best places to eat, drink, and stay.

Ward Lock Regional Guide: Scotland. Frank Thompson. British Tourist Authority/Merrimack Publishers Circle, distr. 1983. A selection of one-day driving tours through the scenic areas of the various regions, including the Highlands and Edinburgh; maps and illustrations clearly delineated for each tour.

Ward Lock Regional Guides to Britain. British Tourist Authority/Merrimack Publishers Circle, distr. Various dates. Selected one-day tours in various regions with full details, clear maps, and illustrations. Titles include: *West Country, The Shakespeare Country and Cotswolds,* and *South East England and East Anglia*.

Audiovisual Materials

Auto Tape Tours. American Automobile Association. 1983. Under the titles, "London to Glastonbury," "Glastonbury to Stratford," and "Stratford to London," gives information on history, folklore, and attractions to be experienced. Includes background music, narration, and sound effects.

Maps

Great Britain Road Map Series. Forsyth Travel Library. Up-to-date, detailed maps showing all important primary and secondary roads in various parts of Great Britain; in color. Separate maps available for Cotswolds and Chilterns, South-West England and South Wales, South-East and Central England,

Devon and Cornwall, Wales and Central England, Northern England, Scotland North and South, and Great Britain (in entirety).

Road maps are also available from AA and RAC and at most gasoline stations.

WALKING TOURS

Walking is not only good exercise—it's fun, especially in Great Britain. Walks there may range in length from those of an hour or two to those lasting a week or even considerably longer. After all, in England and Wales alone there are more than one hundred thousand miles of country paths and many thousands more in Scotland, miles which are for "long distance" travel. Walkers will be pleased to find the paths generally well maintained and free of sogginess. As anywhere, walking alone in isolated country is not recommended, and it is a good idea to leave word, when setting out for a long trip, of the general direction you intend to go and when you expect to return. As for walking anywhere, good shoes, a good map, a compass, and a flask of drinking water are basic equipment; many experienced walkers/ hikers carry stout walking sticks which serve many useful purposes in rough country terrain. Also, you may wish to consider joining one of the walking organizations mentioned below that abound in this land of enthusiastic walkers.

Organizations and Associations

The Backpack Man. 11 Church Street, Moulton, Northampton, Northants, England. Organizes walking tours for private groups.

Countrywide Holidays Association. 338 Cromwell Range, Manchester M14 6HU, England. Organizes walking tours into the English countryside. Write for brochure.

Earthwalk. Pen-y-wern, Kerry, Newtown, Powys, Wales. Johanne and Philip Brachi lead weekend or six-day tours in the hills of Mid-Wales; all equipment is transported ahead so you can walk without carrying packs.

English Wanderer. 13 Wellington Court, Spencers Wood, Reading RG7 1BN, England. Tel: 0734-8825. Offers walking tours in the English countryside; includes accommodations, all meals, and expenses.

Head for the Hills. Leonard Golding. The Recreational Hall, Garth, Builth, Powys, Wales. Offers numerous night walking and camping trips.

London Walks. 139 Conway Road, London N14 7BH. Offers inexpensive guided tours on such topics as "Treasures of the British Museum," "An Historic Pub Walk," "Shakespeare's London," "A Journey through Dickens' London," and many others.

Long Distance Walkers Association. 29 Appledown Close, Alresford, Hants, England. Promotes long-distance walking activities in mountains and undeveloped areas.

Mountain Goat Holidays. Victoria Street, Windermere LA21 1QD, England. Offers information on guided walks in the Lake District.

Mountaineering Council. Crawford House, Precinct Centre, Booth Street East, Manchester M13 9RZ, England. Offers assistance to individuals and groups interested in high country walking.

National Center for Mountain Activities. Plas-y-Brenin, Capel Curig, Betws-y-Coed, Greynedd LL24 OET, Wales. Offers high country walking tour advice and assistance.

Off-Beat Tours of London. 66 St. Michael's Street, London W2 1QR. Organizes unusual walking tours in the London area.

Ramblers' Association. 1-5 Wandsworth Road, London SW8. Organizes walking tours, sometimes in conjunction with rail trips, into the countryside.

Streets of London. 32 Grovelands Road, London N13 4RH. "Street level" exploration of many of the most interesting London streets; small fees charged; twelve different tours offered.

Books

AA Book of Country Walks. M. Davidson. British Tourist Authority/ Merrimack Publishers Circle, distr. 1979. A detailed reference work describing thousands of miles of walking paths in Britain; has detachable walker's kits to carry on the trail.

AA Town Walks in Britain. British Tourist Authority. 1985. Decribes fifty-two town walks, four in London, with map locations, illustrations, and route directions.

Abroad in England. Frank Entwisle. St. Edmundsbury Press/W. W. Norton. 1983. About rambling through provincial England, with emphasis upon the rural scene. Entertaining and humorous.

Activity Holidays in Britain. Farm Holiday Guides. 1985. Annotated, classified listing of hundreds of excitingly different holidays in which one may engage in England, with emphasis upon activities and hobbies.

Along the Green Roads of Britain. J.H.B. Peel. David & Charles. 1982. This well-known English writer describes little known walks in the countryside; also includes walks along the North Cornish Coast, Offa's Dyke, and the old Kennet and Avon Canals.

Another Six English Towns. Alec Clifton-Taylor. British Broadcasting Corp. 1984. Explores Britain's beautiful and historical architecture; takes readers on walks through Bury St. Edmunds, Cirencester, Devizes, Durham, Sandwich, and Whitby.

Backpacker's Manual. Cameron McNeish. Oxford Illustrated Press/ Times Books. 1984. A how-to manual dealing with backpacking equipment, techniques, and recommended trails in England. Includes maps, youth hostels, and guidebooks.

Fellwalking with Wainwright. A. Wainwright. British Tourist Authority/Merrimack Publishers Circle, distr. 1985. Details eighteen walks chosen by an expert who gives practical advice and personal knowledge of each area; illustrated with beautiful photos by Derry Brabbs.

The Footpaths of Britain: A Guide to Walking in England, Scotland, and Wales. Michael Marriott. Salem House/Merrimack Publishers Circle, distr. 1984. Long distance paths, recreational trails, over a thousand miles covered; organized by geographic region; suggests appropriate wearing apparel.

Great Walks of the Yorkshire Dales. Frank Duerden. Ward Lock. 1983. Describes over fifty walks with sights, landmarks, and statistics (length and difficulty) provided for each; useful for all as it is small, light, and easy to read and carry.

Journey Home: A Walk About England. John Hillaby. Holt, Rinehart, and Winston. 1984. An account of a walk from the Lake District of Northwest England to London.

The Kingdom by the Sea. Paul Theroux. Houghton Mifflin. 1984. A narrative of the author's journey by rail and by foot along the coast of Great Britain. Completely readable.

The Lake District. AA/British Tourist Authority. 1985. An ordnance survey of the Lake District including maps, walks, places to stay, scenic drives, and touring guides in the countryside.

Lake District Landscapes. Jo Darke. Batsford/David & Charles. 1983. Paints a picture of the areas in which Wordsworth, Beatrix Potter, and others wrote their famous works.

London Walkabouts with Katie Lucas Top Ten Tourist Attractions.

Katie Lucas. Settle and Bendall/Hippocrene Books. 1985. Organized walking routes through London covering such sights as the Tower of London, Parliament, Westminster Abbey, and St. Paul's Cathedral.

Londonwalks. Anton Powell. Holt, Rinehart, and Winston. 1982. Describes details of five intimate walking tours in London—the London of Dickens, Inns of Court, the Old Palace Quarter, St. James's, and London's Latin Quarter.

Long Distance Paths of England and Wales. T.G. Millar. David & Charles. 1984. Describes waterways for trekking along; includes detailed maps and color photos.

The National Trust Book of Long Walks in England, Scotland, and Wales. Adam Nicolson. Pan Books/Crown. 1981. Delineates ten walks constituting "a discovery of Britain on foot." Contains information about wildlife, history, geology, and archaeology associated with each walk; illustrated with over two hundred color photos.

The New Forest. British Tourist Authority/Merrimack Publishers Circle, distr. 1983. Ordnance survey and walking guide of the New Forest district; includes comprehensive gazetteer, maps, geography, and natural history of the region as well as places to stay and other recreational resources of the area.

On Foot Through Europe: A Trail Guide to the British Isles. Craig Evans. Quill/Morrow. 1982. Lists suggested walks, useful addresses, guidebooks for walking, backpacking, ski touring, and climbing activities.

Scotland: Walks and Trails. Scottish Tourist Board/Merrimack Publishers Circle, distr. 1985. A paperback list of several walks through the Scottish countryside; illustrated with map locations.

Six English Towns. Alec Clifton-Taylor. British Broadcasting Corp./State Mutual Books, distr. 1978. Illustrated architectural walks through six English towns.

Six More English Towns. Alec Clifton-Taylor. British Broadcasting Corp./State Mutual Books, distr. 1981. Architectural walks through Warwick, Berwick-upon-Tweed, Saffron Walden, Lewes, Bradford-upon-Avon, and Beverley.

Strolling Through London. Frank Cook. British Tourist Authority/Merrimack Publishers Circle, distr. 1982. Describes a series of walks through London that cover the best sights and contain many surprises. Includes descriptive maps.

Turn Left at the Pub. George W. Oakes. Congdon and Weed. 1985.

A new paperback version of this classic; details twenty-four walking tours with maps and directions; covers Canterbury, Salisbury, Bath, Oxford, Stratford, and Cambridge areas.

Wales: Walking. Wales Tourist Board/Merrimack Publishers Circle, distr. 1984. Lists the best walks, long and short, through the Welsh countryside.

A Walk around London's Parks. Hunter Davies. Hamish Hamilton/ David & Charles. 1983. Describes walks in several of London's best known parks.

Walker's Britain. Andrew Duncan, ed. Pan Books. 1982. A pocket guide to over 240 walks, arranged by area—Southwest, Wales, Midlands, Northern England, Scotland, and others, with thirty-three sections, maps, and information about how to read them. Sections on clothes to wear, what to see, flora, and wildlife along the way, laws and safety precautions, an index of starting point place names.

Walking Canals. Ronald Russell. David & Charles. 1984. Describes walks along canals in England that can be taken currently.

Walking in the Heart of England. Heart of England Tourist Board. 1985. pamphlet. Key information about various types of walks available in the heart of England country.

Walking Old Railways. Christopher Somerville. David & Charles. 1979. Information about specific sections of old railway lines— most with rails now gone and converted to nature reserves of flora and fauna—that are recommended for exploration on foot.

Walking the Tops: Dartmoor to Scotland. Rex Bellamy. David & Charles. 1984. Walking tours in more than a dozen specific British mountains that require mountain climbing skills.

Audiovisual Materials

Your Personal Guide to London: "Tours by Tape." Nicholson's Publications. 1984. Includes one booklet and two audio cassettes of walking tours of the city; topics covered are Introduction to London, Westminster Walk, Tower of London, Heart of the City Walk, and Fleet Street Walk.

Magazines

WalkWays. 733 15th Street NW, Washington, DC 20005. q. Incorporating *Walking Journal*. Features include an international calendar of walking events, reviews of new books on walking, reports on health and fitness involved with walking, and the "Reading Walker Tours."

HOSTELING

The term "hosteling" is used here to cover opportunities for low-cost overnight accommodations, cultural exchange, and learning. A concept originally thought of exclusively in terms of young students and other traveling youth, it now often relates to older people as well. Youth hosteling is a popular British activity that is widely followed by young visitors to Britain.

The Youth Hostels Association supervises the operation of some 270 hostels in Britain for the use of individuals and groups. It also operates a number of field centers especially equipped for the study of human, plant, and animal habitats, geology, and related subjects. Activities sponsored by the association include walking/hiking trips, cycling, pony-trekking, sailing, and canoeing.

Elderhostel, the address of which, with others, is given below, organizes and manages programs of lifelong learning for senior adults, with courses given in such places as Durham, Birmingham, London, Canterbury, Brighton, and North Wales. Most offerings are for the summer only, but a few are available throughout the year in cooperation with various institutions of higher education. Sample course titles include: "Scotland's Heritage," "Developments in the British Novel," "Celts and Their Culture," "What Is a Village?" and "Roman London."

Some U.S. institutions of higher education also offer summer courses in Britain in cooperation with resident institutions. Universities include some from the California state university system and the University of Pittsburgh, among others.

Organizations and Associations

AFS International/Intercultural Programs, Incorporated. 313 East 43d Street, New York, NY 10017. Applications are received through chapters, but details and costs are available from the headquarters address.

American Youth Hostels. 1332 I Street, Suite 800, Washington, DC 20005, and 132 Spring Street, New York, NY 10012. Eligible individuals may wish to join this organization before leaving for a trip to Great Britain, thus qualifying for reciprocal services from the similar British organization.

British Universities Accommodations Consortium. University Park, Nottingham, England. Assists in locating summer room and board, usually within a British institution of higher education, for foreign students wishing to study there.

Central Bureau for Educational Visits and Exchanges. Seymour Mews, London W1H 9PE. Arranges pen friends links for school classes and individuals.

Elderhostel. 100 Boylston Street, Boston, MA 02116. Enrollment in the programs of this organization is limited to persons sixty years of age or older.

Youth Hostels Association. Trevelyan House, St. Albans, Herts AL1 2DY, England. Promotes appreciation of the British countryside, sponsors learning programs at its field centers, and provides inexpensive overnight rest stops for member travelers.

Books

Britain Youth Accommodation: 1985. British Tourist Authority. 1985. Multi-lingual directory of inexpensive British accommodations for young people.

London Youth Hostels: 1985. Youth Hostels Association. 1985. leaflet, free. Information about how to obtain overnight accommodations in London youth hostels.

Mort's Guide to Low-Cost Vacations on College Campuses. International Edition. CMG Publishing. nd. Offers information regarding summer and vacation accommodations for nonstudents in some thirty or so British colleges and universities.

Young Travellers' Guide: 1985. British Tourist Authority. 1985. Directed toward the purpose of aiding young people in planning interesting and profitable vacations in Britain. Includes information about where to stay, sightseeing, English language instruction, working in Britain, British pen friends, study opportunities, and more.

BICYCLING AND MOTORCYCLING

Britain's well-constructed and maintained road system encourages travel by bicycle or motorcycle. Bicycles are probably the cheapest way to get around the countryside, but if you prefer a little more speed, perhaps the motorcycle may be the way to go. After all, more than a million Britons enjoy recreational cycling; so join up. Remember, you may carry your bicycle free or for a small fee as baggage on public transport units throughout Britain—except during rush hours. Consult British Rail information schedules for full details.

Organizations and Associations

British Cycling Federation. 16 Upper Woburn Place, London WC1H 0QE. An organization which proposes to aid cyclists in their ramblings; publishes a yearly *Handbook.*

Bicycle USA. Suite 209, 6707 Whitestone Road, Baltimore, MD 21207. Distributes ($2/copy) *Tourfinder,* published by the League of American Wheelmen, listing some sixty tour operations which feature trips abroad, including Great Britain.

Country Cycling Tours. 167 West 83rd Street, New York, NY 10024. Offers arrangements for bicycling tours to various countries, including Great Britain.

Cycling Union. 93 Wentwood View, Caldicot, Gwent NP6 4QH, Wales. Organization of amateur cyclists; represents amateur cyclists' interests.

Cyclists' Touring Club. Cotterell House, 69 Meadrow, Godalming, Surrey GU7 3H7, England. A national association devoted to the encouragement of recreational cycling; provides members with useful information and publications as well as other services.

Dial-a-Bike. 18 Gillingham Street, Victoria, London SW1. Rents various styles and makes of bicycles (including tandems and folding types). Requires passport, driving license, student card, or checkbook and bankers card as means of identification.

Highland Cycle Tours. Highland Guides, Aviemore, Scotland. Uses youth hostels for holiday accommodations; participants may join a group or ride alone on new ten-speed bikes.

International Bicycle Touring Society. La Jolla, CA 92038. Organizes bicycling tours to European countries, including Britain; led by volunteers; participants stay in country inns. Caters to experienced cyclists.

London Cycling Campaign. Colombo Street Centre, London SE1 8DP. Promotes cycling in the British capital; distributes cycling-related publications.

Scottish Cyclists Union. 89 Ashley Road, Aberdeen AB1 6RL, Scotland. Represents interests of Scottish cyclists.

Books

Britain: Cycling—1985. British Tourist Authority. 1985. free. Full information about opportunities, regulations, and costs involved in cycling in Great Britain. Includes maps of many suggested itineraries.

Book of Cycling. Peter Knottley. Spurbooks. 1981. General information about the sport of cycling.

The CTC Book of Cycling. John Whatmore. David & Charles. 1983. Official route guide of the Cyclists Club. Offers details of 365 selected routes, with maps, highway information, accommodations; includes organizations.

The CTC Route Guide to Cycling in Britain and Ireland. Christa Gausden and Nicholas Crane. Haynes Publications. 1981. Route guides and tours for hundreds of cycling trips.

Cycle Sport Guide Complete. Peter Konopka. E.P. Group. 1982. General information guide to the cycling sport.

Cycle Touring in Britain and the Rest of Europe. Peter Knottley. Constable. 1981. Guided tours by bicycle in the United Kingdom and on the Continent.

Cycling. Jeanne Mackenzie, ed. Oxford University Press. 1981. More general information about the sport of cycling.

Cycling: A Source Book. Philip Ennis. Pelham Books. 1984. General information about cycling.

Encyclopaedia of Motor-Cycle Sport. rev. ed. Peter Carrick, comp. St. Martin's. 1982. Full details about the sport and necessary equipment for enjoying the ride.

Weekend Cycling: A Selection of Fully Planned Scenic Routes for Easy Touring. Christa Gausden. Automobile Association (AA)/ Merrimack Publishers Circle, distr. 1984. An up-to-date description of routes designed for bicyclists; detailed tours through Britain and Ireland included.

Magazines and Newsletters

Bicycle Magazine. 89-91 Boyham Street, Camden Town, London NW1 0AG. mo. Includes a bicycle buyer's guide, book reviews, test materials and suggestions, and a variety of bicycle trips.

Bike. National Publications Ltd. Bushfield House, Orton Centre,

Peterborough PE3 0UW, England. mo. Book reviews, articles on biking in Britain.

Cyclists Monthly. Specialist and Professional Press Ltd., Surrey House, 1 Throwley Way, Sutton, Surrey SM1 4QQ, England. General articles on British cycling.

Cycling World. Stone Industrial Publications, Limited. 2a Granville Road, Sidcup, Kent DA14 4BN, England. mo. Book reviews, articles on cycling tours, and equipment reviews.

CANAL AND RIVER BOATING

More and more people who vacation in Britain choose canal boats as a mode of travel for at least part of the time they are there. Canal boats provide an easy way to get close-up views of the countryside and fascinating glimpses of industrial cities. The canals make an excellent way to study "industrial archaeology" and offer plenty of opportunities to get well acquainted with people and customs encountered along the way. These trips are not cheap, but considering everything one gets with them they must be regarded as "reasonable." Canal boats range in size from the "skipper-yourself" types accommodating between two and ten passengers on a self-catering basis to those that are fully staffed, contain a number of well-appointed staterooms, and offer excellent gourmet meals. Some of Britain's best known canal-river boat passages include the Trent and Mersey Canal (a 2500-mile network of waterways extending through the English Midlands and the North Country with connections south to London and Oxford); the Thames and Severn Canal; the Grand Union Canal; and the Norfolk Broads of England; the Brecon and Abergavenny Canal of Wales; and the Caledonian Canal of Scotland. The British Waterways Board (see address below) is the single best source of information and assistance to help you plan your trip.

Organizations and Associations

Anglo-Welsh Waterway Holidays. Market Harborough, Leicestershire LE16 7BJ, England. Escorted hotel boat cruises along the Thames from Windsor to Oxford or the reverse; arrangements handled through Esplanade Tours, 38 Newbury Street, Boston, MA 02116.

Blake's Holiday Tours. Wroxham, Norwich NR12 8DH, England. A

British company that specializes in boat trips in the Norfolk Broads (England). U.S. booking agents include Canals Europe, 220 Redwood Highway, Mill Valley, CA 94941; and LeBoat, Inc., Box E, Marywood, NJ 07607.

Boat Enquiries Ltd. 43 Botley Road, Oxford OX2 0PT, England. A booking company for cruises in Great Britain and other European countries as well.

British Waterways Board. Melbury House, Melbury Terrace, London NW1 6JX. Oversees the British waterways, including the many hundreds of miles of canals; maintains publication and public information program pertaining to the waterways.

Charter Cruising Company. Rugby Wharf. Consul Road, Rugby, Warks CU21 1NR, England. Canal and river trips by boat in Britain.

English County Cruises. Station House, Altrincham, Cheshire WA14 1EP, England. Offers catered or self-drive canal cruises in the Chester area, and the Peak National Park and Llangollen canals in Wales.

Esplanade Tours. 38 Newbury Street, Boston, MA 02116. Canal and river tours in Britain began in 1985. Nine passengers are accommodated with all amenities on cruises that ply the upper Thames Valley through Berkshire, Buckinghamshire, and Oxfordshire. Weekly departures leave London from late April through late October.

Floating Through Europe. 271 Madison Avenue, New York, NY 10016. Offers escorted minicruises through Shakespeare country along the River Avon and the Severn; also leads a four-day cruise on the River Thames.

Hoseason's Holidays Ltd. Sunway House, Lowestoft, Suffolk NR32 3LT, England. Manages booking arrangements for a variety of canal boats in the area. Will supply literature describing services.

Inland Waterways Association. 114 Regent's Park Road, London NW1 8UQ. Publishes *Inland Waterways Guide* which gives information on canal and river holidays, including a list of companies that rent boats.

The London Waterbus Co. Camden Lock, London NW1 8AF. Runs waterbuses on the Regent's Canal from Little Venice to Camden Lock and various stops along the way, such as the London Zoo, Regent's Park, and the community of Camden Lock.

Fares and information from above address or the British Waterways Board.

Narrowboat Hotel Co. Ref 1B 12 Sandron Crescent, Little Neston, South Wirral, Cheshire L64 0TU, England. A holiday hotelboat cruise on the canals and waterways of Britain; all services included.

River Barge Holidays, Ltd. R.F.D. No. 1, Lisbon, New Hampshire 03585. Offers escorted tours on the Upper Thames, Oxford, Henley, Royal Windsor, and surrounding village areas; includes food, wine, and shore trips as well.

River Thames Cruising. Ash Island, Hampton Court, Surrey, England. Self-drive luxury cruisers plying the Thames.

Trent Valley Cruising Hotel. 27 St. Aidan's Road, Sheffield S2 2NG, England. Cruises in the East Midlands and Yorkshire country; spacious luxury barges with all amenities.

UK Waterway Holidays Ltd. Penn Place, Rickmansworth, Herts, England. Offers charter and hotel boat cruises on England's canals or skipper-yourself boat trips through the Pennines, Wales, and the North West, the Heart of England, and the Grand Union, Regents, and South Oxford Canals. Also offers trips in Scotland on the Caledonian Canal.

The Waterways Museum. Located beside the Grand Union Canal in Northamptonshire, this exhibit shows working boatmen and their families, traces the architecture of the various canals, and houses a wealth of history of England's industrial past. For further information write to the Curator, Waterways Museum, Stoke Bruerne, Towcester, Northants, England.

Waverly Steam Navigation. Starcross Quay, Glasgow, Scotland. Arranges trips on paddle steamers during the summer season.

Willow Wren Cruising Hotels. Unit 2, Rugby Wharf, Consul Road, Leicester Road, Rugby, Warwickshire, England. Offers cruises on narrow boats on English and Welsh canals; meals, accommodations, and captain provided.

Books

Boating Holidays. British Tourist Authority. 1985. pamphlets. A series of fold-up pamphlets on various waterways boating holiday plans, complete with maps, boat diagrams, information on flora and fauna.

Canal Boat Cookery. Iris Bryce. British Waterways Board. nd. Gives recipes, meal plans, and quantities for family and crew repasts. This author has also written *Canals Are My Home,* and *Canals Are My Life* available from K. Mason Publishers.

Canals and Rivers of Britain. Andrew Darwin. Hastings House. 1977. Accurate pictorial and verbal portrayals of Britain's major navigable rivers, organized by regions—where they go, why the canals were built, features, maps.

The Canals Book. Link House. nd. A guide to two thousand miles of inland waterways; how-to information on operating locks, finding boatyards and services, pump-out stations, shops, pubs, towns, and all waterside facilities.

Canals in Britain. Peter Smith. Discovery Series No. 257. Shire Publications. 1984. Excellent publication with concise information and planning tips. Also available: *London's Canals,* No. 232 in this series.

Canals of the British Isles: An Illustrated History. Charles Hadfield. David & Charles. 1984. Gives a detailed account of the development of the canals in all parts of Britain including South Wales and the Scottish border country.

Discovering Canals in Britain. Peter L. Smith. Shire Publications/ Seven Hills Books. 1984. Covers history of British canals, architecture, museums, and places to visit along the way.

English Rivers and Canals. Paul Atterbury. W.W. Norton. 1984. Written by an expert in this field; describes in detail and gives map locations for many rivers and canals; illustrated with over 190 photos.

A Lazy Man's Guide to Holidays Afloat. Boat Enquiries/British Waterways Board, distr. 1985. Covers self-drive boats, hotel boats, and waterway flora and fauna, character of each inland waterway; great for the neophyte boater.

Lost Canals and Waterways of Britain. Ronald Russell. David & Charles. 1982. Covers waterways in Scotland and Wales as well as England; describes over a hundred derelict canals and rivers for the intrepid explorer.

Narrow Boat. L.T.C. Rolt. Methuen. 1978. A classic story of a man and his boat on a four hundred-mile journey on the inland waterways.

Narrow Boats at Work. M.E. Ware. Moorland Publishing. 1985. A look at the life and work of the narrow boat captains and the areas in which they travel.

Nicholson's Ordnance Surveys, Guides to the Waterways. P. Atterbury and A. Darwin, eds. Robert Nicholson Publications. 1983. Comprehensive guides to the waterways of England and Wales which include strip maps of the various sectors—South, Central, and North. How-to information on facilities, lock operation, cruising details, and places to visit.

Nicholson's Waterways Guides. P. Atterbury and A. Darwin, eds. Robert Nicholson Publications. 1983. Three volumes include descriptions of the waterways in *South, Midlands,* and *North.*

The Royal River: The Thames from Source to Sea. W. Senior et al. Gresham Books/State Mutual Books, distr. 1985. An illustrated history, both pictorial and descriptive of this river; twelve sections of the book cover various stretches of the river, emphasizing the flora and fauna of the area, leisure pursuits on the river, and historical references.

The Shell Book of Inland Waterways. Hugh McKnight. David & Charles. 1981. Describes every aspect of the canals and rivers of Britain from history to architecture with many illustrations.

Stroudwater & Thames and Severn Canals Towpath Guide. Michael Handford and David Viner. Alan Sutton/Humanities. 1984. Details the history of each waterway and today's interest in the preservation of these beautiful areas.

The Thames Illustrated. John Leyland. Town and Country Books. 1983. A picture/text review of the sights and sounds of the Thames River on a journey from Richmond to Oxford.

The Waterways of Britain. Anthony Burton. Collins Willow. 1983. An illustrated description of many of the canals and waterways used by industry or tourist barges.

Audiovisual Materials

Audiovisual Materials. British Waterways Board. Several slide sets are available for purchase from the BWB. Some of the titles are: "Canal Architecture in Britain," "London's Canals," "Maritime England," "In the Steps of Thomas Telford," and "The Birmingham Canal Navigations." Write to the BWB for their "Canal Shop Catalogue."

Canal Maps. Douglas Smith. British Waterways Board. Detailed maps of canals with locks and bridges numbered, location of shops, pubs, and towns along the way, all drawn to scale: ½ inch to a mile. Maps for drivers of the canal boats are available for many sections including "London Waterways," "Upper Trent Valley," "Grand Union Canal," and others.

Films from the British Waterways Board. Central Film Library. The following films are available for rental only: *The World of the Waterways, There Go the Boats, The Gentle Highway, The Maritime Link,* and *Waterways-Our Heritage.* Also available on video cassettes.

Souvenirs for Children. British Waterways Board. Coloring books, cut-out books, games, and jigsaw puzzles available from this source for children to use on canal boat trips. All are related to canal boating and to the sights one sees along the waterways. The Board offers a sales catalog of its publications and other merchandise.

Magazines and Newsletters

Inland Waterways Guide. Inland Waterways Association, 114 Regent's Park Road, London NWL 8UQ. irreg. Offers information on canal and river holidays and lists boat rental companies.

Waterways News. British Waterways Board. 114 Regent's Park Road, London NW1 8UQ. 10/yr. An illustrated newspaper featuring articles on the latest recreational activities sponsored by the Waterways Board. Covers cruising, angling, natural history and industrial archaeology, walking, and boating.

CAMPING AND CARAVANING

British interest in camping and caravaning has recently increased considerably—so much so that today, camp parks are available in all parts of the country. Equipment for camping, widely available on a rental basis, ranges from more or less simple tents to trailers and converted vans (of the type whose tops elevate) to motor homes of various sizes and sophistication. Camping and caravaning give you certain advantages. You may choose where you want to go, do more or less what you want to do, and stay as long as you like—all the while carrying with you the meals and beds you and your family require. Perhaps the chief disadvantage of this recreational mode is that in order to ensure yourself a suitable night's location you must start early to look for a camp spot. But if you have difficulty in finding one, the staff of the nearest Tourist Information Centre will be glad to assist. There are also many unregistered sites (those owned by local farmers, for example) which campers may seek permission to use.

Organizations and Associations

Camping and Caravanning Club of Great Britain and Ireland. 11 Lower Grosvenor Place, London SW1W OEY. Coordinates information about camping and caravaning in Britain and Ireland.

British Caravanners Club. 11 Lower Grosvenor Place, London SW1W OEY. An organization which informs campers about the latest accommodations, equipment, etc. Publishes a biennial book for members; apply to the membership secretary for details.

Caravan Club. East Grinstead House, London Road, East Grinstead, West Sussex RH19 1UA, England. Members exchange information and tips about caravaning in Britain.

National Caravan Council, Limited. 43-45 High Street, Weybridge, Surrey KT13 8BT, England. Coordinates information about the interests of motorhome and trailer hobbyists in Great Britain.

Books

AA Camping and Caravanning in Britain. British Tourist Authority/ Merrimack Publishers Circle, distr. 1986. Lists a thousand campsites in Britain; gives location, prices, and complete information for low-cost travel.

Cade's Camping Site Guide 1985. Reg Cade, ed. Marwain Publishing Co. 1984. Cade's is an authoritative up-to-date guide to everything in the camping world. Other titles include: *Cade's Caravanner's and Camper's Guide 1985, The West Country,* and *Cade's Self-Catering Holiday Guide.*

Scotland: Camping and Caravan Sites. Scottish Tourist Board/ Merrimack Publishers Circle, distr. 1986. Lists nearly 350 sites for tenting, camping, and caravaning, with prices and facilities.

Magazines and Newsletters

Caravan. Link House mo. Evaluates trailer and motorhome equipment; provides buying guides, articles on campsites, and related information.

Farm Holidaying

Scores of the natives as well as American and other tourists find British farm holidays much to their liking. Trading the rigors of daily driving often associated with a typical touring holiday for the quiet of the countryside has much in its favor. The simple, comfortable accommodations to be found on most guest farms invite rest and relaxation. Much of the food of the delicious and bountiful meals is grown on the farms themselves. If you wish to do so, and the season is right, you may be encouraged to help with some of the many tasks associated with farming—harvesting hay, for example. Perhaps best of all, you are really experiencing the daily life of British people as they live it and, once more, the price is right—well within the reach of nearly anyone no matter how limited his or her budget.

Organizations and Associations.

Country-wide Holidays Association. Birch Heys, Cromwell Range, Manchester M14 6HU, England. Seeks to provide recreative, educative, and healthful holidays in Great Britain at lowest possible costs.

National Dairyman's Association. 19 Cornwall Terrace, London NW1 4QP. Coordinates national affairs related to interests of dairymen in the United Kingdom.

Royal Agricultural Society of England. 35 Belgrave Square, London SW1X 8QN. Stimulates attention to agriculture and to agricultural education in England.

Scottish Farmhouse Holidays. Drumtenant, Ladybank KY7 7UG, Fife, Scotland, Scottish farm holiday locations.

Wales Farm Holidays. Owen Glyndwr Centre, Machynlleth, Powys SY20 8EE, Wales. Welsh farm holiday locations.

Books

Britain: Stay on a Farm 1985. British Tourist Authority. 1985. List of accommodations in the countryside, by counties, in the various regions; all pertinent information included.

English Cottages and Farmhouses. Olive Cook. Thames & Hudson. 1984. Describes many farm buildings and cottages throughout England and their rural settings which are rapidly changing and disappearing with the onslaught of the industrial and technological age. Some are still available for viewing and give a glimpse into the social life, skills, and living conditions of the past.

Farm Holiday Guides. Farm Holidays. ann. Produces yearly guide to accommodations in farm locations in England, Scotland, Wales, and Ireland.

Staying Off the Beaten Track. Elizabeth Gundrey. Automobile Association (AA)/Merrimack Publishers Circle, distr. 1986. A guide to moderately priced inns, small hotels, and farm and country houses in England. Provides full information—prices, facilities, and locations. Also available from the BTA.

HOME EXCHANGING

Exchanging your home—and perhaps your car, boat, or other possessions in the United States—for a similar home and possessions in Britain is an arrangement that appeals to many people. The idea is simple: you and your family spend your vacation in the British home, and your British counterparts spend their vacation in your home. It is a basic barter system concept; no rent changes hands. There is a modest fee for the agency that makes the match (unless the arrangement is made privately, which is not usual). Details are worked out before the vacation begins. Inventories of possessions may be exchanged, and pet and plant care in both locations may be involved.

Organizations and Associations

Adventures in Living. Box 278, Winnetka, IL 60093. An annual directory of rentals and exchanges is available at $25/yr., including supplements.

British Tourist Center. 6th Floor, Berkeley Building, 19 West 44th Street, New York, NY 10036. Tel: (800) 225-6577. A British-operated booking agency that handles reservations, usually of a short-term nature (a few days to a few weeks), of well-situated, luxury London apartments that contain full housekeeping facilities and equipment.

Holiday Exchanges. Box 878, Belen, NM 87002. Lists of exchanges available monthly, $20/6 months. Helps to arrange home exchanges on an international basis.

Home Exchange International. 22458 Ventura Boulevard, Suite E, Woodland Hills, CA 91364. International home exchange services.

Home from Home. Oasland's House, 4 Broad Lane, Cottenham, Cambridge CB4 4SW, England. For a fee of $35, one can obtain an application form which will entitle you to a list of properties to fit your needs for a vacation exchange in the British Isles. Over seven hundred homes are available in the U.K., Europe, the U.S., and Canada.

International Home Exchange. Box 3975, San Francisco, CA 94119. Offers about 450 listings; charges a fee.

Vacation Exchange Club. 12006 111th Avenue, Unit No. 12, Youngstown, AZ 85363. Offers about six thousand listings; charges a nominal fee.

Worldwide Exchange. Box 1563, San Leandro, CA 94577. Charges fee when exchange is arranged.

Books

Meet the British: 1985. British Tourist Authority. 1985. Includes names, addresses, and factual annotations of mainly private individuals who are willing to book accommodations for persons wishing to stay as paying guests in British homes.

Travellers' Directory. Tom Linn. Friends General Conference. 1979. An international directory of some eight hundred persons willing to provide short-term hospitality for travelers in return for the same services in this country. International listings.

SELF-CATERING

The British use the term "self-catering" to identify the practice of engaging an apartment, a house, or a cottage in which to live and keep house for a relatively short period of time. In such cases, kitchen and dining equipment is furnished, including a refrigerator, dishes, glassware, pots and pans, and other household paraphernalia. Bed linens and towels are usually, but not always, provided. (Ask.) You have only to buy the groceries and start living there. Maid service for cleaning and bedmaking may or may not be part of the arrangement. People on special diets, or who find it wearing (and expensive) to eat out all the time, find this kind of arrangement especially attractive.

Organizations and Associations

AAD Associates. Box 3927, Amity Station, New Haven, CT 06525. Lists homes in England, Wales, and Scotland, including some in London.

At Home Abroad. 405 East 56th Street, Apartment 6H, New York, NY 10022. Lists British farm and country properties; photos upon request with a payment of $35 fee.

At Home in England. 65 Larchmont Avenue, Larchmont, NY 10535. Lists homes in Wales, Scotland, and England, including London.

Doorways to Britain, Limited. 121 South Royal Street, Alexandria, VA 22314. Serves as a British country homes representative in the United States; provides lists of accommodations; can make advance bookings.

Heart of England Cottages. 215 West First Street, Tustin, CA 92680. Represents the Country Homes Association of Britain in the United States; helps with trip planning and cottage rentals before arrival in Britain.

Home from Home International, Ltd. The Estate Office, Rudgwick Grange, Rudgwick, Horsham, Sussex, England. Manages a program of the rental of British homes for self-catering. Write for booklet, *Self-Catering Holidays in Britain* (free).

In the English Manner. Box 447, Orinda, CA 94563. Tel: (415) 254-6341 or 3986. Christine Campbell, U.S. Manager. A private organization that arranges the rental of homes, apartments, or service flats in London and environs as well as in other parts of England, Scotland, and Wales. Included are some stately homes and castles. Will also arrange tours and trips in Great Britain, including rental of cars, bookings of tours, reservations of theater tickets, rail and air accommodations, and related services. Arrangements may also be made for individuals to stay with families in Britain.

Inquiline, Inc. Cedar Road, Katonah, NY 10536. Has a directory of rentals in London, England, Scotland, and Ireland.

Villas International. 213 East 38th Street, New York, NY 10016. Arranges short- and longer-term rentals of English flats and villas, as well as cottages (principally from one week to a month); typically about $250/week.

Your Home in London. New York, NY (212) 688-2996; Annapolis, MD (301) 261-2233. A new service for travelers to Britain provides apartment rentals in London for stays of three days to three months or longer; cost approximately 30 percent less than comparable hotel rooms and bookings can be made within thirty-six hours or so.

Books

AA Self Catering in Britain. British Tourist Authority/Merrimack Publishers Circle, distr. 1985. Lists approximately fifteen thousand accommodations for rent with cooking facilities; map locations, prices given; AA approved.

Britain: Holiday Homes, 1986. British Tourist Authority. 1986. A helpful guide to what the British call "the self-catering holiday" of the "furnished" facility "with kitchen privileges." Involved are flats, houses, cottages, chalets, or even homes—many converted from barns or cabins. All establishments listed provide linen—some without fee. Each conforms to British Tourist Authority minimum requirements for such facilities. Only those with a minimum of three self-contained rental units are included; those with one or two have been omitted. There are variations in what is provided in the rental fee (gas, electricity, telephone, etc.); inquire in advance for further details.

Scotland: Self Catering Accommodation. Scottish Tourist Board/ Merrimack Publishers Circle, distr. 1986. Lists around two thousand flats, cottages, caravans, and chalets with prices and facility information.

Self-Catering Holidays in England, Wales, Scotland. English Tourist Board. 1984. Where to stay and eat in virtually every part of England. Includes full data on facilities provided.

Wales: Self-Catering. Wales Tourist Board/Merrimack Publishers Circle, distr. 1985. Lists places to rent, camping and trailering sites; gives prices, locations, and facilities available.

BED-AND-BREAKFASTING

Staying overnight in private homes, country inns, and historic hotels that provide both lodging for the night and breakfast the next morning—and sometimes an evening meal, if desired—has become especially popular in Britain. The services of the "B & B" lodgings are available at quite low prices. In them one may have to give up the convenience of a private bath, but that may be more than compensated for by the cozy, homelike atmosphere and the generous breakfast you will be offered. Most of them have "vacancy" and "no vacancy" signs which make it easy to decide which one to stop at. Amost invariably such accommodations are neat and clean and you will save considerably over the price of overnight facilities in a regular commercial hotel.

Books

AA Guesthouses, Farmhouses and Inns in Britain. British Tourist Authority/Merrimack Publishers Circle, distr. 1986. Lists some three thousand bed and breakfast places, inns, and farmhouses with prices and services; carefully checked and approved by AA personnel.

Bed and Breakfast in Britain. 1985. Farm Holiday Guides. British Tourist Authority. 1985. General information and specific listings for bed-and-breakfast establishments in many parts of Britain.

The Best Bed and Breakfast in the World 1985: United Kingdom and Ireland. Sigourney Welles and Jill Darbey. East Woods Press. 1985. Describes bed-and-breakfast accommodations in Britain (England, Scotland, Wales, and Northern Ireland) and offers other useful travel information.

Country Inns and Back Roads of Britain and Ireland. Norman T. Simpson, Berkshire Travellers Press/Harper and Row. 1985. Includes listings for Scotland, Wales, Cornwall, Cotswolds, Highlands, Northern Ireland, and the Lake District. Offers complete directions, addresses, telephone numbers, prices, and locations.

Country Inns and Historic Hotels of Britain: 1985-86. Eileen and Eugene O'Reilly. Burt Franklin. 1985. Organized by geographical region and by town for locations in England, Scotland, and Wales. Provides maps, rates, information about how to get there, and a few historical facts. Full information on facilities offered for more than three hundred selected "best" accommodations, including a drawing or photograph of each.

English, Welsh, and Scottish Country Inns and Castle Hotels. rev. ed. Karen Brown and June Brown. Travel Press. 1985. Describes over a hundred inns and accommodations in these countries with charming sketches of the various lodgings; itinerary suggestions and directions included.

Scotland: Where to Stay—Bed and Breakfast. Scottish Tourist
  Board/Merrimack Publishers Circle, distr. 1986. Lists two thousand bed and breakfast establishments which give good value
  for your money.
Scotland: Where to Stay—Hotels and Guesthouses. British Tourist
  Authority/Merrimack Publishers Circle, distr. 1986. Locations,
  prices, and services of over two thousand places to stay from
  hotels to guesthouses in Scotland.
Wales Hotels and Guesthouses. British Tourist Authority/Merri-
  mack Publishers Circle, distr. 1985. Inexpensive acommoda-
  tions from bed-and-breakfast to inns, hotels, and even campsites.

HOLIDAYS IN THE BRITISH ISLANDS

An island holiday in Great Britain can involve any one of many
outlying islands which are very interesting and very different from
each other. There are several islands in the English Channel, among
them the Channel Islands which are from ten to thirty miles off the
French coast; the Hebrides—themselves divided into Inner and
Outer groups—are off the west coast of Scotland; and the Scilly
Islands lie off the southwestern tip of Cornwall. There is the Isle of
Wight, off the south coast of England; and there is the Isle of Man,
situated in the Irish Sea, equidistant from the coasts of Scotland,
Ireland, and Wales.
  The Channel Islands include Jersey, Guernsey, Alderney, Sark,
and several smaller uninhabited ones. They have the warmest
climate in the British Isles and their chief business—besides tourism—is dairying. They are reached via a five- or six-hour car-
passenger ferry trip from Weymouth or Portsmouth, or by plane.
(Sark accepts no cars, and one must take the ferry from Guernsey.)
The islands are all British dependencies but they have an interesting
sense of independence and laws and customs that are a curious
mixture of Norman French and English. The Hebrides are wilder
and more at the mercy of the sea and the wind—being further
north—but they boast some of the most beautiful scenery in the
world. Sheep herding and fishing are basic to the livelihood of the
natives there, while flower growing for the English markets occupies
many people of the Isles of Scilly.
  The Isle of Wight and the Isle of Man are both popular holiday

destinations for British people. The Isle of Man (home of the Manx cat) has its own parliament, currency, and postage stamps and car ferry connections from Liverpool and other locations, as well as frequent air connections.

Books

Britain's Offshore Islands. Michael Shea. Country Life Books. 1981. Describes not only the islands themselves but the people, their crafts, mountains, wildflowers, and birds; a guide to nearly four thousand islands.

Channel Island Hopping. Mary Fane-Gladwin. Gentry Books/Hippocrene Books. 1984. A handbook for the independent traveler with a short history of each island, places to stay, and detailed maps of sites to visit.

Islands. John Fowler. Little, Brown. 1979. A description of the islands of Britain, especially the Scilly Islands. A personal journey by this author of the *French Lieutenant's Woman;* illustrated with photos.

A Journey to the Western Islands of Scotland. Samuel Johnson and James Boswell. Oxford University Press. 1984. A journal of an early tour of the Hebrides. An interesting glimpse of life on the islands in the eighteenth century.

Scottish Island Hopping. Jemina Tindall. Hippocrene Books. 1983. A revision of this informative book containing hotel, bed-and-breakfast accommodations, services; best ways of getting from island to island via bicycle and ferry or boat.

The Shell Book of the Islands of Britain. David Booth and David Perrott. British Tourist Authority/Merrimack Publishers Circle, distr. 1982. Describes all the British offshore islands along the coast with more than one hundred fifty photographs to guide one in unusual vacations.

Wight: Biography of an Island. Paul Hyland. Gollancz/David & Charles. 1984. Traditional scenic pleasures of this island just off England's south coast.

6 Food and Drink in Great Britain

To many tourists, good food and drink are important to a successful trip abroad. No less important in Britain than elsewhere, food and drink play a significant role in rounding out one's visit. The food there is interestingly good, the pubs attractive and cheerful, the teas unsurpassed anywhere in the world, and the Scotch whisky nothing short of superb. The references and sources that follow will help you to make the most of them.

EATING

At one time it was fashionable to denigrate British cuisine and to compare it unfavorably with the more delicate tastes and greater sophistication of the continental cookery of Europe. Recently, however, there has seemed to be a heightened appreciation of the really good food that is turned out in many British restaurants as well as in private homes. While it may be true that British food has a tendency toward heartiness and is sometimes overcooked for some tastes, the roast meats, game, and fish, especially, are usually delicious. Britain's proximity to the sea at all points highlights the importance of seafood in the diet, and many varieties are eaten: cod, sole, haddock, plaice, bream, halibut, turbot, shrimp, and oysters. Kippered herring is a popular breakfast dish. Cheeses abound, among the best known ones—all named for places in Britain—being

Stilton, Cheshire, Blue Dorset, Caerphilly, Wensleydale, Leicester, Lancashire, Cheddar, and Double Gloucester.

The references that follow, almost all of which have been written or compiled by Britons, provide a broad sampling of the literature of the area that pertains to the preparation and enjoyment of food, and, in some instances, of the entertainment that accompanies its serving in some of Britain's fine restaurants.

Organizations and Associations

British Hotels, Restaurants, and Caterers Association. 13 Cork Street, London W1X 2BH. Looks after the interests of proprietors and others interested in the hotel and restaurant business.

Farm and Food Society. 4 Willifield Way, London NW11 7XT. Encourages ecologically sound agriculture and the production of wholesome food with a fair deal for farmers. Provides general information regarding British food products.

Institute of Food, Science, and Technology of the United Kingdom. 105-111 Euston Street, London NW1 2ED. Encourages applications of science and technology to every aspect of food. Provides scientific information regarding the production, processing, and use of British and other foods.

International Wine and Food Society, Ltd. 66-67 Wells Street, London W1. Promotes the appreciation of wine and food generally; encourages improved standards of cookery.

Books

AA Eat Out in Britain for Around £5. British Tourist Authority/Merrimack Publishers Circle, distr. 1984. Gazetteer format arranged by town with restaurants, pubs, wine bars, and bistros. Includes hours, map locations, addresses, list of gourmet shops, explanation of the "voucher" system, and a detailed map section.

Book of Welsh Food. Bobby Freeman. Image Imprints. 1980.

British and Irish Country Cooking. Tony Schmaeling. Omega Books. 1983. Easy to follow recipes arranged by categories; includes description of restaurant which originated the recipe, the country setting, and color illustrations and photos.

British Cooking: A Complete Guide to Culinary Practice in England, Scotland, Ireland, and Wales. Lizzie Boyd, ed. The

Overlook Press. 1979. A comprehensive guide to English cooking with a brief history, basic methods of cooking, and recipes for everything from jugged hare to meat pies, from tea cakes to jams and jellies. A metric system conversion chart and a glossary of cooking terms are appended.

The Cooking of the British Isles. Adrian Bailey. Time-Life Books. 1983. A classic work on British food from tea through roast beef and lamb to fish, game, and the famous plum pudding; includes introductory sections detailing history, customs, and traditions surrounding British food preferences. Colorfully illustrated with photos; glossary of terms, indexed; recipes at end of each section.

A Cook's Tour of Britain. Michael Smith. Collins/Willow. 1984. A collection of recipes from the Women's Institute groups, arranged by region and compiled by the author with authentic stories, anecdotes, and drawings.

Dining on Show in London. Sara Mengue. British Tourist Authority. 1985. Sponsored by Diners Club. Essential facts about good restaurants in eleven sections of London.

Eating Out in London. London Tourist Board. 1984. An alphabetically arranged compilation (by name) of some seventy London restaurants and places also offering evening entertainment. Intended to meet a wide variety of tastes and budgets. Describes facilities, indicates cost ranges, and identifies menu specialties of the house.

Food and Drink in Britain. Constance Anne Wilson. Penguin. 1984. A history and social commentary on food and drink from early Britain to the eighteenth century.

Great British Cooking: A Well Kept Secret. Jane Garmey. Random House. 1981. A collection of recipes of the best in British home cooking compiled by a native. Includes anecdotes about the history of the dishes, British food lore, and customs. Recipes include Cornish pasties, brown bread, ice cream, crumpets, marmalades; all in easy to follow format using American terms.

A Guide to London's Best Restaurants. Automobile Association (AA)/British Tourist Authority/Merrimack Publishers Circle, distr. 1985. Lists around seven hundred restaurants in the London area with types of food, prices, and location information. Includes breakfast and afternoon tea places, wine bars, and pubs with good food. Indexed by areas of the city.

In Search of Food. David and Richard Mabey. Macdonald and

Jane's. 1979. An informative survey of traditional eating and drinking in Britain, with full details of how to prepare such items as Melton Mowbray pork pie, Yorkshire pudding, Cumberland sausage, and many other items.

The Island Cookbook. Johanna Jones. Arcady Books. 1984. Recipes from the English Isle of Wight area.

Just a Bite: Egon Ronay's Lucas Guide. Mitchell Beazley. Egon Ronay Organization/St. Martin's Press. 1984. For gourmet eating on a budget; covers restaurants throughout Britain including where to eat on and off the motorways. Has an easy "how to use" section; a list of vegetarian places; a list of restaurants, tea shops in London open on Sundays; and town maps of London and other major areas.

London Restaurant Guide. British Tourist Authority. 1984. Regularly distributed throughout London. Contains advertisements of numerous restaurants as well as annotational remarks concerning them. Classified under various ethnic headings.

The National Trust Book of Traditional Puddings. Sara Paston–Williams. David & Charles. 1983. Describes and gives recipes for the centuries old custom of serving English puddings such as "Bedfordshire Clanger" and "Sussex Tipsy Cake."

999 Places to Eat in Britain. Automobile Association (AA)/British Tourist Authority. 1984. A useful guide to planning ahead for your trip to Britain; available from BTA, major bookstores in the U.S., and the British Travel Bookshop.

The Seven Centuries Cookbook: From Richard II to Elizabeth II. Maxime McKendry., McGraw-Hill. 1973. A classic cookbook containing traditional English recipes adapted by the author. Includes a history of English cooking from the fourteenth to the twentieth centuries.

A Taste of England. Josy Argy and Wendy Riches. Sphere Books. 1983. Organized by sections of England (Cumbria, North West, etc.); names restaurants, provides an index for them, and provides recipes of their favorite English foods.

A Taste of Scotland. Scottish Tourist Board. pamphlet. ann. A list of restaurants which serve authentic Scottish dishes such as Scotch salmon, cock-a-leekie soup, clapshot, rumbledethumps, cranachan, and haggis.

A Taste of Wales. Wales Tourist Board. pamphlet. ann. A list of restaurants that serve authentic Welsh dishes such as mutton, lamb, trout, leeks, currant cakes, pancakes, and blueberry pie.

Vegetarian Restaurants in England. Lesley Nelson, ed. Penguin.
1982. A guide to good eating out for vegetarians.
Welsh Fare. Sara Minwell Tibbott. Welsh Folk Museum. nd. A
collection of recipes from all over Wales; authentic old-country
dishes described.

PUB-CRAWLING

Public houses, or "pubs," are characteristic British institutions.
They are more than seventy thousand strong, patronized by men
and women, old and young. Most pubs serve simple, nourishing
food at lunchtime as well as a variety of drinks—mostly alcoholic,
but some nonalcoholic. London pubs open at 11 o'clock A.M.
(exception is 2 P.M. on Sunday), remain open until 3 P.M., reopen at
5:30 P.M., and close for the night at 11 P.M. (with Sunday first and
second closing hours slightly different). There are some variations
depending on area of the city or the country. Legally, no one under
eighteen years of age is permitted to buy alcohol, but it is now
increasingly common for pubs to reserve special family rooms
where the children may be served soft drinks while adults drink
what they please. Although whisky and other hard liquor is served,
the favorite pub drink by far is one or another of the many types of
"brew"—ale, bitter, mild, stout, or lager.

"Pub-crawling"—which means doing the rounds of a series of
drinking establishments—may, after all, not be the best way to enjoy
the uniqueness of British public house culture; settling in for several
hours at one congenial stop may be much more satisfying. Pubs are
essentially neighborhood affairs, centers of sociability and relaxation. Most guidebooks list some favorite pubs and give clues as to
their prevailing atmospheres: literary, artistic, political (and, if so,
what particular stripe), and the like. Pub "regulars" are usually
friendly and welcoming to strangers, and Americans are generally
popular whatever the international political climate of the moment.

Organizations and Associations

International Wine and Food Society, Ltd. 66-67 Wells Street,
London W1. Promotes appreciation of wine and food; seeks to
improve standards of cookery.
National Association of Licensed House Managers. 9 Coombe

Lane, London SW20 8NE. Seeks to improve the status of managers of public houses and to improve the quality of services they offer.

National Association of Wine and Beermakers. 33 Heworth Road, York, England. National association that cares for the interests of entrepreneurs in the field.

National Dart Association of Great Britain. 197 Fulwell Avenue, Clayhail, Ilford, Essex, England. Maintains contact with centers of this sport popularly played in pubs and individuals connected with it.

National Inns and Taverners Association. 36/1 The Market Place, Wokingham, Berks RG11 1AT, England. Seeks to encourage improved services, to instill new ideas, and to improve consumer services in inns and taverns.

Scottish Darts Association. 27 Victoria Street, Rutherglen, Glasgow, Scotland. Collects and distributes unusual facts about the game, which is so often played in pubs.

Books

AA Bistros, Inns, and Wine Bars in Britain. British Tourist Authority/Merrimack Publishers Circle, distr. 1985. Lists a thousand establishments which provide good value for travelers in Britain.

The Best of British Pubs. Peter Earle and David Colbeck, comps. Charles Letts. 1980. Lists over a thousand pubs and restaurants by geographical area and city. Maps included, glossary of terms, food and drink available, whether open to children and dogs or not.

City of London Pubs. Timothy M. Richards and James Stevens Curl. Drake Publishers. 1973. Lists pubs arranged by area with map locations, addresses, description, history of each; illustrated with photos; glossary of architectural terms and bibliography of pub history appended.

The Drinkers' Guide to Walking. Nicola Hodge. Proteus Publishing. 1982. Carefully selected country rambles encompassing historic "watering holes" en route. Includes the northeast, southwest, southeast, London, and Yorkshire.

Egon Ronay's Guinness Pub Guide. Egon Ronay. Egon Ronay Organization/St. Martin's Press. 1985. Lists and annotates good cheeseboards throughout England; pubs for families (by cities);

restaurants and pubs; pubs and restaurants in London and throughout England (by location).

The English Pub. Andy Whipple and Rob Anderson. Thames Hudson/Viking-Penguin. 1985. Includes portraits of publicans, pub signs and their makers, recipes for pub food, a brief history of how beer is made, and why and how the Campaign for Real Ale (CAMRA) was established. Beautifully illustrated with color photos and appended with a short bibliography.

Good Beer Guide. Neil Hanson. Campaign for Real Ale. 1985. Pubs around Europe worth patronizing for their traditionally-brewed (as opposed to commercially manufactured) beer.

A Guide to London's Best Pubs. Martin Green. British Tourist Authority. 1983. A list of 650 best pubs in London, with detailed information on hours, food, drink, and entertainment.

Haunted Pubs in Britain and Ireland. Marc Alexander. Sphere Books. 1984. Where reputedly "haunted" pubs are located; spotted on maps; other details included.

The Inn Explorer's Guide. Frank Bottomley. Kaye and Ward/David & Charles. 1984. Illustrated glossary of terms relating to English inns. History and background of inns generally, by name and location throughout England. Lists seventeen thousand English pubs.

Nicholson's London Pub Guide. Judy Allen. Robert Nicholson Publications. 1981. List of pubs by area and type with a detailed history, facilities, offerings, and easy map locator.

Pub Games of England. Patrick T. Finn. Oleander Press. 1981. Pub games played in several sections of the country: bowls, darts, dominoes, backgammon, skittles, shove half-penny, and more. Interesting commentaries on variations of these games in different parts of Britain. Directions on how to play the games are included, also information about where they are played.

Real Beer in London. Campaign for Real Ale (CAMRA). 1984. English brewers; locations of 2,300 pubs and listings of the beers they serve.

Victorian Pubs. Mark Girouard. Yale University Press. 1984. A profusely illustrated book with photos and drawings of architectural details; covers the development of the pub, history, plans, architecture, fittings, politics, and the demise of many of the establishments. Focuses primarily on London pubs but gives some fine examples of others throughout Great Britain in the final chapter.

TEA IN BRITAIN

The custom of having early morning, midmorning, and afternoon tea is strongly entrenched in Britain. Many people there have early tea to help them get out of bed; you may be served midmorning tea if you are visiting in an office at around 10 o'clock or so, but probably it will be coffee; and afternoon tea is generally had between 4 and 5 o'clock. Afternoon tea can be made into quite a meal; many British people have a "big tea," even a "high tea," if they intend to have dinner, or supper, rather late in the evening. Besides the tea itself (traditionally served with cream or milk rather than lemon), there will be—even for an ordinary run-of-the-mill afternoon tea—thin, delicate sandwiches (watercress, cucumber), scones, little cakes, tarts, toast. There may be a number of other things too, such as egg dishes, small pieces of cold meat or fish, shortbreads and salad, whipped cream, pudding, and jam. High teas often feature something—creamed perhaps—on toast. After a real high tea, you will not want to eat again for some time!

Among western countries, Britain uses by far the most tea; the United States—perhaps surprisingly for such a nation of coffee drinkers—is second. India and Ceylon are the two great producers of tea in the world. Black tea is grown in all tea-growing countries, but most green and Oolong (greenish-brown in color) teas come from China, Japan, and Taiwan.

Organizations and Associations

British Tea Producers Association. 5 High Timber Street, Upper Thames Street, London EC4V 3LE. An organization of companies with overseas tea production interests.

United Kingdom Tea Association. 9 Wapping Lane, London E1 9DA. Promotes consumption of tea; consumer-oriented.

Books

Afternoon Tea in London. London Tourist Board. 1984. A list of London hotels and restaurants where one may have afternoon English tea and in which the menus may consist of choices of "finger" sandwiches (cucumber, cheese, ham, egg, or other), bread and butter, scones or muffins, cakes and pastries, and Indian or China tea.

National Trust Book of Afternoon Tea. Marika Hanbury Tenison.

David & Charles. 1980. Includes, along with numerous "tea-time" recipes, interesting commentaries on the history of afternoon tea, types of tea, and the correct way to make it.

Stop for Tea. English Tourist Board. 1984. Lists more then three hundred English establishments that serve mid-morning and afternoon teas.

WHISKY DISTILLING AND BOTTLING

Observing details of the several steps of producing, distilling, and bottling Scotch whisky (notice the Scottish spelling of "whisky," not "whiskey," as it is with U.S. bourbon or Irish whiskey) is often of great interest to American tourists. Although recent reductions in sales of the beverage have caused some concern in the area, the industry still thrives and shows signs of continuing success. The number of whisky distilleries in Scotland's Grampian region makes it of special interest for a tour. The trail on which six such distilleries are distributed is only seventy miles long. If one allots the minimum recommended one hour of visiting time to each, and includes some travel time between stops, it is easy to see you could use up an entire day in the process. The distilleries involved are Glenlivet, Glenfarclas, Tamdhu, Glenfiddich, Glen Grant, and Strathisia. Known as "the only malt whisky trail in the world," the route provides visual and verbal explanations (and some olfactory as well!) of the several processes involved: *malting* (making barley into malted barley by allowing the grain to germinate which aids in converting its starch into sugar), *mashing* (involving milling and mashing of the malt and mixing it with hot water, forming a sugary liquid which is later drawn off for fermentation), *fermentation* (the liquid is cooled and fermented by yeast into a weak alcohol called wash), *distillation* (the wash is distilled two times to produce the spirit, and it is here, especially, where the stillman's skill is paramount), *maturation* (the newly distilled spirit is placed in oak casks, put in a warehouse, and left for several years to mature and mellow), and, finally, *bottling* (after being reduced—with water—to the proper alcoholic strength, the whisky is filtered, bottled, capped, labeled, and crated for shipment).

It is possible, too, to visit breweries to observe the beer-making process.

Contrary to widespread belief, the British have been producing wines for almost five centuries—largely from grapes grown in the southern parts of Wales and England. The Romans were known to have done the same by planting vineyards around their forts. Today's production, which is not large but is "noticeable," centers on rosés and whites. The latter, especially, are reputed to be "flinty and distinctive." One may call on vineyards in different parts of the country.

Organizations and Associations

English Vineyards Association. The Ridge, Lamberhurst Down, Kent TN3 8ER, England. Publishes a complete list of English vineyards which are open to the public for tours.

International Wine and Food Society, Ltd. 66-67 Wells Street, London, WI. Promotes appreciation of wines and foods; seeks general improvement of cooking standards.

Malt Distillers Association of Scotland. 1 North Street, Elgin, Morayshire 1V30 1UA, Scotland. Cares for national interests in the field.

Scotch Whisky Association. 28 Atholl Crescent, Edinburgh EH3 8HF. Represents whisky producers generally.

Books

English Vineyards. John Bedford. Discovery Series No. 269. Shire Publications Ltd. 1982. Gives practical information on vineyard locations, products, and history. A related book in the series is *Country Winemaking.*

Guide to Visiting Vineyards. Anthony Hogg. Michael Joseph/Merrimack Publishers Circle, distr. 1984. Contains brief chapter materials on English wineries and a valuable guide to Scottish distilleries.

The Malt Whisky Trail. Scottish Tourist Board. nd. Contains printed information, pictures, and a large map portraying locations of most of Scotland's important whisky distilleries.

7 Sports Activities in Great Britain

The British, as a people, love sports of all kinds, and, in fact, all manner of outdoor activity. We have already covered, in the chapter about "getting around," the popular activities of walking and bicycling; we will discuss in another chapter an outdoor activity which engages many British people for countless happy hours—gardening. In this chapter we will look at some of the active sports, many, but not all, which visitors to Britain might be likely to enjoy along with the natives, either by direct involvement or as spectators.

The sports activities we introduce resources for in this chapter are bird-watching and field studies, boating, cricket, croquet, fishing, gliding, golf, horseback riding and trekking, horse racing, hunting, lawn bowling, rugby, sailing, skiing, soccer, and tennis. We have not devoted a separate special section to swimming in Britain even though it is probably the most universally available water sport of all, here as elsewhere in the world, wherever there are rivers, lakes, streams, ponds, or ocean beaches. Like walking, swimming can be done by almost anyone of any age and in any sort of physical condition. However, the chief barrier in Britain—virtually all parts of it—is that the waters both inland and off the coast are *cold*. People do go "bathing," of course, but swimming outdoors cannot be said to be widely popular. A few hotels and motels maintain indoor pools. Recently, many districts have built well-equipped sports centers (often with heated, indoor pools, and sometimes with saunas) catering to sports as varied as badminton and squash, gymnastics, weight training, and indoor bowling.

BIRD-WATCHING AND FIELD STUDIES

Bird-watching is an especially popular diversion in Britain, and the Royal Society for the Protection of Birds, with half a million members, does much to ensure enduring interest in it. The society plans bird-watching holidays in Northern Ireland and in other parts of the United Kingdom, as do several other British organizations. This is a hobby/activity which combines very well with walking and is thus available to people of all ages and physical conditions, including those who cannot participate in more strenuous sports. Flower, plant, tree, insect, and wildlife observation provide, of course, an interesting additional or variational activity in this field.

Visitors to Britain whose interests lie in the areas of bird-watching and field studies will find in the list of organizations and associations, books, and audiovisual materials that follows, helpful clues for ways to capitalize upon their stay.

Organizations and Associations

British Institute of Recorded Sound. 29 Exhibition Road, London SW7. Maintains a national sound archives and serves as a national center for the study of sound and sound recording. Includes an international music collection and the British Library of Wildlife Sounds.

British Natural History Museum. Cromwell Road, London SW7. A collection of over two thousand plants and animals displayed in their natural habitats; includes marshlands, seashore, heath and moors, woodland, freshwater areas, fields, and downlands.

British Trust for Ornithology. Beach Grove, Station Road, Tring, Hertfordshire HP23 5NR, England. Works towards the advancement of the science of ornithology throughout Britain.

The Field Studies Council. 62 Wilson Street, London EC2A 2BU. Arranges studies of conservation, environment, and natural history, and of birds and other animals.

Highland Safaris. Kyle and Glen, Muir of Ord, Ross-shire 1V6 7UQ Scotland. Arranges informal natural history courses including ornithology, botany.

Hobby Holidays. Glencommon, Inchmarlo, Banchory, Kincardineshire, Scotland. Ornithology tours as well as other outdoor activities arranged.

London Natural History Society. 142 Harborough Road, London SW16 2XW. Studies London's natural history within a twenty-mile radius of St. Paul's Cathedral.

Ornitholidays. 1-3 Victoria Drive, Bognor Regis, West Sussex, England. Arranges bird-study holiday trips.

Royal Scottish Geographic Society. 10 Randolph Crescent, Edinburgh EH3 7TU. Sponsors scientific studies of ornithological and other phenomena.

Royal Society for Nature Conservation. The Green, Nettleham, Lincoln LN2 2NR, England. Sponsors scientific studies including those related to natural history.

Royal Society for the Protection of Birds. The Lodge, Sandy, Bedfordshire SG19 2DL, England. Maintains nine regional offices concerned with the conservation of wild birds and their habitats; disseminates related information; conducts literature sales; acquires funds for ornithological programs.

Books

Bird Watcher's Britain. John Parslow. Pan Books. 1983. Outlines fifty bird-watching expeditions in detail; treats some 130 others in less detail. How to sight birds along with maps, drawings of birds, indexes, place names, bird organizations, family names of birds.

Britain's National Parks. William S. Lacey. Windward. 1984. For those wishing an introductory guide to the unspoiled wild places of Britain. Each national park is described and commented upon—beautiful color and black and white photographs.

British Birds: A Field Guide. Alan J. Richards. David & Charles. 1979. Devotes a whole page to each bird type; also includes a full-color photo and drawing of each. Pages can be wiped dry, thus permitting the book to be taken on field trips.

British Birds in Their Habitats. Ron Freethy. Longwood Publishing Group. 1985. A detailed description of the birds of Britain and where to find their nesting areas.

Feathered Friends. Ian Niall. Chatto and Windus. 1985. A detailed look at wild birds in Britain written by an expert ornithologist and lover of birds. Illustrated with line drawings.

A Field Guide to the Birds of Britain and Europe. Roger Tory Peterson, Guy Mountfort, and P.A.D. Hollom. Collins/

Houghton Mifflin. 1983. Describes 635 species, with many color plates and distribution maps; summer and winter ranges shown for 362 species.

Guide to Britain's Nature Reserves. Jeremy Hywel-Davies and Valerie Thom. Macmillan, Ltd. 1984. A reference guide to over two thousand sites of wildlife interest to travelers on the British mainland. Organized by country or region in alphabetical order; includes maps, photos, index of plant and animal life, list of addresses for organizations concerned with conservation of wildlife in England, Wales, and Scotland, and a glossary of naturalist terms.

Guinness Book of Seashore Life. Heather Angel, ed. Guinness. 1981. Overview of the kinds of life to be observed along the seashore; full details on each type.

The Macmillan Guide to Britain's Nature Reserves. Robert Boote. Macmillan Ltd. 1984. Lists over two thousand sites alphabetically by country or region, notes reserves open to the public, and illustrates Britain's plant and wildlife habitats with photos throughout.

The Natural History of Britain and Ireland. Heather Angel. Michael Joseph. 1981. A large format, paperback book, lavishly illustrated; covers these lands from coastlands to highlands, to wetlands, woodlands, lowlands, and grasslands; includes towns and suburbs from heaths to hedgerows.

The National Trust Guide to England, Wales, and Northern Ireland. British Tourist Authority. 1984. An illustrated guide to national trust lands in Britain.

The National Trust Guide to the Coastline of Great Britain. Tony Soper. Webb & Bower. 1984. Similar information regarding coastal lands of the United Kingdom.

The Shell Countryside Book. Richard Muir and Eric Duffey. J. M. Dent and Sons/Biblio, distr. 1984. A broad history of the main outlines of the British countryside, with detailed descriptions of various rural features. Sections on various types of scenery: mountainous, coasts, lakelands, wetlands, and more.

Shell Guide to Britain's Threatened Wildlife. Nigel Sitwell. Collins. 1984. How changes in the environment threaten Britain's wildlife; future options; excellent illustrations of British flora and fauna.

Shell Guide to the Birds of Britain and Ireland. James Ferguson-Lees, et al. Michael Joseph/Merrimack Publishers Circle, distr.

1983. A well-illustrated guide including nesting materials, iden-
tifying characteristics, similar species, voice patterns, and habitats.

Wild Flowers of the British Isles. Daniel Streeter. Macmillan Ltd.
1983. Illustrates and discusses some 1,400 flowers in an attractive and clean format; includes a glossary.

Audiovisual Materials

Wild Wings. International Film Bureau. 1967. 16mm sound film, 35
mins. Activities at an experimental wildbird station in Slim-
bridge, England; movements and habits of ducks, geese, and
other wildfowl.

BOATING

The 2,600 miles of waterways in England alone, plus the many
beautiful lochs in Scotland, make boats and boating almost irresist-
ible for visitors to Britain as well as to the British themselves. The
kinds of boating in which you might engage while in Britain could
involve a canoe, punt, kayak, sculling skiff, or rowboat—that is, in
the do-it-yourself category. You might also, of course, go on a river
steamer, canal boat, ferryboat, or cabin cruiser. In the university
towns of Oxford and Cambridge you will see students punting in flat-
buttomed, pole-propelled boats. You may also see (or use) double-
skulling skiffs which are easy to handle and quite secure in the way
they are managed in the water. Canoes are widely used in faster
waters; establishments that rent them often provide instructions on
how to board, paddle, and steer them.

Organizations and Associations

Amateur Rowing Association. 6 Lower Mall, London W6 9DJ.
Looks after the interests of amateur rowers in the United
Kingdom.
British Canoe Union. Flexel House, 45-47 High Street, Addlestone,
Near Weybridge, Surrey KT15 1JV, England. Provides infor-
mation and advice to canoeists.
National Centre for Mountain Activities. Plas-y-Brenin, North
Wales. Offers courses in canoeing.

Welsh Canoeing Association. Pen-y-Bont, Corwen, Clwyd LL21 ORA, Wales. Information about canoeing in Wales.

Books

Canoeing. Dennis Davis. Hodder. 1981. General treatise on the subject of canoeing; one of the "Teach Yourself Series."

Canoeing Handbook. Geoff Good, ed. British Canoe Union. Hodder, 1983. General information about choosing, handling, and caring for canoes.

Complete Book of Canoeing and Kayaking. Gordon Richards. Batsford/David & Charles. 1981. General information about handling canoes and kayaks.

CRICKET

Cricket is quite a complicated game. It has been played in England since around 1300, and is also played regularly in other Commonwealth countries, notably India, Pakistan, Australia, New Zealand, and the West Indies. Baseball was developed from the British games of cricket and rounders. In cricket, two teams of eleven players take turns in occupying a grassy field (about 400 to 500 feet long and 225 feet wide) and try to prevent their opponents from scoring "runs." There are two wickets, each composed of three wooden stakes driven vertically into the ground and each having two wooden bails set in grooves on top of them. The wickets are some twenty or so yards apart. The bowler (a player of the defending team) throws the ball, without bending his elbow, trying to dislodge the bails atop the wickets. The batsman (of the opposing team) seeks to protect the wicket with his bat, which somewhat resembles a paddle, and at the same time to hit the leather-clad ball and score by running between the wickets. Cricket games can go on for several days and the English can become fanatical about them. A more complete explanation of the game and its rules may be found in the references that follow. While it is essentially an English game, some cricket does go on in Scotland.

Organizations and Associations

Cricket Memorial Gallery. Lord's Cricket Ground, St. John's Wood

Road, London NW8 8QN. Everything connected with the game of cricket on display.

Cricket Society. 11 Clive Court, Babington Road, London SW16 6AL. Promotes interest in and knowledge, love, and appreciation of cricket among persons of all ages.

Marylebone Cricket Association. Lord's Cricket Ground, St. John's Wood Road, London NW8 8QN. Establishes laws of cricket umpiring and scoring services; publishes on the subject.

National Cricket Association. Lord's Cricket Ground, St. John's Wood Road, London NW8 8QN. Provides information on amateur cricket clubs and coaching facilities.

Scottish Cricket Union. 18 Ainslie Place, Edinburgh 3. The controlling body for cricket in Scotland.

Women's Cricket Association. 16 Upper Woburn Place, London WC1. An association of British women's cricket clubs.

Books

Cricket. Barry Richards. Pelham Books. 1975. This well-illustrated booklet shows the techniques of batting, bowling, and fielding in the game of cricket.

Cricket. "Know the Game" Series. E.P. Group. 1983. This complete guide to the game of cricket was produced with the Marylebone Cricket Club's collaboration; incorporates 1980 changes in the Laws of Cricket.

Cricket Country. Edmund Blunder. Pavilion Books. 1985. How village cricket is played; its useful role in the life of rural England; a cricket critic's recollections.

Cricket Fundamentals. Peter Philpott. Batsford/David & Charles. 1982. Basics of the game explained in a clear, concise manner.

Guide to Real Village Cricket. Robert Holles. George Allen & Unwin. 1984. A readable discussion of the way cricket is played in English villages.

John Arlott's Book of Cricketers. John Arlott. Lutterworth Press/ Sphere. 1982. Pictures and commentaries on a gallery of some twenty-five English cricketing stars of recent vintage.

The New Observer's Book of Cricket. Peter Smith. Frederick Warne. 1983. This revised edition includes biographies of players, records of world class play and test matches, a history of the game in England, Ireland, Scotland, and Wales.

Village Cricket. Gerald Howat. David & Charles. 1980. Phases of

change in village cricket; its origins, customs, and eccentrici-
ties; information about some remarkable matches of the past
and of individuals associated with them.

CROQUET

Although croquet is a game that is also played in the United States,
one is likely to encounter it more frequently in Great Britain where it
has been popular for generations. Croquet is usually played by four
persons paired in two teams, although other combinations are also
quite common. Each player has a mallet and one wooden ball
trimmed with a matching color. Players, in turn, try to drive their
balls through hoops (which are wire arches stuck into the ground),
hitting other players' balls out of their good positions as they drive
toward the goal—the wooden stake at the far end of the playing area
(lawn)—hitting it with the ball, and returning through the hoops
again to hit the "home stake" ahead of the other players and win.
The game used to be known as "pall-mall" in England, sharing this
name with a famous London street.

Organizations and Associations

Croquet Association. Hurlingham Club. London SW6 3PR. Governing body for the game of croquet.
U.S. Croquet Association. 635 Madison Avenue, New York, NY
10022. Membership comprised of individuals interested in orga-
nizing and promoting U.S. croquet as a serious national sport.

Books

Croquet: Know the Game. Croquet Association. 1981. General
information about and rules of the game.
Winning Croquet, from Backyard to Greensward. Jack Osborn and
Jesse Kornbluth. Simon and Schuster. 1983. Rules, descriptions of equipment, and game-winning techniques of play.

Magazines and Newsletters

Croquet Gazette. U.S. Croquet Association, 635 Madison Avenue,
New York, NY 10022. semi-ann. News of the sport in the U.S.
and around the world.

FISHING

The British Isles boast superb fishing of many kinds. Particularly outstanding is the fishing for salmon and trout. Numerous "fishing hotels" located near good fishing grounds make it easy to participate in the sport. Instruction is readily available. In England and Wales one needs a license, officially issued by the Water Authority, but usually available without any fuss at fishing hotels in the area where you would like to fish. No license is required in Scotland. The British divide their fishing into three classes: sea fishing; game or sport fishing (as for salmon or trout); and coarse fishing, for freshwater fish other than salmon or trout.

Organizations and Associations

Inquire of local Tourist Boards for information about fishing opportunities and conditions.

British Field Sports Society. 59 Kennington Road, London SE1 7PZ. Affairs relating to British angling, hunting, and shooting.

London Angler's Association. 183 Hoe Street, London E17 3AP. Information on the many fishing clubs in London; has an associate membership plan.

Marine Biological Association of the United Kingdom. The Laboratory, Citadel Hall, Plymouth, Devon PL1 2PB, England. Seeks advancement of zoological and biological science and an increase in knowledge about fishes of the British Isles.

National Anglers' Council. 11 Cowgate, Peterborough PE1, 1LZ, England. Provides information about coarse fishing, sea fishing, and game fishing.

Scottish Anglers Association. 11 Corrennie Drive, Edinburgh EH10 6EQ. Offers information about and assistance to those interested in fishing in Scottish waters.

Books

AA Guide to Angling in Britain. British Tourist Authority. 1984. Lists over three thousand five hundred places to fish in Britain and all the necessary information on accommodations in the areas.

Angling Guide to Wales. Wales Tourist Board. 1974. Information regarding rules and regulations, sites, and types of fishing in Wales.

Compleat Angler. Izaak Walton. Beaufort Books. 1985. Reprint of this famous book which still makes excellent reading and good sense.

The Complete Fisherman. Graham Marsden, Brian Furzer, and John Darling. Ward Lock. 1983. A guide to every facet of this sport from three experts in the field.

The Complete Freshwater Fishes of the British Isles. Jonathan Newdick. A. & C. Black. 1979. Fish listed by type, habitat, diet, size, and spawning grounds; includes fifty-four species of fresh or brackish water fish.

Encyclopaedia of Fishing in Britain and Ireland. 2d rev. ed. Michael Prichard. Collins. 1982. A comprehensive study of fishing in the British Isles arranged in encyclopedic format.

Guinness Guide to Coarse Fishing. Michael Prichard and Michael Shepley. Guiness. 1982. An extensive guide written by two experts in the field covering sea angling, salt water fishing, and freshwater fishing.

Guinness Guide to Game Fishing. William B. Currie. Guinness. 1980. Information about game fishing—equipment, techniques, locations, types of fish, and more.

Hamlyn Basic Guide to Angling. Frances Jones, ed. Hamlyn Publishers. 1983. General book on British fishing.

The Penguin Guide to Freshwater Fishing in Britain and Ireland. Ted Lamb. Penguin. 1984. Lists still rivers, locations, local regulations, and types of fish available; also lists angling associations; area maps appended.

Popular British Freshwater Fish. Ken Smith. British Waterways Board. nd. Describes the common types of fish found in inland waterways of Britain.

Salmon and Trout Fishing Holidays. British Tourist Authority. 1984. A brochure which lists fishing hotels in England, Scotland, and Wales as well as information on seasons, methods of fishing allowed, equipment needed, and advice. Maps of the areas appended.

The Sea Angler's Guide to Britain and Ireland. John Darling. Lutterworth Press/State Mutual Book, distr. 1982. A guide for fishermen listing angling clubs, charter boat services, and touring maps. Written by an expert correspondent for the *Angling Times* and *Angling* magazine.

Shell Book of Angling. Richard Walker, ed. David & Charles. 1979. One of the best coverages of fishing types, sites, and opportunities in the British Isles.

Still-Water Fly Fishing for Young People. Sidney Du Broff. Kaye &

Ward/David & Charles. 1983. Young people's guide to fly fishing in British streams and lakes.

GLIDING

If you are interested in seeing parts of Britain from the vantage point of a noiseless glider, contact the following information sources.

Organizations and Associations

British Gliding Association. Kimberley House, Vaughan Way, Leicester, England. Provides information on holiday gliding courses which are offered weekly from April to October throughout various parts of Britain.

Midland Gliding Club. Lind Mynd, Church Street, Shropshire SY6 6TA, England. Offers gliding courses for beginning or experienced pilots aged sixteen and above.

Scottish Gliding Union, Ltd. Portmonk Airfield, Scotlandwell, Kinross KY13 7JT, Scotland. Promotes gliding, soaring, aerial navigation, study of aeronautics, and the construction of all types of aerial conveyances.

Books

British Gliders. Philip Henry Butler, ed. Merseyside Aviation Society. 1980. Information about British gliding exploits of the past; today's gliding activities.

Glider Pilot. James Webster. Macmillan Co. 1980; what is involved in piloting gliders.

GOLF

It is generally agreed that the game of golf had its beginnings in Scotland about 100 B.C. to 400 A.D., where the Romans played it under the name of *paganica*. In doing this, they employed a bent stick and a leather-covered ball stuffed with feathers. At one time (around 1500 A.D.) golf became so popular that it threatened to reduce interest in archery which at that time was needed for British national defense. The British golf ball is a bit smaller than its American counterpart (1.62 vs. 1.68 inches in diameter). Two of

Britain's top golf courses are St. Andrews and Gleneagles, the former at St. Andrews on the east coast of Scotland, and the latter at Edinburgh. Selsdon Park Hotel (near London) and the St. Nicholas Hotel (in Yorkshire) also offer excellent golfing and accommodations. There are many other hotels that also do, including those at Turnberry, Troon, Carnoustie, and Old Prestwick, in Scotland.

Organizations and Associations

English Golf Union. 12a Denmark Street, Wokingham, Berkshire RG11 2BE, England. An organiztion of thirty-four golf unions; promotes amateur golf in England.

The Golfers' Club. International House, Windmill Road, Sunbury-on-Thames, Middlesex, England. For an annual fee of fifty dollars, golfers can now have special golf tours arranged for them by the club. There are accommodations with members or at the Sloane Club in London available, and special rates are offered for restaurants, hotels, and car rentals.

Golf Holidays and Castle Tours. Major Neil Ramsay & Company, Farleyer, Aberfeldy PH15 2JE, Scotland. Golf holidays in Scotland arranged with one hundred courses to choose from, and recommended accommodations, transportation, games with local players, shopping, and castles as well.

Golf Society of Great Britain. Glen Eagles, Maddox Park, Little Bonkham, Surrey, Bonkham, England. Promotes amateur golf.

Royal and Ancient Golf Club. St. Andrews, KY16 9JD, Fife, Scotland. Oversees this club's golf activities.

Scottish Golf Union. 54 Shandwick Place, Edinburgh EH2 4RT, Scotland. Governing body of amateur golf in Scotland.

Welsh Golfing Union. 2 Isfryn, Burry Port, Dyfed SA16 0BY, Wales. Governing body of amateur golf in Wales.

Books

AA Guide to Golf Courses in Britain. Tony Jacklin. Automobile Association (AA)/Merrimack Publishers Circle, distr. 1986. A comprehensive directory of addresses, facilities, and other facts pertaining to Britain's leading golf courses.

The Golf Course Guide to the British Isles. Donald Steel. Collins. 1982. An up-to-date revised edition listing the major golf courses in the British Isles with all pertinent information such as: length of course, fees, map location, hotel facilities in the area, availability of course play for visitors. Extensive index.

Scotland: Home of Golf. Britain Tourist Authority. 1986. Lists nearly three hundred Scottish golf courses with locations, facilities, and fees; includes maps in color.

Shell Book of Golf. Peter Alliss. David & Charles. 1981. General information about golf, with special attention to the British scene.

HORSEBACK RIDING AND TREKKING

Horseback riding and "trekking" (cross-country trips on horseback) are popular sports with the British; visitors to Britain may enjoy them, too, by taking only a little trouble to set up schedules. If you are completely without skill in handling horses, or if you feel you should have some polishing up before trying your hand with them, any one of the numerous riding stables in the country will oblige with the necessary training. Riding a horse is an excellent way to see back country you would ordinarily miss. Longer trips (up to a week or so) can be arranged.

Organizations and Associations

Association of British Riding Schools. 7 Deer Park Road, Sawtry, Huntington, Cambs PE17 5TT, England. Seeks to raise standards of riding instruction and horsemanship.

Backpackers Club. 20 St. Michaels Road, Tilehurst, Reading RG3 4RP, England. Promotes and protects interests of the lightweight walker/camper, cyclist, canoer, pony trekker, and others.

British Horse Society. British Equestrian Centre, Stoneleigh, Kenilworth, Warwickshire CV8 2LR, England. Oversees, in a general way, various horse-related activities in Britain.

British Show Jumping Association. British Equestrian Center, Kenilworth, Warwickshire, CV8 2LR, England. An association that attends to the interests of horse jumping show enthusiasts in Britain.

The Lilo Blum Riding School. 32a Grosvenor Crescent, London SW1. Assists in the organization of riding instruction sessions for interested individuals.

Tourist Information offices. Local offices will be able to supply information about available horse rentals and trekking opportunities.

Trezaron Pony Trekking Association. 55 East Parade, Harrogate, North Yorkshire HG1 5LQ, England. Promotes pony trekking in Britain.

Books

Riding and Trekking Holidays. British Tourist Authority. 1985. A directory of many locations throughout England, Scotland, Wales, and Northern Ireland where horseback riding and trekking holidays may be booked; all related to the British Horse Society.

Standard Guide to Horse and Pony Breeds. Elwyn Hartley Edwards. Papermac. 1982. Categorizes horses and ponies according to breed.

Maps

Horse and Pony Pictorial Map of Britain. Sandy Ransford, ed. Hamlyn Publications. 1982. Locations of stables and horse collections in Britain.

HORSE RACING

Horse racing appeals enormously to the British, as well as to their visitors. At least a dozen of the world's best race courses are to be found within a sixty-mile radius of London, and there are more than sixty of them in the country as a whole. The two chief forms of racing are flat racing and steeplechasing. Flat racing matches horses for the fastest straight-out running performance; steeplechasing involves top performance in jumping hurdles and other hazards. Race horses are almost always thoroughbreds—horses whose bloodlines go back many generations to only a few Arabian and Moroccan stallions. The most famous flat race in England is Epsom's "Derby" which is run in June. The race at Ascot, in July, is famous for its royal patronage and as a highlight of the social season. Horse racing is known as "the sport of kings" in Britain. Most British horse races are run on grass courses; sufficient time is left between race series to allow the grass to recover for the next use.

Organizations and Associations

British Show Jumping Association. British Equestrian Centre, Kenilworth, Warwickshire CV8 2LR, England. Strives to improve standards of show jumping and to encourage representatives of Great Britain at international shows and jumping contests at home and abroad.

Jockey Club. 42 Portman Square, London W1. Information on horse racing in England.

Racecourse Association. Winkfield Road, Ascot, Berkshire SL5 7HX, England. Seeks to protect interests of race-course owners and to encourage horse racing.

Racing (Horse) Information Bureau. Winkfield Road, Ascot, Berkshire SL5 7HX, England. General information regarding the history of horse racing in the United Kingdom.

Books

Complete Book of the Horse. Carol Foster. Octopus Books. 1983. Gives information about all aspects of horses; illustrated.

Encyclopaedia of Steeplechasing. Patricia Smyly, ed. Robert Hale, Ltd. 1979. The art and practice of steeplechasing as a sport, with special emphasis upon its practice in Britain.

Guinness Guide to Steeplechasing. G. Cranham. Guinness. 1979. Detailed information about the sport of steeplechasing.

History of Horse Breeding. Daphne Goodall. Robert Hale, Ltd. 1977. Thoroughbred horse breeding through the ages.

Horse and Pony Quiz Book. Sandy Ransford, ed. Hamlyn Publications. 1979. Facts and quizzes regarding horses and ponies.

HUNTING

In Britain, "hunting" is defined as "the tracking and taking (killing) of game with the help of hounds that pursue them by scent." There is also "coursing," which is the term used when hunting is done by sight and not by scent—as with the use of greyhounds with hares. The term, "shooting," in Britain refers to the taking of small game and birds with a gun only; repeating or pump guns are not acceptable as sporting weapons. High on the list of available quarry are red grouse, and other favorites include wild ducks, rabbits, pigeons, pheasants, partridges, and woodcock. In certain parts of Scotland one can also stalk red deer, and roe buck and Sika stag are also present.

Unlike the United States, most shooting in Britain takes place on private estates which are managed for just such a purpose. "Shoots" for groups of six or eight persons can be arranged through some of the organizations listed below. Firearm certificates (required of overseas visitors) may also be procured through these same organizations, and require at least thirty days advance notice. Game licenses which are also required may be obtained from post offices. The grouse season begins in August, the partridge season in September, and the pheasant season in October.

If shooting game or birds carries something of the connotation of an "upper class" pastime in Britain, hunting—with its paraphernalia of hounds, horses, and keepers—does so to an even greater extent. The epitome of this is foxhunting, in which most visitors are unlikely to be involved. It is mentioned here because the image of the red coats (referred to as "pink" by those who wear them), the horns, and the "riding to hounds" is so firmly fixed as a British phenomenon. This "sport," which has met with an increasing amount of protest in Britain with the development of greater sensitivity to environmental and cruelty to animals concerns, originated in fifteenth-century England.

Organizations and Associations

Best in Britain. 48 Epple Road, London SW6 4DH. Arranges shooting parties.

British Field Sports Society. 59 Kennington Road, London SE1 7PZ. A source of general information about conditions, sources, and regulations governing hunting and firearms utilization in Great Britain. Encourages the conservation of wildlife and the natural habitat.

League Against Cruel Sports, Limited. 83-87 Union Street, London SE1 1SG. Seeks abolition of the hunting of wild animals, especially of badgers, otters, foxes, hares, and deer.

Macsport, Limited. St. Nicholas House, Banchory, Grampian AB3 3YJ, Scotland. Arranges shooting parties.

Travel Scotland. 10 Rutland Square, Edinburgh EH1 2AE, Scotland. Arranges shooting parties.

Books

Hunting and Stalking Deer in Britain through the Ages. G. Kenneth Whitehead. Batsford/David & Charles. 1980. Interesting historical survey of man's efforts to outwit and bag deer in Britain over the years.

Hunting of the Hare. Lionel R. Woolner, ed. J.A. Allen. 1971. Stories about hare hunting; techniques used by successful hunters.

Peculiar Privilege: A Social History of English Fox Hunting, 1753-1885. David Itzkowitz. Humanities Press. 1977. Historical treatment of the subject of English fox hunting.

Lawn Bowling

Now experiencing something of a comeback, the game of lawn bowling is often to be seen being played in Britain as it has been since at least 100 A.D. It has been played in America since the 1600s. Lawn bowls is played on a bowling green which is about 120 feet square and divided into six rinks, each one 120 by 20 feet. Teams may be made of from one to four men or women. One player throws out a small white ball, called the "jack," at least twenty-five yards down the rink. He follows by rolling a "bowl" (which is about five inches in diameter) in an effort to get it as close as possible to the "jack." Other rollers as they play in turn try to roll their "bowls" so that they dislodge those of the other players in an effort to come closest to the "jack." The contestant or side with a "bowl" closest to the "jack" scores one point; more points are given for each "bowl" which rests closer to the "jack" than the nearest of the opponents' "bowls." A match is usually won by the team first reaching a total of twenty-one points.

Organizations and Associations

English Bowling Association. 2a Iddlesleigh Road, Bournemouth BH3 7JR, England. Information on the 2,600 bowling clubs in England; promotes the game.

Scottish Bowling Association. 50 Wellington Street, Glasgow G2 6EF. An association of 835 amateur bowling clubs in Scotland.

Welsh Bowling Association. 54 Neath Road, Tonna, Neath, West Glamorgan, Wales. Governs the game in Wales.

Books

Bowls for the Beginner. Scottish Bowling Association. 1984. Elementary directions and advice with respect to playing the game.
Guidance for New Bowlers. English Bowling Association. 1983. How to play the game.
Lawn Bowls. J. Jepson. Landsdowne Press. 1983. General information about how the game is played; essential rules.
Laws of the Game. Scottish Bowling Association. 1983. Rules of the game.

RUGBY

Rugby is very much akin to American football; it is a game that involves running, kicking, passing, and tackling. It originated at Rugby School in England. Two teams of thirteen or fifteen players (depending upon the type of rugby being played) are engaged on a field of 110 yards long by 75 yards wide. Following the kickoff, the aim is to score a "try" by touching the ball down behind the opponent's goal line (score four points). Points may also be made by kicking a field goal (three points) or kicking a goal after a try has been scored (two points). Lateral, but not forward, hand passes are permitted, and play is continuous except when a ball goes out of bounds or a rule is violated.

Two types of rugby are commonly played in Britain: Rugby Union, involving fifteen players, is a totally amateur game while Rugby League, with thirteen players, may be amateur or professional. Although there are some differences in the way in which the two versions are organized, both employ the same basic patterns of passing, kicking, and tackling.

Organizations and Associations

British Amateur Rugby League Association. 3 Upperhead Row, Huddersfield HD1 2JL, England. Governing body of amateur Rugby League football in Great Britain.
London Football Association. 88 Lewisohn High Street, London SE13. Provides information on rugby games.
Rugby Fives Association. Fairbourne Lodge, Epping Green, Essex CM16 6PR, Engand. Governing body for British Rugby Five groups.

Rugby Football League. 180 Chapeltown Road, Leeds LS7 4HT, England. Governing body of Rugby League football in England.

Rugby Football Schools Union. Twickenham, Middlesex, England. Promotes the game of Rugby football among English schoolboys.

Rugby Football Unions. Whitton Road, Twickenham, Middlesex TW2 7RQ, Engand. The controlling body of the sport in England.

Books

Focus on Rugby. Carwyn James. An International Coaching Book. Stanley Paul. 1983. This book, based on a BBC series by OPIX Films, tells you all you want to know about Rugby from a coach's point of view.

Guide for Players. Rugby Football Union. 1983. General information about how to play rugby.

Guinness Book of Rugby Facts and Feats. Terry Godwin, ed. Guinness. 1983. Full information about the game of rugby for the beginner and a detailed history of the legends of the game.

How to Play Rugby. David Norrie. Hamlyn Publishers. 1981. The game of rugby for beginners.

Principles of Rugby Football. John Dawes. Allen and Unwin. 1983. A manual for coaches and referees.

Magazines and Newsletters

Rugby. Rugby, 2414 Broadway, New York, NY 10024. 9/yr. In-depth coverage of U.S. and Canadian rugby football matches; news from other parts of the world (New Zealand, France, Great Britain, Argentina, South Africa, and more), tournament coverage, book reviews.

SAILING

Both veteran and inexperienced sailors will be able to find opportunities to engage in their sport in Great Britain. The environment for it is excellent, with some seven thousand miles of coastline and many rivers and lakes at hand for encouragement. Those who feel the need for a little more confidence before setting out will find many schools available. Sources for locating some of them are provided below.

Organizations and Associations

National Sailing Center. Arctic Road, Cowes, Isle of Wight, England. Offers elementary courses in dinghy and board sailing as well as other more advanced courses for experienced persons.

Plas-y-Deri. National Outdoor Pursuits Centre for Wales, Caernarfon, Gwynedd, Wales. Offers various types of accommodations in connection with sailing courses.

Royal Yachting Association. Victoria Way, Woking, Surrey GU21 1EQ, England. Governing body in Britain for sailing sports generally. Will supply names and addresses of certified sailing schools.

Welsh Yachting Association. 86 Sketty Road, Swansea, West Glam SA2 OJZ, Wales. General Information about yachting in Welsh waters.

Books

Complete Book of Boating. Ernest A. Zadig. Prentice-Hall. 1976. Full information about boating.

Family Boating: Guide to Successful Family Cruising. Judy Andrews and Jim Andrews. The Bodley Head/Merrimack Publishers Circle, distr. 1983. Boating, with emphasis upon it as a family sport.

Guinness Guide to Sailing. Peter Johnson. Guinness/ Sterling. 1982. General information about the sport of sailing small boats.

The Past Afloat. Anthony Burton. British Broadcasting Corp. 1982. An illustrated survey of Britain's maritime past, including a list of related museums.

Sailing: A Sailor's Dictionary. Gertrude Beard and Elizabeth C. McKie. Macmillan/Papermac. 1982. Clearly-worded definitions of important sailing-related terms.

Sailing: An Informal Primer. Richard Ulian. Van Nostrand Reinhold. 1982. A beginning presentation about the sport of sailing.

Shell Encyclopedia of Sailing. Michael Rickey. Stanford Maritime/ State Mutual Books, distr. 1981. Full information about most aspects of sailing. An excellent all-purpose sourcebook.

SKIING

Skiing is not a sport that one particularly associates with Britain, and the truth is that the only skiing worthy of the name is to be found in the Scottish highlands, where there are four principal locations: Aviemore, Glencoe, Glenshee, and Lecht. All of these locations are well-developed and maintain full facilities to meet the expectations of even the most demanding skiers. While a tourist with skiing as a primary goal would probably not choose to go to Britain, it is nice to know it is available if desired.

Organizations and Associations

Activity Travel. 12 Raeburn Place, Edinburgh EH4 1HN. Arranges skiing vacations.

Aviemore and Spey Valley Tourist Organization. Aviemore, Inverness-shire, Scotland. Arranges skiing vacations.

National Ski Federation of Great Britain. 118 Eaton Square, London SW1W 9AF. Publishes a list of ski locations.

The Scottish Sports Council. St. Colme Street, Edinburgh EH3 6AA. Organizes instructional courses for skiing and other sports.

Books

Complete Skiing Handbook: A Comprehensive Guide. Mark Heller and Doug Godlington. Mayflower/Smith Publishers. 1979. Information about skiing in the British Isles.

Guinness Book of Skiing. Peter Lunn. Guinness/Sterling. 1984. General information about skiing in the United Kingdom.

Handbook of Skiing. Karl Gamma. Knopf. 1981. Skiing techniques; how-to-do-it.

SOCCER

Soccer (also known everywhere in the world except the United States as "football") is the most popular spectator sport in the world and no less in the United Kingdom. It is capable of drawing crowds of up to a hundred thousand and more at a time. Played largely between September and May, the game elicits great crowd enthusiasm; fans often travel several hundred miles to support their teams in crucial contests. In playing soccer, two teams of eleven persons each seek to score goals by kicking or "heading" a round ball through their opponent's net-covered goal cage. The team with the largest number of goals wins the game. The goalkeeper is the only player who is allowed to touch the ball with his hands. All others must play it with their feet or their heads. Game play is practically continuous, stopped only by a score, a foul, or a serious injury. Games last ninety minutes and are divided into halves.

Organizations and Associations

Football Association, Ltd. 16 Lancaster Gate, London W2 3LW. Attends to promotion, control, and organization of Association (soccer) football in England.

Football Association of Wales, Ltd. 3 Fairy Road, Wrexham, Clwyd LL13 7PS, Wales. Promotes Association (soccer) football in Wales.

Scottish Amateur Football Association. 142 St. Vincent Street, Glasgow G2. Manages amateur soccer football in Scotland.

Women's Football Association. 11 Portsea Mews, Portsea Place, London W2. Some two hundred fifty clubs in twenty leagues, women and girls, play Association football.

Books

Book of Soccer. Laurie McMenemy and Norman Barrett. Purnell. 1981. General information about the game.

Guinness Book of Soccer Facts and Feats. Jack Rollin, ed. Guinness. 1983. Information about the history of the game—outstanding feats of the past.

Soccer (Football Association): Know the Game. Football Association. 1979. General explanation of details of the game.

Soccer Laws Illustrated. Stanley Lover. Pelham Books/ Merrimack Publishers Circle, distr. 1984. Contains the official, approved laws of the game and decisions of the International Football Association board.

Soccer: Skills, Tricks, and Tactics. Simon Inglis. Usborne Publishing. 1981. Specific techniques intended to improve one's skills in playing the game.

You Can Play Football. Gordon Banks. Carousel Books/ Transworld. 1982. Techniques to improve one's abilities to play soccer; also *You Can Play Soccer* by this same author.

TENNIS

Tennis, like golf and football, is reputed to have been developed by the British. It is believed to have stemmed from a handball-like game played in Greece. The all-England championship at Wimbledon, of course, is the contest *par excellence* that continues to earn fame for the game in Britain and throughout the world. It takes place in this London suburb in late June and early July. The current impetus toward leisure in Britain has resulted in the building of thousands of new tennis courts—most of them hard surface, but some of grass. Usually, courts can be rented at a reasonable fee, and vacancies are generally on hand. Tennis holidays, many at five-star hotels, are now quite popular, and offer professional coaching, food, lodging, and other accommodations.

Organizations and Associations

All England Lawn Tennis and Croquet Club. Box 98, Church Road, Wimbledon, London SW19 5AE. Information about tickets to the famous Wimbledon games.

British Association of Tennis Supporters. 58 Exeter Road, Addiscombe, Stanley Road, Croydon, Surrey CR0 6EG, England. Provides informational services for individuals interested in British tennis players and in attendance at tennis tournaments to support them.

International Tennis Supporters. 35 Northcourt Avenue, Reading, Berks RG2 7HE, England. Caters to interests of tennis enthusiasts, especially with respect to tennis tournaments.

Lawn Tennis Association. Baron's Court, West Kensington, London W14 9EG. Will supply information regarding its twenty-five hundred affiliated private tennis clubs where one may set up games.

Scottish Lawn Tennis Association. 7 Albany Street, Edinburgh EH1 3PY. The controlling body for the game of tennis in Scotland.

Tennis and Rackets Association. The Queen's Club, Palliser Road, London W14 9EQ. The central authority in Great Britain for matters connected with games of tennis and rackets associated with them.

Wimbledon Lawn Tennis Museum. Church Road, Wimbledon SW19 5AB, England. Unique museum that tells the story of the game of tennis. Open to the public.

Books

Guinness Book of Tennis Facts and Feats. Lance Tingay, ed. Guinness/Sterling, distr. 1983. Presents the who won what, when and where plus scores, attendance, prize money in the tennis world. Concentrates primarily on competitions in the U.S., Britain, France, and Australia. Illustrated with numerous photos and indexed by subject with pictures of participants.

Tennis, Squash, and Badminton. British Tourist Authority. 1985. Lists hotels and companies in Britain that provide facilities and staff for these sports.

Wimbledon: Centre Court of the Game. Max Robertson. British Broadcasting Corporation/State Mutual Books, distr. 1981. The story of tennis championship matches at Wimbledon from 1877 to the present.

8 The Arts in Great Britain

Britain's achievements in the arts are well-known and respected. The resources presented in this chapter highlight these accomplishments through its art galleries and museums, its arts and crafts, the performing arts of theatre, music, film, and broadcasting, and folk dance and folk music.

FINE ARTS: ART GALLERIES AND MUSEUMS

Britain has some of the finest art galleries and museum collections of beautiful, antique, ancient, and rare objects in the entire world. The government provides support in varying amounts for the development of these exhibits and collections, not only in galleries and museums in London but in many other locations throughout the country. A highly selective (and alphabetical) list of some of the country's best known museums and galleries would include Birmingham Museum and Art Gallery; British Museum (London); Courtauld Institute Galleries (London); Dulwich Picture Gallery (London); Glasgow Museums and Art Galleries; National Gallery (London); National Gallery of Scotland (Edinburgh); National Museum of Wales (Cardiff); National Portrait Gallery (London); Photographer's Gallery (London); Queen's Gallery (Buckingham Palace Road, London); Sir John Soane's Museum; Tate Gallery (London); and Victoria and Albert Museum (London).

Organizations and Associations

Art Galleries Association. Sheffield City Art Galleries, Surrey Street, Sheffield S1 1XZ, England. Seeks to further the exhibition, presentation, and interpretation of British art.

Arts Council Bookshop. 8 Longacre, London WC2. Represents the Arts Council for sale of its publications and reports and other books on the arts.

The Arts Council of Great Britain. 105 Piccadilly, London W1V OAU. Established "to develop and improve the knowledge, understanding and practice of the arts" and to make the arts more accessible to the general British public. Publications include an annual report, *The Arts Council Bulletin,* and reports and monographs in the fields of art, education, information and research, drama, literature, poetry, and music. An extensive system of competitions, awards, scholarships, and grants is in place. Regional arts associations have been established throughout the U.K. The Council organizes touring exhibitions, maintains a traveling gallery, has a permanent collection of works of art and a fund for housing the arts, and offers an advisory service on many aspects of the arts.

British Arts Festivals Association (BAFA). 33 Rufford Road, Nottingham NG5 2NQ, England. A nonprofit organization composed of arts festivals in various parts of Great Britain and Northern Ireland with the primary purpose of encouraging participation and support of arts festivals at home and abroad.

The British Council. 10 Spring Gardens, London SW1A 2BN. Tel: (01) 930-8466. Maintains information offices and libraries in many countries worldwide to promote British culture and literature; also arranges dance, drama, and musical tours of British companies in other countries. Has a special interest in cinema and film appreciation and study.

Contemporary Art Society. Tate Gallery, Millbank, London SW1P 4RG. Seeks to acquire works by leading artists as gifts for public art galleries.

Federation of British Artists, Limited. 17 Carlton House Terrace, London SW1. Provides facilities for exhibiting for member societies and introducing artists to potential patrons.

Books

The Art and Architecture of London: An Illustrated Guide. Ann Saunders. Phaidon Press. 1984. The author, an historian, librarian, and lecturer, describes buildings, monuments, and churches of the Cities of London and Westminster, street-by-street and district-by-district.

Arts Address Book: A Classified Guide to National and International Arts Organizations. Peter Marcan, ed. Peter Marcan Publications. 1983. Covers all areas of the arts including activities of each group and its publications, names, addresses, and telephone numbers.

The British Museum and Its Collections. British Museum Publications. 1984. General review and history of the British Museum, with special attention to its departmental structure and functions.

British Museum Publications: Complete Book List, 1985. British Museum Publications. 1985. General bibliographic listings of publications of the Museum about coins, medals, Egyptian antiquities, ethnography, Greek and Roman antiquities, prints and drawings, Asiatic antiquities, books, and other materials.

Directory of Museums. Kenneth Hudson and Ann Nicholls. Macmillan Ltd. 1981. Covers four hundred museums and galleries in Britain.

Festivals in Great Britain. Arts Council. Offord Publications. ann. A list of arts events in Britain; includes policies statements. Each arts festival receives brief mention and provisional dates for the year.

A Guide to the Transport Museums of Britain. Jude Garvey. Michael Joseph/Merrimack Publishers Circle, distr. 1983. Includes museums in Great Britain and Ireland; indexed; also many maps; written by the former director of the Transport Trust.

Inside the British Museum. Joy Richardson. British Museum Publications. 1984. Puzzles, questions and answers, facts, quizzes, pictures, maps, and fun projects related to contents of the British Museum.

The Knopf Traveler's Guides to Art: Great Britain and Ireland. Michael Jacobs and Paul Stirton. Knopf. 1984. A pocket-sized guide to the paintings, sculpture, and art objects of these countries; includes a city-by-city and regional information guide to museums; location maps, what to see, and fees, opening hours, and facilities. Easy to read and carry; colorfully illustrated.

London Art and Artists Guide. Heather Waddell. Art Guide Publications. 1983. A guide to "what's new" in art and the artistic world of London.

Museums and Galleries in Great Britain and Ireland, 1985. British Tourist Authority. 1984. An illustrated guide arranged alphabetically; also indexed by subject and area.

Museums and Galleries in Scotland. Scottish Tourist Board. British Tourist Authority/Merrimack Publishers Circle, distr. 1985. A guide to all the museums and galleries in Scotland with descriptions, fees, and opening hours.

Museums and Galleries of London. Malcolm Rogers. Blue Guide Series. Benn's Publications/W. W. Norton. 1983. A very informative guide, giving opening times, facilities, and descriptions of the permanent collections of each institution.

Nicholson's London Arts Guide. Robert Nicholson Publications. 1984. A concise guide to museums, galleries, historic houses, theaters, and music and dance festivals; includes all practical information needed for travelers.

100 Things to See. HMSO Books. 1984. For those visiting the Victoria and Albert Museum on a tight time schedule; concisely written description of each of one hundred of the best objects in this vast collection. Also available for purchase at the museum.

Royal Heritage: The Story of Britain's Royal Buildings and Collections. John Harold Plumb and Huw Wheldon. British Broadcasting Corp. 1981. Well illustrated survey of treasures of the British Royal Collection and the history of their acquisition.

The Shell Guide to Country Museums. Kenneth Hudson. Heinemann/David & Charles. 1981. Includes over one hundred "living" museums in Britain and Ireland; alphabetically arranged by towns within regions and nicely illustrated.

Audiovisual Materials

The London of William Hogarth. International Film Bureau. nd. 16mm sound film or video cassette, 26 mins. Views taken from Hogarth's engravings show the character of 18th century London.

Magazines and Newsletters

What's On. Commonwealth Institute. Kensington High Street, London W8. wk. A publication of the Commonwealth Arts Centre which lists current exhibitions, programs of music, dance, drama, programs for children, and others in the visual arts. Available in hotels and tourist offices in Britain or from the Commonwealth Arts Centre Box Office in London—Theatre

Despatch Box 129, London WC2H 9RU. Tickets for events can also be ordered through this office.

ARTS AND CRAFTS IN BRITAIN

Crafts and skilled handwork, often employing simple tools and materials, are important aspects of British artistic development. British handcrafts include work in leather, wood, metal, glass, textile printing, pottery, and porcelain. Craftsmen working on porcelain may be seen at the Wedgwood Centre near Stoke-on-Trent. Here, also, you may see Royal Doulton ceramics being made and potters at work in the nearby Gladstone Museum of British Pottery at Longton. Techniques of glassblowing may be observed and studied at the Caithness Glass Factories in Perth and Wick in Scotland, at Wedgwood's factory near King's Lynn, or at the Pilkington Glass Museum at St. Helen's, east of Liverpool. Laura Ashley's main textile printing plants are located in Wales. Their attractive cloth, characterized by tiny exquisite prints, is sold throughout the world.

Britain offers outstanding opportunities for students and others interested in improving their craft skills to work for short periods of time with established craftsmen and women (see references below). The country is filled with crafts museums, and many fairs are organized to display and sell the wares of the artists and artisans who produce them.

Organizations and Associations

Art Workers Guild. 6 Queen Square, London WC1N 3AR. Advocates education in all the visual arts and crafts and fosters high standards in design and craftsmanship.

Artists League of Great Britain. 48 Hopton Street, London SE1 9JH. Offers advice and assists artist and craftsmen members.

Association of British Craftsmen. 37 Coombs Bridge Avenue, Stoke Bishop, Bristol BS9 2LT, England. Offers vacation arts and crafts instruction in the studios of individual craftsmen. Residential accommodations (rooms and meals) are provided in tutors' own homes, converted pubs, windmills, and cottages located throughout Britain.

British Craft Centre. 43 Earlham Street, London WC2. Holds arts and crafts exhibitions and sells work of local artisans.

Craft Hobby and Industry Association. 89 St. Nicholas Market, Bristol BS1 1JG, England. Coordinates interests of all businesses engaged in buying, selling, or manufacturing craft and hobby merchandise.

Crafts Council. 12 Waterloo Place, London SW1 4AU, England. Tel: (01) 930-4811. Represents craft groups in Great Britain. Will send information materials and answer questions on all phases of crafts in Great Britain.

Craftsman Potters' Association. William Blake House, Marshall Street, London W1V 1LP. Exhibits British pottery; holds sales.

Federation of British Craft Societies. 8 High Street, Ditchling, East Sussex, England. Represents and protects the well-being of the craft movement generally.

Museum and Galleries Gift Selection. North Eastern Road, Thorne, Near Doncaster, England. Lists arts and crafts items available from various museums all over England.

Society of Designer-Craftsmen. 24 Rivington Street, London EC2A 3DV. Promotes professional practices by designer-craftsmen of all types; awards licentiates to last-year students.

Welsh Craft Centre. 36 Parliament Street, London SW1. Displays and sells Welsh textiles and love spoons.

Books

The Additional Crafts in Britain. The Readers Digest Association. 1982. Maps, process drawings, photographs of most traditional crafts practiced in Great Britain. Includes a guide to crafts workshops and museums throughout the area.

British Folk Art. James Ayres. Barrie and Jenkins/Overlook Press. 1977. Review of various types of folk art in the British Isles.

Corn Dollies. Discovering Books Series. Shire Publications. 1983. Techniques of weaving and producing these popular straw figures.

Cottage Industries. Marjorie Filbee. David & Charles. 1982. Details crafts still practiced in British homes: lacemaking, spinning, weaving, pottery making, furniture crafters, leatherworkers, and more.

Country Crafts. Donald John Smith. Discovering Books Series No. 230. Shire Publications. 1980. Practical, concise information on a variety of skills still practiced in England.

Fine English China and Glass. British Tourist Authority. 1982. General information concerning the products and visiting hours and policies for various English china and glass manufacturers, including: Minton, Spode, Wedgwood, and many others.

Lost Country Life: How English Country Folk Lived, Worked, Threshed, Thatched. Dorothy Hartley. Pantheon. 1981. Describes country life in England from the twelfth to the eighteenth centuries; includes arts, crafts, and folk art of the times.

Shell Guide to Country Museums in Britain. Kenneth Hudson. Heinemann/David & Charles. 1980. A detailed run-down of the many craft museums spread throughout the United Kingdom.

Stained Glass. Discovering Books Series. Shire Publications. nd. History, techniques, examples of the art of producing stained glass products.

The Story of English Furniture. Bernard Price. British Broadcasting Corp./Ariel Books. 1982. A history of furniture making in Britain from medieval days to the present.

Textile History and Design. Kenneth G. Ponting. Discovering Books Series. Shire Publications. 1981. The history and techniques of textile design.

Traditional Country Craftsmen. J. Geraint Jenkins. Routledge and Kegan Paul. 1979. A history of the growth of craft specialists in small British communities. Much space devoted to describing the nature of individual crafts, why and how they came about, and what they contributed to community life.

Treasures of Britain and Treasures of Ireland. The Automobile Association/Drive Publications, 1981. A traveler's guide to the many different kinds of riches of Great Britain and Ireland, with emphasis upon the artistic and products of handicrafts of the countries. Items are shown to have come from some four thousand locations—all man-made wonders of national importance.

Yorkshire Craftsmen at Work. David Morgan Rees. Dalesman Publications. 1981. An illustrated story about traditional craftspeople and their works: wheelwrights, rugmakers, walking stick carvers, horn cutters for cutlery handles, blacksmiths, and many others.

Magazines and Newspapers

Crafts Magazine. Crafts Council, 8 Waterloo Place, London SW1Y 4AU. 6/yr. A calendar of events, by British region, featuring current exhibitions for a large variety of crafts.

THE PERFORMING ARTS: THEATRE

Britain's, and particularly London's, preeminence in the field of live theatre is acknowledged the world over. British theatre as an institution has produced a formidable cadre of leading actors and actresses who carry on the profession and set the highest standards for it in productions around the world in all the media. Indeed, Britain contributes more than its share of outstanding practitioners in all the theatre arts: directing, set designing, lighting, costuming, and the rest. Today, some four hundred years after the construction of the old Globe Theatre on the south banks of the Thames, there are thirty-seven commercial theatres in the "West End" (London's entertainment center) as well as two major subsidized theatres, the National Theatre and the Royal Shakespeare Company (at the Barbican), making London the theatrical capital of the world. There are notable theatres in other parts of the United Kingdom as well, including the Royal Shakespeare Theatre at Stratford-upon-Avon; the Theatre Royal at Richmond in Yorkshire; the Repertory Theatre in Birmingham; the Royal Exchange Theatre in Manchester; and the Belgrade in Coventry. Scotland has excellent theatres in Edinburgh, Glasgow, Aberdeen, Sterling, and elsewhere. In fact, almost every large city in Great Britain has at least one.

Obtaining Theatre Tickets

Here is a list of names and addresses of theatre ticket agencies from which London/Britain theatre tickets may be ordered before leaving on your trip. A surcharge may be expected for this service.

Brewer and Brewer. 10222-B Westheimer, Houston, TX 77042. Tel: (713) 780-1730.
British Banqueting and Entertainment Center. 1202 Meramac Heights Drive, Manchester, MO 63011. Tel: (314) 394-3552. Will work through travel agents.
Edwards & Edwards. 226 47th Street, New York, NY 10036. Tel: (212) 944-0290 or (800) 223-6108. London Theatres, Edinburgh International Festival, Stratford's Shakespeare plays, sports, ballet, opera, concerts, and special events (for example, Wimbledon Tennis matches).
Keith Prowse. 234 West 44th Street, New York, NY 10036. Tel: (212)

398-1430 or (800) 223-4440. Makes bookings for London and advertises that they sell "only the best seats." Tickets, sometimes available on short notice, are non-refundable.

London Stages. 9763 West Pico Boulevard, Suite 100, Los Angeles, CA 90035. Tel: (213) 879-4997. Specializes in obtaining tickets to West End shows in London, to the Royal Shakespeare Company productions at the Barbican Theatre, and to the Stratford Shakespeare productions. A small fee is charged for the convenience of having the tickets before you go.

Buying theatre tickets in London is not difficult. There is a half-price ticket office in Leicester Square at which you can, by standing in line and paying cash, purchase tickets for that day only. As in other big cities you may order tickets from a theatre ticket agency or through your hotel concierge (usually the more expensive tickets and with an added service fee), or you can of course go to the box office yourself. Some people who are very sure of their plans purchase tickets for particularly-hard-to-get shows before they leave on their trip.

Organizations and Associations

British Theatre Association. 9 Fitzroy Square, London W1P 6AE. Seeks "to develop the art of the theatre."

British Theatre Institute. 30 Clareville Street, London SW7 5AW. Seeks "the creation and proper funding of a professional institute for the theatre."

National Drama Festivals Association. 24 Jubilee Road, Formby, Liverpool L37 2HT, England. Assists amateur theatrical activities of groups throughout the United Kingdom.

Society of West End Theatres (SWET). Bedford Chambers, Covent Garden, London WC2E. Organizes theatre tours; gives discounts to hotels, restaurants; publishes *West End Theatre Magazine* which gives current information on all productions in the theatres comprising the society.

Theatre Arts Society. Wyndhams Theatre, Charing Cross Road, London WC2 ODA. Encourages theatre-going by providing reduced-price reservations for some West End shows.

Theatre Museum. Victoria and Albert Museum, London SW7. Displays memorabilia of the British theatre.

Books

British Alternative Theatre Directory. Catherine Itzin, ed. J. Offord Publications, 1984. A directory of theatres in Britain that are known as "alternative" types.

British Theatre Directory: 1984-85. J. Offord, ed. J. Offord Publications. 1983. Full information about theatres all over the United Kingdom.

London IS Entertainment. British Tourist Authority. 1984. map and guide, free. An excellent map of Central London showing cinemas, theatres, concert halls, musical venues, night spots, and general transportation centers; includes an underground map, booking information, London transport, tourist centers, and more.

The London Theatre Scene. Susan Elms, ed. Society of West End Theatres/Merrimack Publishers Circle, distr. 1986. This updated version provides a history of London theatres, seating charts for each, and tips on theatre going, dining, or shopping in the theatre district.

London Theatre Today. Mildred Fischer. Golden West Publishing, 1981. This paperback is a comprehensive guide to London entertainment for travelers.

The Playgoers' Companion. Barry Turner and Mary Fulton. Virgin Books. ann. Includes a calendar of plays by titles with a brief synopsis of each; offers information about purchasing theatre seats, and provides an alphabetical listing and description of London and regional theatres. Also features profiles of actors and actresses and some critiques of recent productions.

The Royal Shakespeare Company. Sally Beauman. Oxford University Press. 1982. A history of 100 years of the Royal Shakespeare Company, the theatres in which it has been housed, and the many talented performers it has brought forth.

Theatre London. London Transport. 1980. A helpful theatre guidebook compiled by the British Centre of the National Theatre Institute in association with UNESCO. Contains an index to London theatres and full directions as to how to get to them, also general theatre information.

Audiovisual Materials

Theatre in Shakespeare's Time. BFA Films. 1973. 16mm sound film, 14 mins. Facets and traditions of the Elizabethan theatre, emphasizing its spectacle and exuberance and its place in society of the time.

William Shakespeare (1564-1610). History Maker Series. Jeffrey Norton Publishers. nd. audio tape, 60 mins. An audio biography that relates Shakespeare's works to the conditions of his time and also to the Elizabethan theatre; includes music and dramatizations.

Magazines and Newsletters

London Events and Entertainment. London Tourist Board. Urban and Provincial Advertising. bi-wk., free. Published on behalf of the London Tourist Board and London Transport. Information of special interest to tourists regarding what is going on in London.

Plays and Players. Brevet Publishing, Ltd., 43B Gloucester Road, Croydon, Surrey, CRO 2DH, England. mo. Reviews the latest productions in the theatre world in Britain.

Stage and Television Today. Carson and Comerford, Ltd. Stage House, 47 Bermondsley Street, London SE1 3XT. wk. A tabloid which contains book, play, and television reviews.

West End Theatre Magazine. Society of West End Theatres, Bedford Chambers, Covent Garden, London WC2. Latest information on shows, forthcoming productions, stars, eating out, and other related articles and features. Subscribers are also eligible for discounts in restaurants, hotels, BritRail, some shows, first night previews, and visits with stars, directors, and writers of West End productions.

THE PERFORMING ARTS: BALLET, MUSIC, OPERA

London is the home of five world-class symphony orchestras and a generous helping of chamber groups, and symphony orchestras have been independently established in Bournemouth, Liverpool, Manchester, and Birmingham. There are national orchestras in Wales and Scotland. The British Broadcasting Corporation (BBC) maintains a network of regional symphony orchestras.

Britain also maintains six major opera companies, two of them in London: one at the Royal Opera House, Covent Garden, and another at the English National Opera at the Coliseum Theatre. The others are: Glyndebourne Festival Opera in Sussex; the English National Opera (North) headquartered at Leeds; the Welsh National Opera of Cardiff; and the Scottish National Opera based in Glasgow.

Ballet in Britain is presented by the Royal Ballet (world class, and preeminent in the field); the Ballet Rambert (smaller, experimental); Sadler's Wells Royal Ballet (another major company famous throughout the world); the Festival Ballet (still another major company); and several smaller ones such as the new London Ballet, the prestigious London Contemporary Dance Theatre, and the Scottish Ballet.

Organizations and Associations

Association for British Music. Flat 11, 19 Hanson Street, London W1P 7LN. Seeks to educate the public to a greater knowledge, interest in, and appreciation of its heritage of music.

British Country Music Association. Box 2, Newton Abbot South, Devon TQ12 4HT, England. Promotes and seeks general acceptance of country music in Great Britain.

British Music Hall Society. 1 King Henry Street, London N16. Seeks to stimulate interest in music hall and variety entertainment.

Royal Musical Association. British Library, Great Russell Street, London WC1B 3DG. Studies the science and history of music.

Scottish Amateur Music Association. 7 Randolph Crescent, Edinburgh EH3 7TH. Encourages amateur music-making in Scotland.

Books

The Beatles: An Illustrated Record. Roy Carr and Tony Tyler. Crown. 1980. Events in the lives of the Beatles from 1960 to 1980. Fully illustrated.

A Book of British Music Festivals. Richard Adams. Robert Royce. 1986. Britain's music festivals are described as taking place between March and October in towns and cities famed as tourist venues. This profusely illustrated guide gives details of the music—classic, opera, jazz, folk—to be heard in places as far-flung as St. Magnus in the Orkneys, Fishguard in West Wales, and Aldeburgh on the Suffolk coast, together with accounts of recent performances and the special atmosphere that is to be encountered in concert halls, cathedrals, and village squares at festival time. There are separate chapters on London, England, Scotland, and Wales.

British Music Hall: An Illustrated Who's Who from 1850 to the Present Day. Roy Busby. Elek Publishers. 1976. People, places, and programs of the phenomenon known as the "British music hall."

The Complete Gilbert and Sullivan Opera Guide. Alan Jefferson. Facts on File. 1984. Detailed information on fourteen operas, plus texts of songs and dialogs. Data on sound and visual recordings; excellent bibliography.

Complete Opera Book. Gustav Kobbe. Bodley Head. 1976. A comprehensive book of operatic stories, performers, composers, music, companies, and opera locations.

Covent Garden Album. Lord Drogheda, et al. Routledge and Kegan Paul. 1982. An account of 250 years of theatre, opera, and ballet at this famous London location.

Critic at the Opera. Dennis Arundell. Da Capo Press. 1980. Comments by contemporary critics on operas performed in London during the past three centuries.

Gilbert and Sullivan: The Official D'Oyly Carte Picture History. Robin Wilson and Frederick Lloyd. Knopf. 1984. Concerning the D'Oyly Carte years. Excellent bibliography and index of operas and plays. Highly illustrated; notes on actors and performances.

History of Music in England. 3d ed. Ernest Walker. Da Capo Press. 1978. Historical development of music, composers, and instruments in England.

Music Festivals in Europe and Britain. Carol Price Rabin. Berkshire Travellers Press. 1984. Annotations of 105 music festivals in twenty-three European countries and in Britain.

Oxford Anthology of Medieval Music. W. Thomas Marrocco and Nicholas Sandon, eds. Oxford University Press. 1977. A classic treatise on music which is often performed on today's circuit.

Sounds British: Music in Britain Today. Jane Pettigrew. Harrap Publishers. 1980. Overview of types of British music in the modern world.

Story of Sadler's Wells, 1683-1977. Dennis Arundell. Rowman. 1978. Historical review of the development and accomplishments of this famous British ballet group.

Magazines and Newsletters

Music and Musicians. Brevet Publishing Ltd., 43B Gloucester Road, Croydon, Surrey CR0 2DH, England. mo. Incorporates *Records and Recording;* includes illustrated reviews, articles and more.

The Musical Times. Novello and Company, Limited, 8 Lower James St., London W1R 4DN. mo. Contains book, music, and record reviews and articles on the present musical scene.

Opera. Seymour Press Ltd., 336 Woodland Rise, London N10 36H. mo. Contains book and music reviews, new recording reviews, and illustrated articles.

The Performing Arts: Film and Broadcasting

Even before going to Great Britain you will have little trouble in locating, viewing, and listening to products of British film and broadcasting production. Probably you are already familiar with many of them, since numbers of Britain's best films come to U.S. theatres, and many of its best radio and television programs are aired on the Public Broadcasting System and National Public Radio. Also, you need not leave the country to listen to British radio broadcasts. If you are interested in "DX" (long distance) radio listening, you can without difficulty obtain a shortwave receiver and schedules giving times and frequencies of British radio broadcasts (especially the BBC's World Service) which may be heard in your part of the United States.

If you are further interested in the film and broadcasting aspects of the performing arts in Britain, other opportunities are open to you in the country itself—after you arrive there. But as in any country, you will need a legitimate reason and proper introductions to get "on the inside" in the studios or administrative offices of the British Broadcasting Corporation or any major film studio or production unit (except possibly for organized public group tours or as a member of a live telecast studio audience). The following organizations may be contacted regarding tickets for various live British television broadcasts:

ATV Ticket Office. Eldon Avenue, Borehamwood, Herts, England. Tickets to live radio and television shows.

BBC Ticket Unit. Broadcasting House, Portland Place, London WI. Tickets to live BBC radio and television programs.

London Weekend TV Ticket Unit. South Bank Television Centre, Kent House, Upper Ground, London SE1. Television program tickets available.

Thames TV Ticket Office. 306 Euston Road, London NW1. TV tickets available.

However, much research and study may be pursued through one or more of the organizations whose names appear in the list below. An advance telephone call (or even a letter before your arrival in London) stating your specific interests in films and broadcasting, particularly as educative and communications arts, may help to insure that you may set up arrangements to obtain the kinds of information you need.

Organizations and Associations

British Broadcasting Corporation. Broadcasting House, London W1A 1AA. Operates two national television networks in Britain; also provides a national radio network and regional services; operates thirty local radio stations in the United Kingdom. Maintains an extensive book publishing program with outlets in London and elsewhere.

British Council. 10 Spring Gardens, London SW1A 2BN. Promotes understanding and appreciation of Great Britain in other countries through cultural and educational cooperation. Organizes exhibitions of British art, books, drama, dance, and music abroad; recruits teachers and others for professional educational and cultural assignments abroad. Much of its work is performed through activities of the British Media Council.

British DX Club. 55 Boundary Road, Worthing, Sussex BN11 4LL, England. Encourages amateur long-distance radio listening.

British Federation of Film Societies. 81 Dean Street, London W1V 6AA. Attempts to extend the range and availability of all types of visual media through film societies operating throughout the United Kingdom.

British Film and Television Producers' Association. Paramount House, 162-170 Wardour Street, London W1V 4AB. Helps to coordinate and represent needs and interests of its commercial members.

British Film Institute. 127 Charing Cross Road, London WC2H OEA. Encourages development of the art of British film; promotes its use as a record of contemporary life and manners; fosters public interest in the study of film as art.

British Industrial and Scientific Film Association. 120 Longacre, London WC2E 9PA. An association of companies and individuals in industry, commerce, government, science, education, and the film industry; aims to assist in achieving effective internal and external communication through the use of audiovisual techniques and media.

British Kinematograph, Sound, and Television Society. 110-112 Victoria House, Vernon Place, London WC1B 4DJ. Offers courses in film; publishes technical manuals in the audiovisual communication field.

British Media Council. 10 Spring Gardens, London SW1A 2BN. Promotes effective use of radio, television, audiovisual media, distance learning systems, and information technology for developmental and educational purposes.

British Universities Film and Video Council. 55 Greek Street, London W1V 6AA. Fosters use of audiovisual media for teaching and research in universities and similar institutions throughout Britain and the world.

DX Association of Great Britain. Five Acres, Whereditch, Newport, Saffron, Walden, Essex CB11 3UD, England. Encourages long-distance (mostly short-wave) radio listening.

Independent Film Makers Association. 79 Wardour Street, London W1V 3PH. Supports professional independent film makers' efforts in the United Kingdom; also includes attention to video production.

Institute of Amateur Cinematographers. 63 Woodfield Lane, Ashstead, Surrey, Kent KT21 2BT, England. Supports the interests and work of amateur cinematographers throughout the United Kingdom.

International Shortwave League. 88 The Barley Lee, Coventry CY3 1DY, England. Encourages amateur short-wave radio listening.

National Film Archives. 81 Dean Street, London W1V 6AA. Acquires and makes available for study a national collection of film and television programs.

National Film Theatre. South Bank, London SE1. Offers inexpensive memberships in a film club (weekly or yearly basis). Its two cinemas show a wide range of films—foreign and domestic. The theatre also sponsors film festivals and other film-related activities.

National Sound Archives. 29 Exhibition Road, London SW7 2AS. A division of the British Library; formerly the British Institute of Recorded Sound. For thirty-five years this organization has gathered and preserved a collection reflecting the development of sound recording from wax cylinders to compact discs. Services available to students, composers, critics, radio and film producers, and the general public.

Radio Society of Great Britain. 35 Doughty Street, London WC1N 2AE. Encourages amateur radio activities in Great Britain.

Society for Education in Film and Television. 29 Old Compton Street, London W1V 5PM. Concerned especially with uses of films, television, and other media in visual literacy.

Telecom Technology Showcase. Baynard House, 135 Queen Victoria Street, London EC4. Historically oriented collection of communication equipment and procedures.

Television Gallery. IBA, 70 Brompton Road, London SW3. History of radio and television broadcasting is displayed and explained.

Books

The British Film Collection 1896-1984. Patricia Warren. Merrimack Publishers Circle, distr. 1984. A history of the British cinema in pictures with a foreword by Richard Attenborough. Arranged by decades, this story is told in black and white photos; it traces the rise, fall, and regeneration of the British cinema. Includes a bibliography, index of films, and a general index.

British Film Institute Film and Television Yearbook. Mundy Ellis, ed. British Film Institute. ann. Information for individuals as well as students and film-TV buffs interested in the British film and television industries. Includes information on all theatrical film releases for the year, lists film societies, identifies TV courses in higher education, and provides a professional trade directory.

Goodnight Children-Everywhere. Ian Hartley. Midas Books. 1983. An informal history of children's broadcasting by the British Broadcasting Corporation. Amusing glances behind the scenes.

Great British Films. Jerry Vermilye. Citadel Press. 1980. Detailed information about many so-called "great" British films of the past.

Guinness Book of Film Facts and Feats. Patrick Robertson. Guinness/Sterling. 1985. Anecdotal facts, characters, themes of films; different types of films made in the United States and Britain in each ten-year period, 1918-1984.

History of Broadcasting in the United Kingdom. Asa Briggs. Oxford University Press. 1979. A thorough review of the history of British broadcasting.

The Illustrated Who's Who of the Cinema. Ann Lloyd and Graham Fuller, eds. Macmillan Ltd./Orbis Publications. 1983. Descriptions of film personalities—players, producers, or directors who have participated in British cinema over the past years.

Radio: The Great Years. Derek Parker. David & Charles. 1977. History of radio during its peak years, with emphasis upon the work of the British Broadcasting Corporation.

Radio Comedy: Informal History of British "Laughter in the Air." Barry Took. Robson Books/British Broadcasting Corp. 1981. A detailed history of British radio comedy presentations.

Magazines and Newsletters

Film. British Federation of Film Societies. 81 Dean Street, London W1V 6AA. 10/yr. News of film society activities in England, Wales, Scotland, and Northern Ireland.

The Listener. British Broadcasting Corp., Broadcasting House, London W1A 1AA. wk. Presents interviews and feature articles on significant BBC television and radio programs and the broadcasters responsible for them.

London Calling. British Broadcasting Corp., Broadcasting House, London W1A 1AA. (BBC External Services.) mo. A magazine of special interest for short-wave listeners to BBC broadcasts in all parts of the world. Copies are mailed six weeks before they are needed.

Radio Times. British Broadcasting Corp., Broadcasting House, London W1A 1AA. wk. Conveniently displays all British Broadcasting Corporation radio programs available to British listeners. Includes notes on many of them.

World Service Quarterly Guide: North and Central America. British Broadcasting Corp. Box 76, Bush House, London WC26 4PH, England. q., pamphlet, free (apply to British Tourist Authority for copies). A schedule (printed in Greenwich Mean Time) of BBC broadcasts to North and Central America.

FOLK DANCE AND FOLK MUSIC

Speak of folk dance in the British Isles and the thoughts of many people will turn first to Scotland and such dances as the Highland Fling (named for the flinging action of one foot of the dancer). "Shabby trousers" is the English name for another favorite Scottish dance, and the Papa Stour sword dance is still performed in Scotland. The bagpipe, though known to the ancient world, India, and other countries, has achieved its greatest appeal as an instrument of martial and folk music in Scotland.

Morris dances, which originated as part of country festivals for such occasions as May Day or Whitsunday, are still performed in some parts of England, particularly in the Cotswolds. There are sword dances in the northeast which are thought to date back to Roman customs. There is a Hobby Horse ceremony and procession which occurs in connection with May Day in Cornwall and Somerset; Abbots Bromley (in Staffordshire) has a horn dance related to the traditions of the deer hunt.

A good deal of Welsh folk dancing may be seen at the International Musical Eisteddfod held in July in Llangollen (North Wales) or at the Royal National Eisteddfod of Wales held alternately, in August, in North and South Wales.

Organizations and Associations

English Folk Dance and Song Society. Cecil Sharp House, 2 Regent's Park Road, London NW1 7AY. Collects information about British folk dances, songs, concerts, and festivals. Maintains a library and bookshop. Works with organizations throughout England and has regular evening classes and social gatherings.

Royal Scottish Country Dance Society. 12 Coates Crescent, Edinburgh, EH3 7AH. Information on Scottish dances and festivals.

Scottish Tourist Board. 23 Ravelston Terrace, Edinburgh EH4 3EU. Will provide information about Scottish dance festivals.

Wales Tourist Board. 3 Castle Street, Cardiff CF1 2RE, Wales. Will provide information regarding Welsh dance festivals.

Books

Discovering English Folk Song. Michael Pollard. Discovering Books Series No. 270. Shire Publications/Seven Hills Books.

1982. Another in this series giving a brief history and background of the subject with examples of familiar songs.

English Folk Dance. Hugh Rippon. Discovering Books Series. Shire Publications. 1981. A review of various types of folk dancing among the English.

English Folk Dancing. Jack Hamilton. Charles River Books. 1974. Detailed explanations of the movements in several basic English folk dances. One of the series, "Know the Game."

Observer's Book of Folk Songs in Britain. Fred Woods. Observer's Pocket Series. Frederick Warne. 1980. Examples of British folk songs with lyrics and music.

Penguin Books of English Folk Songs. Ralph Vaughan Williams and Albert Lloyd, eds. Penguin. 1968. Compilation of well-known English folk songs with a brief history of each.

Audiovisual Materials

A British Sampler: A Souvenir in Sound of England, Scotland, Wales, and Northern Ireland. British Travel/BBC. 1981. phonograph recording (two sides). Presents a musical tour of Britain sampling some of the audio fare the tourist is likely to find in traveling around the four countries. Included are Westminster chimes, barrel pianos, music hall numbers, fishing songs, chorus songs, and much more.

Special Interest
Activities
9
in Great Britain

We end our book with a chapter on "special interest activities" in which travelers may engage while in Britain. The activities we discuss and present information resources for include such various topics as tracing one's ancestral heritage, archaeology, brass rubbing, cathedrals and churches, collecting, gardens, castles, and stately homes, literary "site-sleuthing," young people's attractions and opportunities in London and elsewhere in Great Britain, and photographing, recording, and videotaping one's trip to Britain.

ANCESTORS: TRACING YOUR HERITAGE

Although much of the work of tracing one's British ancestry may be performed at home in the United States, opportunities for doing this are vastly expanded by going to Britain. Of course, you may hire professionals to carry out the search for you, but doing it yourself will yield more satisfactions. Finding out "who you are," even if only partially, and even if based on findings that are quite ordinary, offers food for thought and appreciation. Fortunately, British officialdom and volunteer organizations are well set up to serve the needs of persons seeking to research their roots. Commercial organizations, too, offer their services for the task, addresses for several of which are listed below.

Organizations and Associations

Association of Genealogists and Record Agents. "Oakdene," 64 Oakleigh Park North, London N20 9AS. A professional organization which promotes high standards in this field; maintains a list of approved researchers.

The British Museum. Great Russell Street, London WC1. Contains a great amount of British genealogical material housed in the Museum's British Library.

Burke's Peerage Research, Ltd. 1 Hay Hill, London W1X 7LF. Professional genealogists who will trace your family history, do legal searches, trace corporate history, or do heirloom research for a fee. Brochure available describing various services.

Debrett Ancestry Research, Ltd. Gordon Road, Winchester SO23 7DD, England. Also maintains offices at Court House Road, Accomac, VA 23301. Performs (for fee) ancestry research for persons of English, Scottish, and Irish backgrounds. Offers free booklet describing services.

Federation of Family History Societies. The Drovers, Gloucester GL2 7AN, England. A worldwide group of family history societies that maintains a family reference collection, publishes *Family History News and Digest* (2/yr.), and produces low-cost pamphlets for beginners in family history studies.

General Register Office. St. Catherine House, 10 Kingsway, London WC2. Where one can look up records of British ancestors, marriage, and death certificates.

Heraldry Society. 28 Museum Street, London WC1A 1LH. Concerned with details of heraldry, armory, chivalry, and genealogy. Helpful in tracing possible family coats of arms.

Heraldry Society of Scotland. National Museum of Antiquities of Scotland, Queen Court, Edinburgh EH2 15D. Conducts continuing studies of heraldry in Scotland.

Institute of Heraldic and Genealogical Studies. Northgate, Canterbury, Kent CT1 1BA, England. Involved in training, study, and research in family history.

Registrar-General. New Register House, Princes Street, Edinburgh. Maintains records of Scottish ancestors.

Scots Ancestry Research Society. 20 York Place, Edinburgh EH1. A nonprofit group that assists those seeking to trace their ancestral lines; registration fee is $12.50; costs rarely exceed $100 per search.

The Scottish Genealogy Society. 21 Howard Place, Edinburgh EH3
5JY. Publishes *The Scottish Genealogist* (q.), free to members;
also maintains a list of researchers who will work on genealogies for a fee.

Society of Genealogists. 37 Harrington Gardens, London SW7. A
private association which publishes *The Genealogists Magazine* (q.), and houses a valuable library open to non-members
for a fee.

Somerset House. Principal Registry of the Family Division, Strand,
London WC2R 4LB. Provides probate and divorce records as
well as wills, all of which may be inspected for a small fee.

Books

America's British Heritage. British Tourist Authority. 1978. free. A
general overview of the subject of ancestral heritage, with
special reference to individuals in the United States whose
forebears may have come from the United Kingdom.

The Clans and Tartans of Scotland. Robert Bain. Fontana. 1981.
Describes various Scottish clans with septs (branches) evolved
over the centuries. Includes family histories, information on
133 clans; includes color illustrations of tartans; gives place
names.

Discovering Your Family Tree. David Ireland and John Barrett.
Discovering Books Series. Shire Publications/Seven Hill
Books. 1985. A pocket guide to tracing one's English ancestors.
Directs attention to and explains uses of registers, census
records, probate records, town books, quarter session records,
estate papers, government documents, newspapers, school records, heraldry, and more. Lists important U.S. sources for
amateur genealogists and lists of genealogies already compiled.
Also available are these related publications in the series:
Christian Names No. 156, *Local History* No. 158, and *Surnames* No. 125.

Family Historian: A Guide to Tracing Your Ancestry. Noel Currer-
Briggs and Royston Gambier. Debrett's Peerage Publishers.
1981. A practical guide of "how to" information—sources and
records and where to find them; also chapters on heraldry,
surnames, and family trees.

Family History in Focus. Don Steel and Lawrence Taylor. Lutterworth Press. 1984. Practical advice and sources of information for everyone interested in tracing ancestors.

Homeland of the Scots. British Tourist Authority. 1984. A new guide to tracing one's Scottish ancestry; includes history of the clans and places in Scotland connected with each family.

In Search of Your British and Irish Roots. Angus Baxter. Morrow. 1982. A complete guide to tracing English, Welsh, Irish, and Scottish ancestors.

The International Genealogical Index (Computer File Index). Genealogical Society of Utah, comp. Contains records of births from 1538-1875 with some coverage of English parishes; available at chapels and public libraries.

Scots Kith and Kin. Albyn Press. 1978. Information to assist in tracking one's clan, family, and tartan. Includes more than four thousand Scottish names.

Step-by-Step Guide to Tracing Your Ancestors. D. M. Field. British Tourist Authority/Merrimack Publishers Circle, distr. 1983. Complete information on how to trace your British ancestors with sample family tree, parish record pages, and a list of names and addresses in Britain, the U.S., Canada, Ireland, and Australia for ideas for further research.

Tartans: Their Art and History. Ann Sutton and Richard Carr. Arco. 1984. An encyclopedic revelation of the history of tartans, their manufacture, their designs, and patterns. Illustrates over 300 different designs for weavers to copy and 150 two-color designs to enjoy. Bibliography and index appended.

Tracing Your Ancestors 1984/85. British Tourist Authority. 1984. free. Tells genealogical researchers what information to gather before coming to Britain, organizations to contact in Britain, and reference materials available. Covers England and Wales, Scotland, Northern Ireland, Channel Islands, and the Isle of Man.

Tracing Your Ancestry. F. Wilbur Helmhold. Oxmoor House. 1978. A step-by-step analysis and guide to the processing of research on one's own family tree.

Magazines and Newspapers

The Genealogists' Magazine. Society of Genealogists, 37 Harrington Gardens, London SW7 4JX. q. This society journal is free to members. It is valuable as a tool for researchers.

The Scottish Genealogist. Scottish Genealogical Society, 16 Charlotte Square, Edinburgh EH2 4YS. q. The quarterly journal of the society; a research tool for tracers of their ancestry.

ARCHAEOLOGY

Almost anywhere you go in Britain, you are likely to encounter impressive archaeological ruins that span many centuries, from prehistoric to recent times. The New and Old Stone Ages are represented; the Bronze Age, which witnessed the arrival of the Celts; the Roman period from about 55 B.C. to after 400 A.D.; the arrival of the Angles, the Saxons, and the Jutes, from about 450 A.D.; the Norsemen and the Danes, about 800 A.D.; and finally, in terms of early, successful invaders who stayed, the Normans, in 1066. There were wars between royal houses, between England and Scotland, between parties and factions, and most recently, the World War II blitz (of England especially) by the Nazis, in their attempt to conquer Britain. All of these events have left scars and ruins, as has the simple passing of time. The British government has made a great effort to develop, and in some places to restore, archaeological sites, and has helped to make them a valuable and effective educational force as well as a strong tourist attraction.

Organizations and Associations

British Archaeological Association. 61 Old Park Ridings, Winchmore Hill, London N21 2ET. Engages in the study of archaeology and the preservation of national antiquities.

British Museum. Great Russell Street, London WC1. A world-famous, outstanding collection of Greek, Roman, and Egyptian antiquities, as well as much more—including displays related to Stone Age Man, and Near- and Far-Eastern cultures. Maintains an extensive publication program.

Council for British Archaeology. 112 Kensington Road, London SE11 6RE. Publishes *Newsletter and Calendar of Excavations* listing conferences, courses, and archaeological digs the year around. Personal participation in digging is usually limited to individuals aged sixteen years and older.

Institute of Archaeology. University of London, 31-34 Gordon Square, London WC1H OPY. Archaeology of Europe, Western Asia, and Latin America; world prehistory.

Royal Archaeological Institute. 304 Addison House, Grove End Road, St. John's Wood, London NW8 9EL. Maintains archaeological records and files; sponsors research.

Books

Archaeology in England and Wales. Discovering Books Series No. 46. Shire Publications. nd. Excellent little publication packed with practical information on the subject.

Arthur's Britain: History and Archaeology, A.D. 367-634. Leslie Alcock. Penguin. 1970. An illustrated exposition which attempts to present a scholarly approach to the question of Arthur's existence in his legendary Camelot.

Dark Age Britain: What to See and Where. Robert Jackson. Salem House/Merrimack Publishers Circle, distr. 1984. Evidence of Dark Age ancestral presence in modern-day stone and wood and in the vague outlines of fields and roadways.

In Search of the Dark Ages. Michael Wood. British Broadcasting Corp./Ariel Books. 1982. Information about Boadicea, Offa, Ethelred, and others from the period.

The National Trust Book of Ruins. Brian John Bailey. British Tourist Authority/Weidenfield and Nicolson. 1984. An illustrated guide to castles, monasteries, palaces, and other edifices, their histories and locations.

National Trust Guide to Our Industrial Past. Anthony Burton. British Broadcasting Corp./George Philip and Son. 1983. An introduction to major industrial archaeological sites of England and the industries they represent.

National Trust Guide to Prehistoric and Roman Britain. Richard Muir and Humphrey Welfare. Sheridan. 1983. An illustrated guide to this early period in British history and its historic remains.

Prehistoric England. Richard Cavendish. Weidenfield and Nicolson. 1983. Contains over ninety color photos plus nearly one hundred black and white illustrations, with maps and diagrams picturing prehistoric remains.

The Prehistoric Stone Circles of Britain and Ireland. Aubrey Burl. Shire Publications/Seven Hills Books. 1983. A theory and explanation of these early remains with illustrations.

The Quest for Arthur's Britain. Geoffrey Ashe. Academy Chicago. 1980. An examination of Britain in the time of King Arthur; a discussion of the reality of this personage and the times in which he lived; includes an extensive bibliography, illustrations, and drawings.

Riddles in the British Landscape. Richard Muir. Thames & Hudson. 1981. An exploration of the ruins and remains of prehistoric times including the famous Stonehenge.

Roman Britain. David E. Johnstone, ed. Discovering Books Series. Shire Publications. 1983. A pocket guide to the study of ancient ruins.

Roman Britain: History and Sites. Plantagenet Somerset Fry. Barnes and Noble Imports. 1984. For history buffs who want facts and details about this period in Britain's history.

Roman England. John Burke. W. W. Norton. 1984. Profusely illustrated with color and black and white photos, this story of early England gives historical and archaeological data.

The Secret Country: More Mysterious Britain. Janet Bord and Colin Bord. Granada/Academy Chicago. 1981. A journey into the past with descriptions of archaeological sites and ancient ruins and the legends that have perpetuated from these mysterious remains.

Stone Villages of Britain. Geoffrey Wright. David & Charles. 1985. A new chapter in the search for ancient remains of Roman and prehistoric ruins, many of which are still to be viewed today.

Stonehenge and Its Mysteries. Michael Balfour. Hutchinson. 1983. A detailed story of the eighth wonder of the world, scientifically compiled and illustrated with over two hundred diagrams, maps, charts, and photographs.

Stonehenge Complete: Archaeology, History, Heritage. Christopher Chippindale. Cornell University Press. 1983. An entertaining and well-illustrated collection of everything that has been written or painted, of any consequence, about Stonehenge; selected by the author, these works present an introduction to this phenomenon with an annotated bibliography appended of further readings.

Audiovisual Materials

Before the Romans. International Film Bureau. nd. 16mm sound film or video cassette, 22 mins. Views of selected prehistoric sites in Britain, all dating before the Romans. Included are settlements, ritual centers, flint mines, burial places, and mysterious monoliths.

Cracking the Stone Age Code. Time-Life Multimedia. 1971. 16mm sound film, 52 mins. Dramatizes the work and theories of Alexander Thom and his studies of megalithic stone structures found throughout Britain and Brittany. Attempts to validate Thom's theory that they were, in effect, astronomical observation areas.

Exploring the Unwritten Past. International Film Bureau. nd. 16mm film and video cassette, 22 mins. Stratification and carbon 14 are used to date excavated objects in Britain; other analyses identify characteristics of the civilizations in which they existed. Significant cultural changes, as related to these objects, are discussed.

Mystery of Stonehenge. McGraw-Hill Films. 1965. 16mm sound film, 57 mins. Considers legends surrounding England's Stonehenge monuments (on Salisbury Plain); reenacts the best-known religious ceremonies of the Druids.

Roman Britain. Ordnance Survey Engineers. British Tourist Authority. nd. A hard-cover publication with explanatory material and detailed information on the Roman archaeological sites in Great Britain.

BRASS RUBBING

Brass rubbing as a special interest and hobby activity grows increasingly popular in Britain as more people learn how to practice the art successfully. Most of the really interesting rubbings are done in cathedrals and churches, especially in England where there are more monumental brasses than anywhere else in Europe. Many of these brasses are set into stone slabs marking graves. In order to make a brass rubbing, one must place a sheet of paper (preferably one of sturdy texture) over the area of the brass where the inscription or design to be copied is incised, and rub over it with a hard wax crayon-like or chalk substance. Marks will occur where the paper comes in contact with the metal with the exception of the engraved areas themselves. The result can be a near-perfect copy of the brass engraving, rather like a photographic negative, which is quite suitable for framing as a decorative piece. A good place to start with this hobby is the London Brass Rubbing Centre, St. James's Church, Piccadilly, London W1. Westminister Abbey Cloisters also have very good brasses. Reproductions of original brasses are available here and in various other rubbing centers throughout England where, for a small fee, one may make copies of them in black and white or color on various types of paper.

Organizations and Associations

Academy of Monumental Brass Rubbing. Queen Street, Lynton, Devon EX35 6AA, England. Offers courses in brass rubbing history, procedures, and teaching techniques on a year-round basis.

All Hallows by the Tower. Byward Street, London EC3. Brass rubbings available from historic brass portraits and figures. Materials and instruction are supplied for a small fee.

Cambridge Brass Rubbing Centre. The Wesley Church Library, King Street, Cambridge, England. Offers an excellent collection of English and continental brasses of medieval knights and ladies, children, dogs, and gruesome skeletons.

London Brass Rubbing Centre. St. James's Church, Piccadilly, London W1. Outstanding brass rubbing facility in which one may make beautiful pictures to retain as wall hangings or framed examples of the art. Instruction is provided; a small fee is charged.

Westminster Abbey, London. Maintains a brass rubbing facility within the Westminster Abbey Cloisters where, in twenty-five minutes or so, one may make a brass rubbing to keep as a souvenir of a visit there.

Books

Brass Rubbings in Yorkshire. H. Chadwick and Gilbert Wild. Dalesman Books. 1975. Brief history of brass rubbing, with special emphasis upon the Yorkshire area. Names and identifies locations of significanty important brasses. Explains how to do brass rubbings.

Brasses and Brass Rubbings. Malcolm Cook. Discovering Books Series. Shire Publications. 1976. Where to find some of Britain's best monumental brasses; practical hints about how to do successful brass rubbing.

CATHEDRALS AND CHURCHES

Major cathedrals, minsters, and other types of church-related edifices continue to fascinate large numbers of visitors to Great Britain. Familiar names abound: Westminster Abbey, St. Martin-in-the-Fields, St. Paul's Cathedral in London; Canterbury Cathedral, Coventry Cathedral, Durham Cathedral, Ely Cathedral, Exeter Cathedral, Lincoln Cathedral, York Minster, Wells Cathedral, and many others in the English countryside; as well as others in Scotland and Wales. The books and audiovisual materials cited here deal at length with such structures, often illustrating them in full color as well.

Books

The Abbey Explorer's Guide to England, Scotland and Wales. Frank Bottomley. David & Charles. 1981. Over eight hundred entries arranged alphabetically covering all aspects of abbeys and religious houses in these countries. Includes a glossary and gazetteer; illustrated with diagrams and plans of the buildings; locations, types, and the extent of the remains.

Cathedrals and Abbeys of England and Wales. Keith Spencer and Shawn McVeigh. Blue Guides Series. W. W. Norton. 1984. A narrative description of all buildings and ruins accessible to the explorer; includes plans and drawings, times of opening, and locations.

Cathedrals in Britain and Ireland. William Anderson and Clive Hicks. Macdonald and Jane's/Scribners. 1978. A lavish study of the cathedrals of Britain and Ireland before the Reformation—from early times to the reign of Henry VIII.

The Cathedrals of England: Midland, Eastern, and Northern England. Nikolaus Pevsner and Priscilla Metcalf. Viking. 1985. Scholarly treatment of cathedrals of England—thirty-eight in all.

The Cathedrals of England: Southern England. Nikolaus Pevsner and Priscilla Metcalf. Viking. 1985. Colorful pictures, drawings, and textual descriptions of some twenty-five cathedrals of note in southern England.

Discovering English Churches: A Beginner's Guide to the Story of the Parish Church from Before the Conquest to the Gothic

Revival. Richard Foster. Oxford University Press. 1982. Illustrated study of the development of the English parish church; glossary of terms included.

English Cathedrals. Patrick Cormack. Crown. 1984. Describes in detail many pre-Reformation cathedrals, those with ancient foundations and restorations, as well as modern English cathedrals; illustrated with numerous photos, maps, and diagrams.

English Church Architecture. Mark Child. Batsford/David & Charles. 1981. Illustrated with drawings and photographs, this authoritative guide classifies churches by Norman, Transitional, Early English, Decorated, Renaissance, Perpendicular, Classical, and Victorian periods.

The Good Church Guide: A Church-goers Companion. Audrey Rich and Anthony Kilmister, eds. Blond and Briggs/Penguin. 1982. Describes over 450 Anglican churches in England with notes on history, architecture, and more.

A Guide to the Cathedrals of Britain. Anthony S. B. New. Constable/State Mutual Books, distr. 1981. Includes many Church of England, Scottish Episcopalian, Greek Orthodox, Ukrainian, Church of Wales, and ruined and vanished cathedrals in Britain. Written by a church architect.

Audiovisual Materials

Canterbury Pilgrimage. Encore Visual Education, Inc. 1980. 35mm sound filmstrip. Highlights of a journey to Canterbury Cathedral, with music recorded on location. History, aspects of the architecture, stained glass artifacts; problems caused by time and neglect of the building and air pollutants; current restoration program.

Exeter. International Film Bureau. nd. 16mm film or video cassette, 29 mins. Story of the building and use of Exeter Cathedral in Devonshire, England.

From Every Shires Ende. International Film Bureau. nd. 16mm sound film, 38 mins. A film about the world of Chaucer's pilgrims, during a 14th century pilgrimage to Canterbury Cathedral. Castles, churches, and cottages reveal the character of the people; wooden misericords and illuminated manuscripts provide pictures of daily life.

The History of Westminster Abbey. International Film Bureau. nd. 35mm sound filmstrip (with cassette). Development of the

Abbey Church of Westminster from a simple monastery to its current status. Recalls some important historical events associated with it.

In Britain Christian Heritage. British Tourist Authority. 1984. map leaflet, free. Sketches places of historical interest covering their Christian heritage which are available for viewing by tourists; map locations given in this colorful capsule of church growth and development through the ages.

COLLECTING: ANTIQUES AND OTHER ARTIFACTS

Antique collecting has been an especially important hobby activity in Britain since the early 1800s when it became fashionable to want to buy old objects for their beauty and historical importance. Other kinds of collecting have been in vogue for an even longer time, such as stamps, coins, lead soldiers, and toys. Objects that are not old enough to be rightfully called "antiques" are often known as "collectibles" and there is hardly any kind of object, from buttons to bottle tops, that does not have its avid collectors. Nostalgic appeal and design quality both play a part in attracting collectors, and hunting for bargains in the favored object to start or round out a collection is exciting and satisfying to many people. London is an antique hunter's dream! There are permanent antique and collectibles markets there and in many other locations throughout Britain. The listings below will suggest organizations and associations as well as many publications related to this field which is of considerable interest to many persons who visit Britain.

Organizations and Associations

Antique Collectors Club. 5 Church Street, Woodbridge, Suffolk IP12 1DS, England. Publishes *Guide to the Antique Shops of Britain*.

British Numismatic Trade Association. Box 52c, Esher, Surrey KT10 8PW, England. Commercial group behind the organization of coin fairs, exchanges, and publicity efforts.

British Philatelic Federation, Ltd. 1 Whitehall Place, London SW1A, 2HE, England. Organization that sponsors activities in support of British philatelists and philatelic groups.

British Toy and Hobby Manufacturers Association (BTHA). 80 Camberwell Road, London SE5 0EG. A British association which organizes trade fairs for those involved in the toys, games, and hobby field.

Fenton House. The Grove, London, NW3. Collection of porcelain and furniture; early keyboard instruments.

Imperial Collection. Central Hall, Westminster, London. Replicas of many famous pieces of royal jewelry.

International Philatelic Press Club. Philatelic Press Club, Box 114, Richmond Hill, NY 11419. Offers membership list (names, addresses, affiliations) available to members of the Universal Postal Union.

The London Toy and Model Museum. 23 Craven Hill, London W2. Located near London's West End, this museum houses rare toys and models of boats, trains, airplanes, and other entertaining creations.

National Postal Museum. King Edward Building. King Edward Street, London EC1. A large postal and postage stamp collection.

Postal History Society. Lower Street Farmhouse, Hildenborough, Tonbridge, Kent TN11 8PT, England. Concerned with the history of British and international postal communications.

Royal Numismatic Society. British Museum, Great Russell Street, London WC1B 3DG. Official stamp collecting association in the United Kingdom.

Veteran Car Club of Great Britain. Jessamine House, High Street, Ashwell, Herts, England. Interested in the restoration and preservation of pre-1919 automobiles.

Vintage Sports Car Club. 121 Russell Road, Newbury, Berks RG14 5JX, England. Gives special attention to sports cars in the "vintage" category.

Books

British Toy and Hobby Fair: 1985 Buyers Guide. British Toy Fairs. 1985. Lists trade fairs for the current year and the associations involved; also includes an alphabetical list of brand names, game titles, BTHA members, and products.

Collecting Now: Know Your Picture. John Fitzmaurice Mills. British Broadcasting Corp./Ariel Books. 1984. Surveys methods and pigments used by artists throughout the centuries. Gives pratical advice for looking after and restoring pictures.

Guide to the Antique Shops of Great Britain 1986. Rosemary

Ferguson and Stella King, eds. Antique Collectors Club. 1985. Annual list of sources for antiques in Great Britain.

Toy Armies. Peter Johnson. Doubleday. 1982. Since the mid-1960s lead soldiers were no longer produced, creating a market for the collector of these fascinating toys. History of this industry, well-illustrated and clearly written.

Magazines and Newsletters

Antique Collector. National Magazine Co., 72 Broadwick Street, London W1V 2BP. mo. Heavy with antique collector-type advertisements; content articles on British antiques and the antique market.

Coin and Medal News. Token Publishing Ltd. Wheelhouse, 5 Station Road, Liphook, Hants GU30 7DW, England. Contains a helpful advertising section which will serve to direct American coin collection enthusiasts to product outlets in Great Britain; up-to-date and historical coin news and analyses.

Coin Monthly. Numismatic Publishing Co., Sovereign House, Brentwood, Essex CM14 4SE, England. mo. General information on British coin collecting; helpful advertisements.

Connoisseur. Hearst Magazines Co., 250 W. 55th Street, New York, NY 10019. mo. A periodical for serious collectors of antiques.

Gibbons Stamp Monthly. Stanley Gibbons Magazines, Ltd., 399 Strand, London WC2R 01S. mo. A stamp collectors' journal with worldwide coverage.

New Collecting Lines. Kollectarama Publications, 9 High Street, Bembridge, Isle of Wight, England. bi-mo. Information about collecting (in Britain) postcards, bottles, cigarette cards, tins, old toys, and more.

Stamp News. Stamp News Ltd., 100 Fleet Street, London EC4Y 1DE. 2/mo. An international magazine with contributions about stamps from and about England as well as other countries. Incorporates *Philately, Stamp and Postal History News,* and *Philatelic Magazine.*

GARDENS, CASTLES, AND STATELY HOMES

Some of Great Britain's most famous parks are to be found in London. They are royal parks—those which have been owned by the Crown as early as the sixteenth century, of which examples are:

St. James's Park, Hyde Park, Kensington Gardens, Regent's Park, Greenwich Park, Richmond Park, Hampton Court Park, Hampstead Heath, the Royal Botanic Gardens (Kew Gardens), and Battersea Park. A few private gardens may be visited. Many "stately homes" which may be visited have most exquisite gardens. See references (below) for locations of both types.

There are also many beautiful gardens throughout other parts of Britain, including: The Shakespeare Knott Garden at Stratford-upon-Avon; Levens Hall, Cumbria; Chatsworth in Derbyshire; Blenheim Palace (a Capability Brown triumph); the botanic gardens at Oxford University, Bath, Edinburgh; on Scotland's warmer Gulf Stream section of northwest coast, at Gairloch and Kyle of Lochalsh. Two examples of Welsh gardens are found in Bodnant Gardens (rhododendrons and more), and Dyffryn Gardens (with orchids, cycads, and giant banana trees).

There are many avid gardeners among the British. Flowers are important to them. Gardens, gardening, and flowers are great conversational ice breakers for the visiting tourist with such interests. Numerous gardening references—both organizations and books—appear in the lists that follow.

Organizations and Associations

Gardener's Sunday Organization. White Witches. 8 Mapstone Close, Glastonbury, Somerset BA6 8EY, England. A specialized gardeners' group.

Museum of Garden History. St. Mary at Lambeth, Lambeth Palace Road, London SE1. A gardening museum.

National Garden Scheme. 57 Lower Belgrave Street, London SW1W 0LR. Provides information about dates of openings of private gardens in Great Britain.

The National Trust. 36 Queen Anne's Gate, London SW1H 9AS. The trust cares for historic buildings, gardens, and half a million acres of country and coast lands. Membership provides free admission to all Trust properties, a 224-page guide, and a magazine (3/yr.) at a cost of $15 for individuals and $32 for families. Activities include summer camps, concerts, festivals, and drama.

Orchid Society of Great Britain. 28 Felday Road, London SE13 7HJ. An orchid growers' association.

Royal Botanical and Horticultural Society. 55 Brown Street, Man-

chester M2 5DS, England. Specialized amateur gardeners and
students of botanical and horticultural matters.
Royal Gardenia Horticultural Society. 1 West Newington Place,
Edinburgh EH9 1QT. Amateur gardeners who specialize in
gardenias.
Royal Horticultural Society. Vincent Square, London SW1P 2PE.
Interested in the cultivation of plants and trees; encourages
every branch of horticulture.
Royal National Rose Society. Chiswell Green Lane, St. Albans,
Herts AL2 3NR, England. Amateur rose growers.

Books

Architecture of Southern England. John Julius Norwich. Macmillan
Ltd. 1985. A personal selection of 1,200 of southern England's
finest and most fascinating buildings, each of which is described
in authoritative detail.
Capability Brown: And the Eighteenth Century English Landscape.
Roger Turner. Rizzoli International. 1985. Handsomely illustrated for those interested in gardening history and design of
garden settings for stately homes, by one of the all-time great
innovators in this art.
Castles in Wales. Automobile Association/Merrimack Publishers
Circle, distr. 1983. Features eighty of the most famous Welsh
castles with history, color photos, atlas, and eighteen special
one-day driving tours to castles in the countryside.
Celebration of English Gardens. English Tourist Board. 1984. Cele-
brates the heritage of English gardens with an enumeration and
annotation of many garden-related events and visitor trails.
Cottage Homes of England. Helen Allingham and Dick Stewart.
Bracken Books. 1984. How life was lived in cottage homes of
England in Edwardian days.
English Castles. Richard Humble. Crown. 1984. Describes in detail
historic castles in Britain; illustrated with color and black and
white photos; maps and diagrams show locations and floor plan.
The English Country House: An Art and Way of Life. Olive Cook.
Thames & Hudson. 1984. English country houses as works of
art are displayed along with the kinds of people for whom they
were built, the rituals of their pursuits and lives, and the
professional development of their architects.
The English Garden. Laurence Fleming and Alan Gore. Michael

Joseph/Merrimack Publishers Circle, distr. 1983. Herbs and
roses in the English garden, garden design, lake additions, color
factors, chronological list of gardens, gardeners, and garden
authors, and the origins of various garden plants are all included
in this comprehensive volume.

English Stone Building. Alec Clifton-Taylor and A.S. Ireson. Gol-
lancz/David & Charles. 1983. A comprehensive guide to English stone building: types of stone, decorative uses of stone,
present-day stone work, and implications for the future.

*The English Vision: The Picturesque in Architecture, Landscape
and Garden Design.* David Watkin. Harper & Row. 1982. A
discussion of the picturesque movement in landscape design
perpetuated by Capability Brown and carried through to the
present day; also covers architects such as John Vanbrugh and
John Nash who tried to blend the design of buildings with their
surroundings.

Gardens Open to the Public in England and Wales. National Garden
Scheme. 1984. Details of London's private gardens and those in
other parts of England and Wales, all of which may be visited.

Great Britain and Ireland: A Phaidon Cultural Guide. Phaidon/
Prentice-Hall. 1985. A comprehensive guide to both countries
with detailed explanations of important art and architecture and
one hundred photos and ground plans; index of places appended.

Great English Houses. E. Russell Chamberlin. Crown. 1983. Contains over ninety-full-color photographs and more than a hundred black-and-white illustrations as well as maps and diagrams. Gives descriptions of and locates these beautiful homes.

Guide to National Trust Properties in Britain. Automobile Associa-
tion/Merrimack Publishers Circle, distr. 1984. Covers nearly
eight hundred castles, houses, gardens, and properties in Britain managed by the National Trust including places in Scotland
and Northern Ireland. A full-color, large-format publication
with hundreds of photos and many regional maps.

Historic Houses and Castles Handbook. Neil Burton. Sunday Telegraph (London). 1984. Gives factual data about historic houses
and castles, country by country, all of which belong to the
National Trust.

Historic Houses, Castles, and Gardens in Great Britain and Ireland.
Patricia M. Wickens, ed. ABC Travel. 1984. Includes advertisements, locates most of the habitable castles of Great Britain

open to the public, contains an alphabetical index, tells how to gain access to the sites, and describes the properties.

Life in the English Country House. Mark Girouard. Penguin. 1980. A social and architectural history of the English country house and its occupants.

The National Trust for Scotland Guide. Robin Prentice, ed. W.W. Norton. 1981. An official guide to all the trust properties in Scotland; includes buildings, gardens, and country estates.

National Trust Book of British Castles. Paul Johnson. Granada/ Academy Chicago. 1983. Specific information regarding castles under the aegis of the National Trust management.

The National Trust Book of Great Houses of Britain. Nigel Nicholson. Granada/Academy Chicago. 1983. Directory of National Trust homes complete with factual information about each.

The Queen's Hidden Garden. David Bellamy. Salem House/Merrimack Publishers Circle, distr. 1985. See Buckingham Palace's treasury of wild plants on a tour through these gardens; illustrated with color and black-and-white photos.

The Smaller English House: An Introduction to Its History and Development. Lyndon F. Cave. Robert Hale. 1981. Informational notes on early English housebuilders; the medieval and timbered tradition, stone and brick tradition; houses in various English regions; Georgian houses, Regency and Victorian houses.

Stately Homes, Castles and Gardens in Britain 1985. Automobile Association/British Tourist Authority. 1985. A guide to more than two thousand sights in Britain with operating times, dates, fees of places mentioned plus locations and directions for travel given.

Stone Villages of England. Brian John Bailey. Robert Hale. 1982. A leisurely ramble through English lanes in search of stone in its various forms; stone for housebuilding, stone for other uses—fences, gates, walls.

The Victorian Country House. rev. and enlarged ed. Mark Girouard. Yale University Press. 1985. A collection of articles (most of which were originally published in *Country Life*) about large manor houses which were built from 1840 to 1890 and centered on country estates. These homes, surrounded by carefully planned gardens, are in various parts of Great Britain. Illustrated with photos, floor plans, and sketches. An alphabetical list of country houses with architect's name and short biography, present status of occupancy, and important features of each is appended.

Visit an English Garden. English Tourist Board. 1983. Descriptions of over five hundred gardens open to the public in the English countryside.

The Victorian Garden. Tom Carter. Salem House/Merrimack Publishers Circle, distr. 1985. Presents a picture of the Victorian garden through the use of photos and excerpts from contemporary writers' works.

Audiovisual Materials

The Hand of Adam. International Film Bureau. nd. 16mm sound film or video cassette, 35 mins. Dramatizes the life of Robert Adam, the Scottish urban architect who made significant contributions to the London landscape.

Let's Look at Castles. International Film Bureau. nd. 16mm film or video cassette, 32 mins. Traces the development of the castle in England from the eleventh century to the beginning of the fourteenth century. Details of construction; methods of defense; brief histories of castles.

Magazines and Newsletters

Country Life. Country Life, King's Reach Tower, Stamford Street, London SE19. wk. Availabilities of high quality real estate (large homes, estates, castles) in Britain; news and views concerning real estate in particular areas; living conditions and advantages. Heavily illustrated (large number of pictures in full color).

LITERARY SITE-SLEUTHING

Many visitors to Britain will go there with a highly individualized list of places they want to be sure to see. Often, the best and most highly anticipated of these will be related to literary characters in books that brought them so vividly to life—as well as to films, plays or television programs—and to the work of well-loved British novelists, poets, playwrights, and historians. A great number of works are identified with districts in Britain, with certain streets in London, perhaps, or with particular churches, villages, castles, or landscapes.

The listings in this section will lead you to specific materials by or about such people and thus encourage you to read more about them before you leave on your trip. You are advised to check with the National Trust Guides or local tourist bureaus to obtain times of opening and other information about the particular locations in which you are interested. The associations and organizations, books, and audiovisual materials mentioned in the lists that follow will offer useful resources for your efforts.

Books

America's British Heritage. British Tourist Authority. 1978. free. A listing of places in Great Britain connected with America's heritage and the literary and historical figures associated with the areas; illustrated with maps and drawings; a complete index of names and places appended.

Authors and Places: A Literary Pilgrimage. Roger Lancelyn Green. Putnam Publishing Group. 1964. Intended as a special aid to individuals in visiting places where British authors were born and raised. Includes data for such authors as Beatrix Potter, Sir Walter Scott, A. Conan Doyle, Lewis Carroll, Charles Dickens, J.M. Barrie, Charles Lamb, Kenneth Grahame, John Milton, Shakespeare, T.L. Peacock, Shelley, and others.

Betjeman's Country. Frank Delaney. Hodder and Stoughton/David & Charles. 1984. Glimpses, in words and pictures, of places in the Cornwall area from which Betjeman's poetic inspirations sprang.

The Game Is Afoot: A Travel Guide to the England of Sherlock Holmes. David L. Hammer. Gaslight Publications. 1983. A description of Sherlock Holmes' England, locating the "scenes of the crimes" in Sir Arthur Conan Doyle's stories; an engrossing armchair "read" with ninety-three photos and fourteen maps to help one visualize the locales.

Guide to Literary London. George Guion Williams. Hastings House. 1973. Arranged in three parts of "best" tours, "excellent" tours, and "good" tours with an index of persons and places. Each tour lists major literary figures included, then offers a map and walking directions; also included are short bits of history, background, and events of the times.

How the Heather Looks. Joan Bodger. Viking. 1965. "A joyous journey to the British sources of children's books." Descriptions of settings and locales for many British stories for children such as Caldecott country, Narnia, Camelot, Robin Hood's Forest, King Arthur's castle remains, *Johnny Crow's Garden,* the moors, gardens, and the banks of the Thames—setting for *Alice in Wonderland* and *Wind in the Willows;* a marvelous compendium of British connections in children's literature.

The Illustrated Wordsworth's Guide to the Lakes. William Wordsworth. Peter Bicknell, ed. Congdon and Weed. 1984. The original "guide to the lakes" by Wordsworth, vintage 1810, plus color photos, engravings, and watercolors.

James Herriot's Yorkshire. James Herriot. St. Martin's. 1981. A guided tour of the countryside well-known to followers of this popular television (and real life) veterinarian. Fully illustrated in color.

The Landscape of Thomas Hardy. Dennis Kay-Robinson. Salem House/Merrimack Publishers Circle, distr. 1984. A tour of Hardy's literary haunts, illustrated with many photographs taken in recent times. Supplemented by a listing of Hardy's novels with page references to scenes in the writings and the photographs, this book is described as "an enormous feat of detective work."

A Literary Atlas and Gazetteer of the British Isles. Michael Hardwick. Gale Research. 1973. Gives 4,500 short sketches of authors keyed to detailed maps with literary associations. Arranged by country—England, Scotland, and Wales—and by shires with an index by personal name as well.

Literary Britain: A Reader's Guide to Its Writers and Landmarks Frank Morley. Moyer Bell. 1985. Arranged in six sections, this book is a narrative account of English writers, their connections with various areas of the country, and the influence of those areas upon their writings. Indexed by place names and personal names; area maps included.

Literary Britain and Ireland. Ian Ousby. Blue Guides Series. W.W. Norton. 1985. One hundred and eighty poets and novelists arranged by author, with a comprehensive index of places. It offers driving and walking tours with topographical and literary references, gives streets and house numbers for birthplaces and residences as well as chapter numbers for novels and line numbers for poetry references.

Literary Landscapes of the British Isles: A Narrative Atlas. David
Daiches and John Flower. Facts on File. 1978. Gives short,
literary profiles of over 225 British authors from Chaucer to
Woolf; written by a literary scholar and cartographed by an
expert in the field. Each entry is keyed to excellent maps which
give birthplace, where each one lived and wrote, death and
burial place, and an indication of whether a house, a museum,
or a memorial to the author still exists.

Literary Lodgings. Elaine Borish. Constable. 1984. A listing of
thirty-seven hotels in Britain which have associations with
famous literary personalities, many of which were dwelling
places for notable writers in their creative time. Written by an
American English literature professor, this account gives location and a few critical comments on each of the establishments.

*A Literary Pilgrim: An Illustrated Guide to Britain's Literary Heri-
tage.* Edward Thomas. Salem House/Merrimack Publishers
Circle, distr. 1985. A record of "wanderings" through England
seeking out birthplaces and familiar grounds of some of England's most celebrated writers and poets, with a short biography of each.

A Literary Tour Guide to England and Scotland. Emilie C. Harting.
Morrow. 1976. Lists sites to visit connected with authors in
England and Scotland. Includes a special section on London
walking tours. Gives information on locations, visiting hours,
directions, and historical as well as literary connections.

London and the Famous. Kathy Carter. British Tourist Authority/
Merrimack Publishers Circle, distr. 1982. A guide to fifty famous British personalities and their homes in London which
can still be viewed; includes maps, tours, and illustrations of
historic London.

*The London Yankees: Portraits of American Writers and Artists in
England 1894-1914.* Stanley Weintraub. Harcourt, Brace,
Jovanovich. 1979. Discusses the intellectual life in London and
the homes and haunts of these famous personages: Mark Twain,
Bret Harte, Stephen Crane, Whistler, Jacob Epstein, Robert
Frost, Amy Lowell, Ezra Pound, Henry James, and others.

The Oxford Literary Guide to the British Isles. Dorothy Eagle and
Hilary Carnell, eds. Oxford University Press. 1977. Lists cities,
towns, villages, homes, castles, schools, and inns connected
with the writings of more than 900 authors—from Bede to
Tolkien. Gives hours of opening for buildings available to the

public. Fictitious names of real places are cross-indexed. Biographical index gives brief outline of authors' lives relating to places mentioned in the text.

Poet's London. Paddy Kitchen. Longman Group. 1980. A guide to the habitats and neighborhoods of many English poets during their lives in London. Poems are included in a separate listing at the back of the book.

Walking Through Literary Landscapes. Richard Shurey. David & Charles. 1984. A series of rambles through country associated with 19 British writers; includes, in alphabetical order by author, biographical sketches, line drawings, and excerpts from each writer's works. Complete walking itineraries, maps, and notes also included.

Where They Lived in London: A Guide to Famous Doorsteps. Maurice Rickards. Taplinger. 1972. Shows the location of forty homes of the famous—writers, artists, statesmen, and explorers in London. Extensive illustrations of people, buildings; map locations and additional addresses of notables appended.

Wordsworth and the Lake District: A Guide to the Poems and Their Places. David McCracken. Oxford University Press. 1985. A thorough examination of Wordsworth's poetry, journals, and letters resulting in a detailed map of Wordsworth's Lake District with images and associations located exactly.

Writer's Britain: Landscape in Literature. Margaret Drabble. Knopf. 1979. How fifty British writers felt about their land with 150 color and black-and-white photos. Includes impressions of Henry James, Tolkien, Spenser, Shakespeare, and others.

Audiovisual Materials

Behind the Scenes: Three Views of Shakespeare. National Public Radio. nd. audio cassette, 1 hr. Three tapes covering Shakespeare's life and times, his works: "Shakespeare the Man," "Shakespeare in Our Time," and "Shakespeare and His Theatre."

The Brontë Sisters. International Film Bureau. nd. 16mm sound film, 19 mins. Set in Yorkshire, England, the film tells the story of the lives of the Brontë sisters, Charlotte, Emily, and Anne. Places are shown that are described in *Jane Eyre* and *Wuthering Heights.* Each of the sisters reads from her work.

Shakespeare's Britain. National Geographic Society. Map, 19″ x 25″, 1981. Features forty-five sites from Shakespeare's plays.

YOUNG PEOPLE'S ATTRACTIONS AND OPPORTUNITIES: LONDON

London offers a great variety of interesting and educational things for children and young people to do while on vacation. The following sources suggest many possibilities.

Books

A Capital Guide for KIDS: A London Guide for Parents with Small Children. Vanessa Miles. Allison and Busby/Schocken. 1983. For parents with preschoolers touring London; covers cinema, puppets, river trips, sightseeing, parks, books and toys, restaurants, and free entertainment.

Children's London. London Tourist Board. 1984. Intended to eliminate (or reduce) some of the headaches of planning a visit to London with children. Information on things to do and see, opening hours, availability of children's discounts, information on disabled access facilities, and more.

A Child's History of London. Nicholas Whines. British Broadcasting Corp. 1984. This attractive history shows the "great fire," London Bridge, the Tower of London, and other places of significance in the city's story with associated facts.

Discovering London for Children. rev. ed. Margaret Pearson. Shire Publications/Seven Hills Books. 1984. A sightseeing guide for parents who have the interests of their children in mind; basic information about dozens of worthwhile London sightseeing locations.

London for Children. Margaret Pearson. Discovering Books Series No. 110. Shire Publications. 1985. Lists attractions available for children.

London in Your Pocket. Reginald Hammond. Ward Lock. 1984. A concise guide to London including a good section on Children's London.

London Is for Children. London Tourist Board. 1985. Sites and activities of London that will be of special interest to children.

Young London. Keith Blogg. London Transport. 1982. Day-by-day schedules of significant sites of London which young people would be interested in visiting. By the same author, titles of similar interest: *Free (or Nearly Free) London, Family London,* and *Royal and Historic London,* all available from London Transport.

YOUNG PEOPLE'S ATTRACTIONS AND OPPORTUNITIES: ALL
AROUND BRITAIN

A few other special attractions in various parts of Great Britain are
rated as being of considerable interest to children and young people.
The books and audiovisual materials listed below deal with a number of them.

Books

Activity and Hobby Holidays. English Tourist Board. 1984. A classified listing of various types of hobby and activity holidays in
which young people may choose to engage in the United
Kingdom.

Britain: Four Countries, One Kingdom. Jean Ellenby and Suzy
Siddons. Dinosaur Publications/British Tourist Authority, distr.
1980. An illustrated children's history of life in the United
Kingdom.

Cambridge Topic Books. Trevor Cairns, ed. Lerner Publication Co.
1982. Well-illustrated, informative books for children on various aspects of English history. Titles include *Life in a Medieval
Village, Christopher Wren and St. Paul's Cathedral, Building
Medieval Cathedrals,* and *The Murder of Archbishop Thomas.*

Children's History of Britain. Neil Grant. Hamlyn Publishing
Group. 1977-1983. Covers two thousand years of British history
from the Stone Age to the present day; updated and revised
periodically; for ages seven and up.

The Family Welcome Guide. Jill Foster and Malcolm Hamer. Sphere
Books. 1985. The best pubs, restaurants, and hotels for parents
visiting England with children. Also inventories stately homes
and other places of interest and lists 400 British pubs, hotels,
and restaurants.

Fielding's Europe with Children. 2d rev. ed. Leila Hadley. 1984.
Morrow. Why children should be taken along on trips to Europe
explained: full facts about baby-sitting and childcare services
and camps, family accommodations, zoos, and other family
attractions.

Getting to Know Britain. B. Elizabeth Pryse. Basil Blackwell. 1984.
A student guide to life in the British Isles.

Great Britain. Francis Coleman. Macdonald Countries Series. Macdonald Educational. 1979. A nicely produced history for children; simple maps, diagrams, drawings; a ten-page reference
section including facts on history, geography, and the economy.

Audiovisual Materials

Authors of the Ages. National Center for Audio Tapes. nd. audio cassette, 30 mins. each. "Canterville Ghost" (Oscar Wilde), "Ivanhoe" (Sir Walter Scott), "A Picture of Dorian Gray" (Oscar Wilde), "She Stoops to Conquer" (Oliver Goldsmith), "Wuthering Heights" (Emily Brontë).

A Child's Christmas in Wales. Dylan Thomas. Minnesota Public Radio. 1984. audio cassette, one hr. An unabridged reading by the author of his best known Christmas story and also of five of his poems.

Then and Now Series. National Center for Audio Tapes. nd. audio cassettes, 15 mins. each. A series of dramatizations stressing that history is more than a series of events in the past. Rather, it is the result of what people have said and thought in the past. Titles pertaining to Great Britain: "Cedric Goes to a Fair," "Cedric Goes to a Tournament," "Cedric Goes to School," "A King Signs: Magna Carta," "Medieval England: A Famous Pilgrimage," and "The People Build a Cathedral: Canterbury, England."

The Secret Garden. Frances Hodgson Burnett. Minnesota Public Radio. 1984 audio cassettes (two), 2½ hrs. An abridged version of the author's story of friendship set in the English countryside; read by actress Gwen Watson.

The Wind in the Willows. Kenneth Grahame. Mind's Eye. 1985. audio cassettes (three). A dramatization of this popular children's story set partly on the River Thames.

Magazines and Newsletters

Young Visitors to Britain. British Tourist Authority. ann., free. Lists various types of schools, hostel groups, camps, museums, children's and young people's activities of various types throughout Britain.

PHOTOGRAPHING, RECORDING, AND VIDEOTAPING

Recording the highlights of your trip in Britain in still or motion pictures, on video tape, or on audio tape requires some advance planning and decision-making. You should ask yourself—and answer—the following questions somewhat in the order in which they are presented here:

• *What principal uses will you make of the recorded material?* Will still photos go into a paper-print album? Will you want to project them as 2 x 2-inch slides? Might you want to put either still pictures or motion pictures into video cassette format to save as part of your private travel collection? Are you audiorecording to capture documentary sounds (church bells, street noises)? For interviews? Are you getting sounds on tape simply to jog your own memory of pleasant experiences, or do you expect to dub them into slide, movie, or video tape presentations you will develop?

• *How much time and attention do you expect to devote on your trip to your recording activities?* Are they a side-line, incidental to your interest in sightseeing, or a main reason for going to particular places?

• *How much money are you willing to spend on materials and processing?* This question applies primarily to film and video tape. You would probably be wise to decide to specialize in one format and to carry only the type of camera gear and film you need for that (35mm Kodacolor or similar for prints, 35mm Kodachrome or similar for slides, video tape, or motion picture film). If you have a choice of film speeds, take a slower one for outdoor use and a faster one for indoor natural light shots, as recommended.

Most films are readily available in Great Britain, so you do not need to carry a full supply for your whole trip. You may wish to take an extra set or two of the batteries that work best in your audio recorder, some ninety-minute blank tapes, and a separate microphone. The results of the separate mike will be better under travel conditions than the built-in one (trying to record the choir in a cathedral, for example).

The 35mm single lens reflex camera is a recommended format for filming in that medium. Selecting one with a flexible zoom camera lens with, say, 40mm to 105mm range, simplifies picture-taking and reduces carrying bulk.

Organizations and Associations

British Institute of Recorded Sound. 29 Exhibition Road, London
   SW7 7AS. A national archive of recorded sound items (250,000
   tapes, discs, cylinders), as well as a library of books, micro-
   films, and other publications relating to sound.

Federation of British Tape Recordists and Clubs. 20 Plantation Close, Saffron Walden, Essex CB11 4DS, England. Furthers the interests of amateur tape recordists; sponsors conferences and meetings; publishes *Recording News.*

Kodak Museum. Headstone Drive, Harrow, Middlesex, England. History of photography portrayed in exhibits; reconstruction of Victorian photo studio.

Oral History Society. Department of History, University of Essex, Colchester, Essex, England. Concerned with the study and writing of history through words of people who have experienced it.

Radio Society of Great Britain. 35 Doughty Street, London WC1N 2AE. Encourages amateur radio activities in Great Britain.

Books

Everything You Always Wanted to Know about Portable Video Tape Recording. Don Harwood. VTR Publishing. 1983. A simply written, down-to-earth discussion of equipment, procedures, and techniques of producing video tapes, using portable amateur equipment.

Guide to Filmmaking. Edward Pincus. New American Library/ Signet Books. 1972. Beginner's book on 8mm and 16mm film use, movie cameras and lenses, lighting, color, sound, editing, printing, and projection.

John Hedgecoe's Photographic Workbook. John Hedgcoe. Simon and Schuster. 1985. Choosing still cameras, taking pictures, darkroom techniques, common errors, pages on which to record notes for pictures taken.

John Hedgecoe's Pocket Guide to Practical Photography. John Hedgecoe. Simon and Schuster. 1979. Similar to the preceding book, but in a briefer format. Handy size for carrying in the field.

Kodak Pocket Guide to Great Pictures. Editors of Eastman Kodak. Simon and Schuster. 1984. Simple camera systems, tips for making better pictures, what to photograph, using flash, making outdoor shots, traveling with a camera, basic cameras, films.

The New Joy of Photography. Editors of Eastman Kodak. Addison-Wesley. 1985. Presented in five sections: (1) "The Vision: Elements of Good Photography"; (2)"The Tools"; (3)"The Image"; (4)"The Process"; and (5)"The Joy."

Oral History. Thad Sitton et al. University of Texas Press. 1983. The pleasures and techniques of collecting oral history through effective use of audio tape recorders; kinds of hardware and reference tools required.

Planning and Producing Instructional Media. Jerrold E. Kemp and Deane K. Dayton. Harper and Row. 1986. While this is a college text, its down-to-earth and very clear presentation of audio, video, and photography materials is useful to all amateurs.

Single Camera Video Production. Barry J. Fuller et al. Prentice-Hall. 1982. Full information, with clear diagrammatic presentations, about how to produce simple television tapes using just one camera.

Television Production Handbook. William McCavitt. Intertec. 1983. A beginner's introduction to amateur television production. Topics include production, cameras, audio, lighting, graphics, special effects, projection, scenery, direction, scripting, editing, and video tape recorders.

The Videotaping Handbook. Peter Lanzendorf. Harmony Books. 1983. Nontechnical treatment of videotaping equipment and various techniques for using it; video recorders, cameras, and sound equipment; tips for using it.

Directory of
Publishers and Producers

AA (Automobile Association). See
Automobile Association (AA).

ABC Historic Publications. See
ABC Travel Guides.

ABC Travel Guides
World Timetable Centre
Dunstable, Beds LU5 4HB,
England

Harry N. Abrams, Inc.
100 Fifth Ave.
New York, NY 10011

Abson Books
Abson, Wick
Bristol BS15 5TT, England

Academy Chicago Publishers
425 N. Michigan Ave.
Chicago, IL 60611

Addison-Wesley Publishing, Co.,
Inc.
General Books Division
1 Jacob Way
Reading, MA 01867

Adler & Adler Publishers, Inc.
4550 Montgomery Ave., Suite 705
Bethesda, MD 20814

Albyn Press
2 Caversham St.
London SW3, England

J.A. Allen and Co. Ltd.
Sporting Book Centre, distr.
Canaan, NY 12029

George Allen and Unwin Ltd.
40 Museum St.
London WC1A 1LU, England

Allison and Busby Ltd.
6A Noel St.
London W1Y 3RB, England

American Automobile Association
(AAA)
811 Gatehouse Rd.
Falls Church, VA 22047

American Express
6 Haymarket
London SW1, England

American Library Association
50 E. Huron St.
Chicago, IL 60611

Anchor. *See* Doubleday & Co.,
Inc.

Antique Collectors Club
5 Church St.
Suffolk 1P12 1DS, Woodbridge,
England

Arcady Books Ltd.
2 Woodlands Rd.
Ashurst, Southampton SO4 2AD,
England

Arco Publishing, Inc.
215 Park Ave. S.
New York, NY 10003

Ariel Books
820 Miramar Dr.
Berkeley, CA 94707

Arrow Books Ltd.
Hutchinson House
17-21 Conway St.
London W1P 6JD, England

Art Guide Publications
28 Colville Rd.
London W11 2BS, England

Arts Address Book
31 Rowcliff Rd.
High Wickam, Bucks, England

Atheneum Publishers
597 Fifth Avenue
New York, NY 10017

Automobile Association (AA)
Fanum House, Basingstoke, Hants
RG21 2EA
England

John Baker Pubs. Ltd. *See* A & C
Black.

Bantam Books, Inc.
666 Fifth Ave.
New York, NY 10103

Barnes and Noble Imports
Div. of Littlefield, Adams & Co.
81 Adams Dr.
Totowa, NJ 07512

Barrie and Jenkins
Hutchinson House
17-21 Conway St.
London W1P 6JD, England

Barron's Educational Series, Inc.
113 Crossways Park Dr.
Woodbury, NY 11797

John Bartholomew and Son Ltd.
12 Duncan St.
Edinburgh EH9 1TA, Scotland

B. T. Batsford Ltd.
4 Fitzhardinge St.
London W1H 0AH, England

Battle of Britain Prints
International Ltd.
3 New Plaistow Rd.
London E15 3JA, England

Beaufort Books, Inc.
9 E. 40 St.
New York, NY 10016

Berkshire Traveller Press
Pine St.
Stockbridge, MA 01262

BFA Films
2211 Michigan Ave.
Santa Monica, CA 90406

Biblio Distribution Center
81 Adams Dr.
P.O. Box 327
Totowa, NJ 07511

A. & C. Black, Ltd.
35 Bedford Row
London WC1R 4JH, England

Basil Blackwell, Inc.
432 Park Ave. S.
New York, NY 10016

Boat Enquiries. See British
  Waterways Board.

The Bodley Head Ltd.
30 Bedford Sq.
London WC1B 3EL, England

R. R. Bowker Co.
205 E. 42 St.
New York, NY 10017

Bracken Books
24/28 Friern Park
London N12 9DA, England

Bradt Enterprises, Inc.
93 Harvey St.
Cambridge, MA 02140

British Broadcasting Corp. Pubs.
35 Marylebone High St.
London W1M 4AA, England

The British Council
Publications Dept.
65 Davies St.
London W1Y 2AA, England

British Film Institute
81 Dean St.
London W1V 6AA, England

British Gifts
P.O. Box 26558
Los Angeles, CA 90026

British Hotels, Restaurants, and
  Caterers Assn.
40 Duke St.
London W1M 6HR, England

British Library Publications
Boston Spa, Wetherby
W. Yorkshire LS23 7BQ, England

British Museum Publications Ltd.
40 Bloomsbury St.
London WC1B 3QQ, England

British Tourist Authority
40 W. 57 St.
New York, NY 10019
    or
John Hancock Center
Suite 3320
875 N. Michigan Ave.
Chicago, IL 60611
    or
612 S. Flower St.
Los Angeles, CA 90017
    or
Plaza of the Americas
750 N. Tower LB 346
Dallas, TX 75201

British Toy Fairs Ltd.
British Toy and Hobby Mfrs. Assn.
80 Camberwell Rd.
London SE5 0EG, England

British Travel Bookshop
40 W. 57 St.
New York, NY 10019

British Travel International
630 Third Ave.
New York, NY 10017

British Waterways Board
Melbury House, Melbury Terrace
London NW1 6JX, England

John Gordon Burke, Publisher, Inc.
P.O. Box 1492
Evanston, IL 60204

Cambridge University Press
32 E. 57 St.
New York, NY 10022

Cameron & Co.
543 Howard St.
San Francisco, CA 94105

Campaign for Real Ale (CAMRA)
Ltd.
34 Alma Rd.
St. Albans, Herts AL1 3BW,
England

Carousel Books Ltd.
Century House
61-63 Uxbridge Rd.
Ealing, London W5 5SA, England

Carousel Films, Inc.
241 E. 34 St.
New York, NY 10016

CBD Research Ltd.
154 High St.
Beckenham, Kent BR3 1EA,
England

Central Film Library
Chalfont Grove, Gerrards Cross
Bucks SL9 8TN, England

Chatto and Windus Ltd.
(The Hogarth Press)
40 William IV St.
London WC2N 4DF, England

Citadel Press
120 Enterprise Ave.
Secaucus, NJ 07094

Clarion Books. *See* Houghton
Mifflin Co.

CMG Publishing Co.
P.O. Box 630
Princeton, NJ 08540

William Collins Sons & Co. Ltd.
8 Grafton St.
London W1X 3LA, England

Collins Willow. *See* William Collins
Sons & Co. Ltd.

Colour Library International Ltd.
86 Epsom Rd.
Guildford, Surrey CU1 2BX,
England

Communications House
Dobbs Ferry, NY 10522

Congdon and Weed, Inc.
298 Fifth Ave.
New York, NY 10001

Constable Publications
19 Stephenson Dr.
E. Grinstead, W. Sussex RH19
4AP, England

Thomas Cook Ltd.
1085 Avenue of the Americas
New York, NY 10019
and
Box 36, Thorpe Wood
Peterborough PE3 6SB, England

Cornell University Press
124 Roberts Pl.
P.O. Box 250
Ithaca, NY 14851

Council on International
Educational Exchange
205 E. 42nd St.
New York, NY 10017

Country Life Books. *See* Newnes
Books.

Country Road Press
414 W. Jonquil Road.
Santa Ana, CA 92706

CRM/McGraw-Hill Films
110 Fifteenth St.
Del Mar, CA 95014

Croquet Assn.
Hurlingham Club
London SW6 3PR, England

Crown Publications
66 Queens Rd.
Watford, England

Crown Publishers, Inc.
1 Park Ave.
New York, NY 10016

Da Capo Press, Inc.
233 Spring St.
New York, NY 10013

Dalesman Publishing Co. Ltd.
Clapham
Lancaster LA2 8EB, England

David & Charles Ltd.
Brunel House
Newton Abbot
Devon TQ12 4PU, England
and
P.O. Box 57
North Pomfret, VT 05053

Debrett's Peerage Publishers
73/77 Britannia Rd.
London SW6 2JR, England

Dell Publishing Co., Inc.
One Dag Hammarskjold Plaza
New York, NY 10017

J. M. Dent and Sons Ltd.
Aldine House
33 Welbeck St.
London W1M 8LX, England

Distribution Services Corp.
131 N. Ludlow, Suite 750
Dayton, OH 45402

Dodd, Mead and Co.
79 Madison Ave.
New York, NY 10016

Doubleday & Co., Inc.
245 Park Ave.
New York, NY 10167

Drakes Printing and Publishers
225 Magnolia Ave.
Orlando, FL 32801

Drive Publications
Box 222
7/10 Old Bailey
London EC99 1AH, England

E. P. Dutton, Inc.
2 Park Ave.
New York, NY 10016

The East Woods Press
429 East Blvd.
Charlotte, NC 28203

Elek. *See* Granada Publishing Ltd.

Encore Visual Education, Inc.
1235 S. Victory Blvd.
Burbank, CA 91502

Encyclopaedia Britannica
Educational Corp.
425 N. Michigan Ave.
Chicago, IL 60611

English Tourist Board. *See*
Automobile Association (AA) for
orders.

E. P. Group. *See* A. & C. Black.

Eurail Guide Annual
27540 Pacific Coast Highway
Malibu, CA 90265

Expediters of the Printed Word
Ltd.
527 Madison Ave.
New York, NY 10022

Facts on File, Inc.
460 Park Ave. S.
New York, NY 10016

Fairleigh Dickinson University
Press
285 Madison Ave.
Madison, NJ 07940

Farm Holiday Guides Ltd.
Abbey Hall Business Centre
Seedhill, Paisley
Renfrewshire PA1 1JN, England

Fielding/Morrow. See Morrow
Publishing Co.

Films, Inc.
733 Green Bay Rd.
Wilmette, IL 60091

Fisher Travel Guides, Inc.
Suite 2300
401 Broadway
New York, NY 10013

Fodor's Travel Guides
2 Park Ave.
New York, NY 10016

Fontana. See William Collins Sons
and Co. Ltd.

Football Association
16 Lancaster Gate
London W2 3LW, England

Forest Press, Inc.
Lake Placid Club
Lake Placid, NY 12946

Forsyth Travel Library
P.O. Box 2975
Shawnee Mission, KS 66201

Burt Franklin and Co., Inc.
235 E. 44 St.
New York, NY 10017

Freelance Publications Ltd.
P.O. Box 1385
Meredith, NH 03253

Friends General Conference
1520-B Race St.
Philadelphia, PA 19102

Frommer-Pasmantier
1230 Avenue of the Americas
New York, NY 10020

Futura Publications. See
Macdonald and Co. Ltd.

Gabbitas-Thring
Broughton House
6/7/8 Sackville St.
Piccadilly, London W1X 2BR,
England

Gale Research Co.
Book Tower
Detroit, MI 48226

Gaslight Publications
112 E. Second
Bloomington, IN 47401

Genealogical Society of Utah
Genealogical Institute/Family
History World
57 W. South Temple, Suite 255
Salt Lake City, UT 84101

Gentry Books. See Haynes & Co.
Ltd.

Geographers A-Z Map Co.
Ventry Rd.
Sevenoaks, Kent TN14 5EP,
England

Gill and Macmillan Ltd.
Goldenbridge, Inchicore
Dublin 8, Irish Republic

Golden West Publishing
4113 N. Longview
Phoenix, AZ 85014

Victor Gollancz Ltd.
14 Henrietta St., Covent Garden
London WC2E 8QJ, England

Granada Publishing Ltd.
8 Grafton St.
London W1X 3LA, England

Grand Circle Travel
555 Madison Ave.
New York, NY 10022

Greenwich Bookshop
37 King William Walk
London SE10 9HU, England

Gresham Books Ltd.
Box 61, Henley-on-Thames
Oxon RG9 3LQ, England

Grosset and Dunlap, Inc. *See*
Putnam Publishing Group.

Guinness Superlatives Ltd.
2 Cecil Ct., London Rd.
Enfield, Middlesex EN2 6DJ,
England

Robert Hale Ltd.
Clerkenwell House
45-47 Clerkenwell Green
London EC1R 0HT, England

Hamish Hamilton Ltd.
Garden House
57-59 Long Acre
London WC2E 9JZ, England

Hamlyn Paperbacks. *See* Arrow
Books Ltd.

Harcourt Brace Jovanovich, Inc.
1250 Sixth Ave.
San Diego, CA 92101
and
111 Fifth Ave.
New York, NY 10003

Harmony Books. *See* Crown
Publishers.

Harper and Row, Publishers, Inc.
10 E. 53 St.
New York, NY 10022

Harrap Ltd.
19-23 Ludgate Hill
London EC4M 7PD, England

Hastings House, Publishers, Inc.
10 E. 40 St.
New York, NY 10016

J. H. Haynes and Co. Ltd.
Sparkford, Yeovil
Somerset BA22 7JJ, England

Haynes Publications, Inc.
861 Lawrence Dr.
Newberry Park, CA 91320

Heart of England Tourist Board
Old Bank House
Bank St.
Worcester WR1 2EW, England

William Heinemann Ltd.
10 Upper Grosvenor St.
London W1X 9PA, England

Her Majesty's Stationery Office
Publications Centre
51 Nine Elms Lane
London SW8 5DR, England

Hippocrene Books, Inc.
171 Madison Ave.
New York, NY 10016

HMSO Books. *See* Her Majesty's
Stationery Office.

Hodder and Stoughton Ltd.
47 Bedford Sq.
London WC1B 3DP, England

Holt, Rinehart & Winston, Inc.
521 Fifth Ave.
New York, NY 10175

Houghton Mifflin Co.
One Beacon St.
Boston, MA 02108

Humanities Press, Inc.
171 First Ave.
Atlantic Highlands, NJ 07716

Hutchinson Publishing Group Ltd.
Hutchinson House
17-21 Conway St.
London W1P 6JD, England

Image Imprints. *See* Image
Publishers.

Image Publishers
Ty'r Cwm, Llangoedmor
Cardigan, Dyfed SA43 2LE, Wales

Indiana University Audiovisual
Center
Bloomington, IN 47409

International Film Bureau, Inc.
332 S. Michigan Ave.
Chicago, IL 60604

International Video Network
3744 Mt. Diablo Blvd.
Lafayette, CA 94549

Intertec Publishing Corp.
P.O. Box 12901
Overland Park, KS 66212

Michael Joseph Ltd.
44 Bedford Sq.
London WC1B 3DU, England

Kaye and Ward Ltd.
10 Upper Grosvenor St.
London W1X 9PA, England

Kensington Publishing Co.
P.O. Box 10058
Berkeley, CA 94709

Alfred A. Knopf, Inc.
201 E. 50 St.
New York, NY 10022

Lansdowne Press, Australia
5 Great James St.
London WC1N 3DA, England

Learning Corporation of America
1350 Avenue of the Americas
New York, NY 10019

Lerner Publications Co.
241 First Ave. N.
Minneapolis, MN 55401

Charles Letts and Co. Ltd.
3 Woodhollow Lane
Huntington, NY 11743
and
Charles Letts and Co. Ltd.
Diary House, Borough Rd.
London SE1 1DW, England

Link House Magazines. *See* Link
House Publications.

Link House Publications
Link House, Dingwall Ave.
Croydon CR9 2TA, England

J. B. Lippincott Co. *See* Harper
and Row.

Little, Brown & Co., Inc.
34 Beacon St.
Boston, MA 02106

London Regional Transport
55 Broadway
London SW1H 0BD, England

London Tourist Board
26 Grosvenor Gardens
London SW1W 0DU, England

Longman Group Ltd.
Subscription Dept.
Pinnacles, Fourth Ave.
Harlow, Essex CM19 5AA,
England

Longwood Publishing Group, Inc.
51 Washington St.
Dover, NH 03820

Lutterworth Press
7 All Saints Passage
Cambridge CB2 3LS, England

Macdonald and Co. Ltd.
Maxwell House
70 Worship St.
London EC2A 2EN, England

Macdonald and Jane's Publishers
Ltd. *See* Macdonald and Co.
Ltd.

Macdonald Educational Ltd. *See*
Macdonald and Co. Ltd.

Macmillan Publishing Co.
866 Third Ave.
New York, NY 10022

Macmillan Publishers Ltd.
4 Little Essex St.
London WC2R 3LF, England

Peter Marcan Publications
31 Rowliff Rd.
High Wycomb, Bucks, England

Marwain Publishing Ltd.
245 Queensway
Bletchley, Milton Keynes, England

Keith Mason
36 Grange Rd.
Albrighton, Wolverhampton WV7
3LD, England

Mayflower Books Ltd. *See*
Granada Publishing Ltd.

McGraw-Hill Book Co.
1221 Avenue of the Americas
New York, NY 10020

McGraw-Hill Films. *See*
CRM/McGraw-Hill Films.

David McKay Co., Inc.
2 Park Ave.
New York, NY 10016

Meadowbrook Books
18318 Minnetonka Blvd.
Deephaven, MN 55391

Merrimack Publishers Circle
47 Pelham Rd.
Salem, NH 03079

Merseyside Aviation Society Ltd.
Rm 20, Hanger 2, Liverpool
Airport
Liverpool L24 8QE, England

Methuen & Co. Ltd.
11 New Fetter Lane
London EC4P 4EE, England

Michelin Tyre Public Ltd. Co.
81 Fulham Rd.
London SW3 6RD, England

Midas Books
c/o Baton Press Ltd.
44 Holden Park Rd.
Southborough, Tunbridge Wells
Kent TN4 0ER, England

Mind's Eye
P.O. Box 6727
San Francisco, CA 94101

Minnesota Public Radio
45 East 8th St.
St. Paul, MN 55101

Moorland Publishing Co. Ltd.
9/11 Station St.
Ashbourne, Derbyshire DE6 1DE,
England

William Morrow & Co., Inc.
105 Madison Ave.
New York, NY 10016

Moyer Bell Ltd.
R.F.D. 1, Colonial Hil
Mt. Kisco, NY 10549

Frederick Muller Ltd. *See* Muller, Blond, and White Ltd.

Muller, Blond, and White Ltd.
55 Great Ormond St.
London WC1N 3RZ, England

National Center for Audio Tapes
Educational Media Center, Stadium
   Bldg.
University of Colorado
Boulder, CO 80309

The National Gardens Scheme
57 Lower Belgrave St.
London SW1W 0LR, England

National Geographic Society
17th and M Sts. N.W.
Washington, D.C. 20036

National Information Center for
   Educational Media (NICEM)
P.O. Box 40130
Albuquerque, NM 87196

National Public Radio
Customer Service
Box 55417
Madison, WI 53705

National Textbook Co.
4255 W. Touhy Ave.
Lincolnwood, IL 60646

National Trust
36 Queen Anne's Gate
London SW1H 9AS, England

National Video Clearinghouse, Inc.
100 Lafayette Dr.
Syosset, NY 11791

The New American Library, Inc.
1633 Broadway
New York, NY 10019

New Enterprise Publications
212 Broad St.
Birmingham BI5 1AY, England

The New York Times Co.
229 W. 43 St.
New York, NY 10036

Newnes Books
84-88 The Centre
Feltham
Middlesex TW13 4BH, England

Robert Nicholson Publications Ltd.
Hutchinson House
17-21 Conway St.
London WLP 6JD, England

Nomadic Books
401 N.E. 45 St.
Seattle, WA 98105

Jeffrey Norton Publishers
On-the-Green
Guilford, CT 06437

W. W. Norton & Co., Inc.
500 Fifth Ave.
New York, NY 10110

Octopus Books Ltd.
59 Grosvenor St.
London W1X 9DA, England

Official Airlines Guides
2000 Clearwater Dr.
Oak Brook, IL 60521

John Offord Publications
12 The Avenue, Eastbourne
Sussex BN21 3YA, England

Oleander Press
210 Fifth Ave.
New York, 10010

Omega Books Ltd.
1 West St.
Ware, Herts SG12 9AB, England

The Overlook Press
12 W. 21 St.
New York, NY 10010

Oxford. *See* Oxford University
Press.

Oxford Illustrated Press Ltd.
Sparkford, Yeovil
Somerset BA22 7JJ, England

Oxford University Press
Walton St.
Oxford OX2 6DP, England
and
200 Madison Ave.
New York, NY 10016

Oxmoor House, Inc. *See* Harper
and Row.

Paladin Books. *See* Granada
Publishing, Ltd.

Pan Books Ltd.
Cavaye Pl.
London SW10 9PG, England

Pantheon Books, Inc.
201 E. 50 St.
New York, NY 10022

Papermac. *See* Macmillan
Publishers, Ltd.

Partners Press
181 Canal Rd.
R.D.1
Princeton, NJ 08540

Passport Books, *See* National
Textbook Co.

Stanley Paul & Co., Ltd. *See*
Hutchinson Publishing Group,
Ltd.

Pavilion Books Ltd.
196 Shaftesbury Ave.
London WC2H 8JL, England

Pelham Books Ltd.
44 Bedford Sq.
London WC1B 3DM, England

Penguin Books, Inc. *See*
Viking-Penguin, Inc.

Penguin Books Ltd.
Bath Rd.
Harmondsworth, Middlesex
UB7 0DA, England

Phaidon Press Ltd.
Littlegate House
St. Ebbe's St.
Oxford OX1 1SQ, England

George Philip and Son Ltd.
12-14 Long Acre
London WC2E 9LP, England

Pitkin Pictorials Ltd.
11 Wyfold Rd.
London SW6 6SG, England

Prentice-Hall, Inc.
P.O. Box 500
Englewood Cliffs, NJ 07632

Proteus Publishing Co., Inc.
9 W. 57 St.
New York, NY 10019

Purnell Books
Paulton, Bristol
BS18 5LQ, England

The Putnam Publishing Group, Inc.
200 Madison Ave.
New York, NY 10016

Quill Trade Paperbacks
105 Madison Ave.
New York, NY 10016

Rand McNally & Co.
P.O. Box 7600
Chicago, IL 60680

Random House, Inc.
201 E. 50 St.
New York, NY 10022

Reader's Digest General Books
750 Third Ave.
New York, NY 10017

Readers Digest Assn. Ltd.
25 Berkeley Sq.
London W1X 6AB, England

Rizzoli International
    Publications, Inc.
712 Fifth Ave.
New York, NY 10019

Egon Ronay Organization Ltd.
Greencoat House
Francis St.
London SW1P 1DH, England

Rothmans Publications Ltd.
Box 103, Oxford Rd.
Aylesbury, Bucks
HP21 8SZ, England

Routledge & Kegan Paul
14 Leicester Sq.
London WC2H 7PH, England
    and
9 Park St.
Boston, MA 02108

Rowman and Allanheld, Publishers
Division of Littlefield,
    Adams & Co.
81 Adams Dr., P.O. Box 368
Totowa, NJ 07512

Royal Automobile Club (RAC)
100 RAC House
RAC Publications
Landsdowne Rd.
Croydon CR9 2JA, England

Robert Royce Ltd.
93 Bedwardine Rd.
London SE19 3AY, England

St. Edmundsbury Borough Council
Thingoe House
118A Northgate St.
Bury St. Edmunds, Suffolk
IP33 1HH, England

St. Martin's Press, Inc.
175 Fifth Ave.
New York, NY 10010

Salem House, Ltd. *See* Merrimack
    Publishers Circle.

Schocken Books, Inc.
200 Madison Ave.
New York, NY 10016

Scottish Bowling Assn.
50 Wellington St.
Glasgow G2 6EF, Scotland

Scottish Genealogy Society
9 Union St.
Edinburgh EH1 3LT, Scotland

The Scottish Tourist Bureau
23 Ravelston Ter.
Edinburgh EH4 3EU, Scotland

Charles Scribner's Sons
597 Fifth Ave.
New York, NY 10017

Seabury Press, Inc.
810 Second Ave.
New York, NY 10017

Martin Secker and Warburg Ltd.
54 Poland St.
London W1V 3DF, England

Settle and Bendall
32 Saville Row
London W1X 1AG, England

Seven Hills Books
519 W. Third St.
Cincinnati, OH 45202

Severn House Publishers Ltd.
4 Brook St.
London W1Y 1AA, England

Sheridan House, Inc.
145 Palisade St.
Dobbs Ferry, NY 10522

Shire Publications Ltd.
Cromwell House, Church St.
Princes Risborough, Aylesbury
Bucks HP17 9AJ, England

The Shoe String Press, Inc.
P.O. Box 4327
Hamden, CT 06514

Signet Books. *See* New American
Library.

Simon & Schuster, Inc.
1230 Avenue of the Americas
New York, NY 10020

Simon and Schuster
Communications. *See* Simon and
Schuster.

W. H. Smith and Son Ltd.
Strand House
New Fetter Lane
London EC4A 1AD, England

Society for Visual Education, Inc.
1345 Diversey Pkwy.
Chicago, IL 60614

The Society of Genealogists
37 Harrington Gardens
London SW1, England

Society of West End Theatres
(SWET)
Bedford Chambers
Covent Garden
London WC2, England

Sphere Books, Inc.
940-950 N. Shore Dr.
Lake Bluff, IL 60044
and
30-32 Gray's Inn Rd.
London WC1X 8JL, England

Spurbooks Ltd. *See* Frederick
Warne.

Stanford Maritime Ltd.
12-14 Long Acre
London WC2E 9LP, England

State Mutual Book and Periodical
Services Ltd.
521 Fifth Ave.
17th Fl.
New York, NY 10017

Sterling Publishing Co., Inc.
2 Park Ave.
New York, NY 10016

Summit Books. *See* Simon and
Schuster.

Sunday Telegraph
135 Fleet St.
London EC4P 4BL, England

Alan Sutton Publishing Ltd.
30 Brunswick Rd.
Gloucester GL1 1JJ, Scotland

Taplinger Publishing Co., Inc.
132 W. 22 St.
New York, NY 10011

Thames & Hudson Ltd.
30 Bloomsbury St.
London WC1B 3QP, England

Ticknor and Fields
52 Vanderbilt Ave.
New York, NY 10017

Time-Life Books, Inc.
777 Duke St., Rm 204
Alexandria, VA 22314
and

Time-Life Books
Time-Life Internatioanl
153 New Bond St.
London W1Y 0AA, England

Times Books
130 Fifth Ave.
New York, NY 10011

Tours by Tape Ltd.
500 Fifth Ave.
New York, NY 10110

Town and Country Books Ltd.
Coombelands House
Addlestone, Weybridge
Surrey KT15 1HY, England

Transatlantic Arts, Inc.
P.O. Box 6086
Albuquerque, NM 87197

Transworld Publishers Ltd.
Century House
61-63 Uxbridge Rd.
Ealing, London W5 5SA, England

Travel Information Bureau
44 County Line Rd.
Farmingdale, NY 11735

Travel Press
16 E. Third Ave.
San Mateo, CA 94401

Traveler's Bookstore
75 Rockefeller Plaza
22 W. 52 St.
New York, NY 10019

U.K.H.M. Publishing Ltd.
165 Cromwell Rd., Suite 2
London SW5 0SH

U.S. Customs Service
Department of the Treasury
Washington, DC 20229

U.S. National Audiovisual Center
8750 Edgeworth Dr. SE
Capitol Heights, MD 20027

Universe Books
381 Park Ave. S.
New York, NY 10016

University of California Press
2120 Berkeley Way
Berkeley, CA 94720

University of Chicago Press
5801 Ellis Avenue
Chicago, IL 60637

University of Texas Press
P.O. Box 7819
Austin, TX 78713

Unwin Brothers Ltd.
The Gresham Press
Old Woking, Surrey GU22 9LH,
England

Usborne Publishing Ltd.
20 Garrick St.
London WC2E 9BJ, England

Vacation-Work
9 Park End St.
Oxford OX1 1HJ, England

Van Nostrand Reinhold Co., Inc.
135 W. 50 St.
New York, NY 10020

Verbatim Books
P.O. Box 668
Essex, CT 06426

Video Publications
P.O. Box 1507
Santa Barbara, CA 93102

Viking Penguin, Inc.
40 W. 23 St.
New York, NY 10010

Virgin Books
328 Kensall Rd.
London W10 5XJ, England

VTR Publishing Co.
23 Eaton Rd.
Syosset, NY 11791

Waldenbooks Video Film Classics
201 High Ridge Rd.
P.O. Box 10218
Stamford, CT 06904

Waldentapes
201 High Ridge Rd.
Box 10218
Stamford, CT 06904

Wales Tourist Board
Davis St.
Cardiff CF1 2FU, Wales

WalkWays
733 15th St. NW
Washington, DC 20005

Ward Lock, Ltd.
82 Gower St.
London WC1E 6EQ, England

Frederick Warne Ltd.
536 Kings Rd.
London SW10 0UH, England

Webb and Bower Ltd.
3 Colleton Crescent
Exeter EX2 4BY, England

George Weidenfeld and Nicolson
 Ltd.
91 Clapham High St.
London SW4 9TA, England

J. Whitaker & Sons Ltd.
12 Dyott St.
London WC1A 1DF, England

Wildwood House Ltd.
Jubilee House
Chapel Rd., Hounslow
Middlesex TW3 1TX, England

The H. W. Wilson Co.
950 University Ave.
Bronx, NY 10452

Windward
WHS Distributor
St. John's House, East St.
Leicester LE1 6NE, England

Yale University Press
302 Temple St.
New Haven, CT 06520

Youth Hostel Assn.
Trevelyan House, St. Albans
Herts AL1 2DY, England

Zebra Books
475 Park Ave. S.
New York, NY 10016